MP5129

# PASSPORT SERIES
## Western Europe

Author: Heather Knowles
Contributors: Ellen M. Dolan (England, Ireland, Italy),
  Ann Edmonds (France), Kelly Herrenkohl (Spain), PJ Lents (Germany), Susan D. Royals (Sweden)
Editor: Jonathan Gross
Original Illustrations: Ada K. Hanlon, Kathy Mitter, Larry Nolte, Joan C. Waites
Design and Layout: Jeff Richards

Copyright: 2011 Lorenz Educational Press, a Lorenz company, and its licensors.
All rights reserved.

Permission to photocopy the student activities in this book is hereby granted to one teacher as part of the purchase price. This permission may only be used to provide copies for this teacher's specific classroom setting. This permission may not be transferred, sold, or given to any additional or subsequent user of this product. Thank you for respecting copyright laws.

Printed in the United States of America

ISBN 978-1-4291-2255-9

**BRIDGING the Gaps in Education**™
Lorenz Educational Press
P.O. Box 802 • Dayton, OH 45401-0802

for other LEP products visit our website
www.LorenzEducationalPress.com

*All statistics are based on information from 2010.
*** For further information on pronunciations, research foreign language dictionaries and/or the Internet.

# Metric Conversions

The purpose of this page is to aid in the conversion of measurements in this book from the English system to the metric system. Note that the tables below show two types of ounces. Liquid ounces measure the volume of liquids and have therefore been converted into milliliters. Dry ounces measure weight and have been converted into grams. Because dry substances such as sugar and flour may have different densities, it is advisable to measure them according to weight rather than volume. The measurement unit of the cup has been reserved solely for liquid, or volume, conversions.

## Conversion Formulas

| when you know | formula | to find / when you know | formula | to find |
|---|---|---|---|---|
| teaspoons | × 5 | milliliters | × .20 | teaspoons |
| tablespoons | × 15 | milliliters | × .60 | tablespoons |
| fluid ounces | × 29.57 | milliliters | × .03 | fluid ounces |
| liquid cups | × 240 | milliliters | × .004 | liquid cups |
| U.S. gallons | × 3.78 | liters | × .26 | U.S. gallons |
| dry ounces | × 28.35 | grams | × .035 | dry ounces |
| inches | × 2.54 | centimeters | × .39 | inches |
| square inches | × 6.45 | square centimeters | × .15 | square inches |
| feet | × .30 | meters | × 3.28 | feet |
| square feet | × .09 | square meters | × 10.76 | square feet |
| yards | × .91 | meters | × 1.09 | yards |
| miles | × 1.61 | kilometers | × .62 | miles |
| square miles | × 2.59 | square kilometers | × .40 | square miles |
| Fahrenheit | (°F − 32) × $5/9$ | Celsius | (°C × $9/5$) + 32 | Fahrenheit |

**Equivalent Temperatures**
- 32°F = 0°C (water freezes)
- 212°F = 100°C (water boils)
- 350°F = 177°C
- 375°F = 191°C
- 400°F = 204°C
- 425°F = 218°C
- 450°F = 232°C

**Common Cooking Conversions**
- 1/2 cup = 120 milliliters
- 12 fluid ounces = 354.88 milliliters
- 1 quart (32 ounces) = 950 milliliters
- 1/2 gallon = 1.89 liters
- 1 Canadian gallon = 4.55 liters
- 8 dry ounces (1/2 pound) = 227 grams
- 16 dry ounces (1 pound) = 454 grams

# Table of Contents

| | |
|---|---|
| England | 4 |
| France | 27 |
| Germany | 50 |
| Iceland | 74 |
| Ireland | 86 |
| Italy | 107 |
| Spain | 126 |
| Sweden | 143 |
| Switzerland | 164 |
| Answer Key | 176 |
| Additional Resources | 178 |

# England

# Welcome to England!

For many centuries England has been one of the most influential and important countries of Europe. In spite of its relatively small size, England has produced many hardy explorers. These adventurers helped to create the world's largest empire, which stretched into many parts of the world. At home, English workers built the first industrial communities in Europe. England joins the smaller countries of Wales, Scotland, and Northern Ireland to form the United Kingdom of Great Britain.

**Official Name:** England

**Location:** Off the coast of Western Europe (northwest of France), between the Atlantic Ocean and the North Sea; England is an island that includes roughly one-sixth of north Ireland's land.

**Population:** 61,113,205 (2010 estimate)

**Capital City:** London

**Area:** 50,400 square miles; England is a little smaller than the state of Alabama.

**Major Language:** English. Many regions have their own dialects, which are frequently used to identify a person's background and social class.

**Major Religion:** Christianity: 71.6 %; though all religions are accepted, the Protestant Church of England has been the country's official religion since the 1500s.

**Currency:** The English unit of currency is the pound sterling (£), with 100 pence in one pound. Coins are minted in 1, 2, 5, 10, 20, and 50 pence and 1 pound pieces. Paper currency is printed in 5, 10, 20, and 50 pound notes, which are designed in different sizes and colors and etched with portraits of the queen or other famous historic figures. A pound is often called a "quid" in everyday conversation, much as the U.S. dollar is called a "buck." People often refer to their pound notes, such as tens or fives, as "tenners" or "fivers." The British pound is worth, on average, between 1.5 and 2 U.S. dollars.

**Climate:** Temperate, due to warm ocean currents and winds; more than half of the year's days are overcast.

**The Land:** England is characterized by rugged hills and low mountains, with flat and rolling plains in the east and southeast.

**Government:** A constitutional monarchy with a parliamentary government; Parliament consists of two chambers: the House of Lords and House of Commons.

| | | |
|---|---|---|
| **Flag:** |  | The Union flag, which combines the red cross of England's St. George, the Scottish diagonal blue and white cross of St. Andrew, and the Irish red diagonal cross of St. Patrick; when flown on an English ship it is often called the "Union Jack." |

**Royal Banner:** The banner contains the royal arms of England, three golden lions arranged vertically. The lions have blue tongues and claws, and are set against a deep red background.

**National Flower:** Rose

**Motto:** "God and my right"

## Natural Environment

England, one of the smallest countries of Europe, was once part of the mainland. At the end of the last Ice Age, temperatures warmed and ice began to melt. This caused flooding, which covered the shallow shelf that is now the North Sea to the east and the English Channel to the south. England, Scotland, and Wales became an island with a jagged coastline. No part of England is more than 70 miles from the coast. The Isle of Wight near the southern coast is the most important English offshore island. A strait called the Solent separates the island from the mainland.

The Straight of Dover became the scene of a historic rescue mission during World War II. Over 350,000 Allied soldiers were trapped in Dunkirk, a city on the French coast opposite Dover. Germany staged a massive air strike on the unprotected troops. The English, using all sorts of crafts—yachts, cruisers, row boats, destroyers, and gunboats—rushed to Dunkirk to evacuate the soldiers. Most of the troops were saved by the operation, which lasted three days and was later called "one of the best-ordered military movements in history."

England's lowland area covers the central, southern, and eastern parts of the country. Much of the soil has generous amounts of limestone and chalk. This chalk forms the famous White Cliffs of Dover. The western coast of the country extends to the tip of Cornwall and Land's End.

Much of the fertile land is used for farming and yields wheat, barley, oats, beets, and potato crops. The highland area includes the hills along the Welsh border, the Pennine mountain range to the north, and the beautiful "Lake District," which inspired the work of many poets and authors, such as William Wordsworth and Samuel Taylor Coleridge. Lake Windermere is the largest of the 16 lakes.

Industrial cities have developed near large coal and iron ore mines. England's rivers are the main industrial shipping routes that bring products to the coasts. The Thames and Severn rivers are the longest. Others are the Tyne, Tees, Avon, and Trent rivers.

The fishing industry off the east coast brings cod, haddock, herring and mackerel to the cities. Cockles, mussels, and other small fish are also sold from barrows in the cities.

Since the 1970s, oil and gas fields in the North Sea have helped England meet its own energy needs. Some of the country's electricity has been generated by nuclear power since 1988.

The many forests and wooded areas provide habitats for deer, otters, rabbits, songbirds, and the endangered owl. Fox hunting remains a royal pursuit. Cattle, sheep, pigs, and poultry are raised on the farms.

## UNESCO World Heritage Sites in England

England has a long list of UNESCO World Heritage Sites, which isn't surprising, given the country's long history. Stonehenge, a gathering of earthworks and standing stones that dates back thousands of years, is one such site. Other sites around the country include the Tower of London, the cities of Bath and Liverpool, and the ruins of Hadrian's Wall.

*Stonehenge*

## In Your Classroom

Show the students a large scale map of England. Point out the mountain ranges, forests, and rivers. Ask them to compare its size and location to the United States. For example, both of them are part of a larger land mass.

Using plaster of Paris, or a mixture of flour, water, and salt, help students make a relief map of England. Have students use the map to explain the importance of rivers in English commerce. Do England's largest cities have access to major water routes?

Ask students to research "Robin Hood," who lived in Sherwood Forest. Was he real? Was the story based on truth?

Locate the "White Cliffs" of Dover. Have students discover why they are white. Listen to or sing traditional songs related to England, such as "The White Cliffs of Dover."

Show students photos of English paper money or have real currency available. Ask them to design their own paper money. What color would they use? How much would it be worth? What picture would it feature—a family name, symbol, or local landmark?

Ask students to look up the terms "moor" or "heath." Read *Hound of the Baskervilles*, by Arthur Conan Doyle, or *Jane Eyre*, by Charlotte Brontë, both of which are set on a moor, or *King Lear*, by William Shakespeare, much of which takes place on a heath.

# A History of England

## Early History and Occupations

In prehistoric times, England was a country of thick forests, dank swamps, and barren land. Its earliest inhabitants were known as Beaker people because of their pottery skills. They crossed the sea from the Iberian Peninsula and North Africa and arrived about 3000 BCE Many centuries later, tribes of Celts came from central Europe. "Stonehenge," a mass of gigantic stones set in a circle, dates from 1500 BCE and was likely used for religious ceremonies.

When the Romans arrived, Boudicca, the female leader of the Celts, unsuccessfully tried to drive them out. Hadrian was the Roman ruler from CE 117— 38. As a defense from Northern tribes he built Hadrian's Wall, which stretched across northern England from the Solway Firth to the Tyne River. Its length was about 75 miles.

The Romans brought Christianity and peace to the country. The monk Augustus became the first Archbishop of Canterbury. When the Romans returned home to protect their own country in CE 400, Germanic tribes—Angles, Saxons, and Jutes—invaded and settled. Alfred the Great, the Anglo-Saxon king from CE 871–899, had the monks draw up a code of written laws.

Viking warriors began a series of attacks in later centuries. They conquered and settled every area but Wessex. Alfred drove them out, but they eventually returned. The Normans, in 1066, under William the Conqueror, invaded, conquered, and united England. William's religion, Catholicism, became widespread among the English.

## The Many Monarchs of England

Democratic ideals began to strengthen in the next centuries. In 1215 King John was forced to sign the Magna Carta (Great Charter), which promised certain rights to all free men. Under the rule of Henry III, Simon de Montfort formed a council which became Parliament. In the 1300s the country waged a series of battles with France, known as the Hundred Years War. As a result, England lost all of its land possessions in France except Calais.

Under Henry VI's reign in the 1400s the nobles divided into two groups: the House of Lancaster and the House of York. When Yorkist King Edward died in 1483, his brother, Richard of York, seized the throne. Henry Tudor unseated Richard in 1485, married Elizabeth of York to end the feud, and ruled until 1509.

His son Henry VIII succeeded to the throne. In the early 1500s Henry wished to divorce his wife, but could not under Roman Catholic laws. So he formed his own religion, the Church of England. He married six times, divorcing or even executing most of his wives. As a result, the country was divided between two religions, Catholic and Protestant.

During the reign of Henry's daughter, Elizabeth I, the country prospered. England's naval forces defeated the huge Spanish Armada, sent to conquer England in 1588. In 1625 Charles I became King. He ignored Parliament, raised taxes, and made life difficult for religious groups like the Puritans. Oliver Cromwell, a Puritan, led an army against Charles' forces in 1642 and defeated them. Cromwell became the Lord Protector of the Republic. After Cromwell died in 1658, the Republic fell apart.

England and Scotland had been ruled by the same monarchs for more than a century. But the two kingdoms quarreled over many issues. King William III planned to unite the two countries, but died before he accomplished it. However, Parliament passed the Act of Union in 1701, joining Scotland, England, and Wales under one kingdom—the United Kingdom of Great Britain.

## Expansion at Home and Abroad

In the 1700s England began to extend its territories, founding colonies in North America, India, Africa, Asia, Australia, and the Caribbean. The American Colonies were being heavily taxed, but were not allowed either a voice or vote in Parliament. The Americans rebelled and won their independence from England in 1781.

The Industrial Revolution of the mid-1700s changed England from an agricultural to a manufacturing country. The English developed a talent for machinery and built many factories. Cities grew around these bustling factories.

## A Time of Wars

Under the command of Napoleon Bonaparte, France began an expansion that threatened England's empire. However, in 1815 the British defeated the French army in the Battle of Waterloo. Queen Victoria, who was proper, serious, and pious, became monarch in 1837 when she was 18 years old, and ruled until she died in 1901. During the Victorian Age industry prospered, railroads developed, and literature flourished. In 1860 the two-party system began in Parliament with Benjamin Disraeli as the Conservative representative, and William Gladstone as the Liberal representative.

The Crimean War (1854-56) against Russia was waged during Victoria's reign. It was the first war in which newspaper reporters sent "on the scene" news by telegraph directly from the battlefield. Florence Nightingale reorganized the medical service during the conflict and achieved respect for nursing as a profession.

World War I broke out in 1914. England, France, Russia, the U.S., and other Allied forces defeated the Central Powers of Germany, Austria-Hungary, Bulgaria, and the Ottoman Empire. Twenty-five years later Adolf Hitler led Germany and other Axis countries into World War II against England and its Allies. In 1945 England and the Allied countries defeated Germany.

## After the Wars

Elizabeth II became Queen of England in 1952. Her husband, Prince Phillip, is also called the Duke of Edinburgh. The eldest of their four children is Prince Charles, heir to the throne. Members of the royalty participate at traditional and ceremonial functions and govern in conjunction with Parliament.

Many Prime Ministers throughout history have served their monarchs and country well. Among the most recent are: Sir Winston Churchill, a brilliant military strategist who served during World War II; Margaret Thatcher, the first female Prime Minister; John Majors, who worked closely with President George H. Bush during the Gulf War; Tony Blair, whose term coincided with America's War on Terror; Gordon Brown, who reformed England's financial policies; and David Cameron, who took office in 2010.

## Modern England

In 1993 England joined the European Union (EU). Their alliance with the EU is still very controversial. Many English people feel that people from other parts of Europe are taking their jobs away from them. However, being a member of the EU benefits English citizens as well. Most countries in the EU use the Euro as currency, while England still operates on the pound.

England continues to be a major player in the world-at-large. The country took part in the liberation of Kuwait in the early nineties. In 1997, Diana, Princess of Wales, was killed in an automobile accident. An extremely popular public figure, her death was a somber event around the world.

The early 21st century presented England with challenges. Global economic conditions worsened, and England worked internally (and externally) to improve the situation. After the tragic events of September 11, 2001, England became a major supporter of United States military involvement in the Middle East. In 2005, terrorists detonated bombs on London's transportation system, killing 52.

England continues to play a major role in the European Union, working for the betterment of all its member states. Coupled with their involvement in global affairs, England's contributions to the world are numerous. England has been an important country for thousands of years, a fact that isn't likely to change in the future.

## In Your Classroom

Divide the class into thirds. Have each group choose a prominent historical figure to research. Have them contrast their lifestyles with our modern way of life. Examples: How did they dress? What did they eat? What did they do for entertainment? Have them draw a mural of a typical day.

Have students research knights. How did a young squire become a knight? What weapons did knights use in a joust? Have them describe a tournament.

Ask students to discover more about Parliament. Have them follow a day in the life of the Prime Minister. Discuss how he or she represents a certain party, but must work for the good of all. Candidates for the office belong either to the Conservative (Tory) Party, which generally represents the upper and middle classes, or the Labor Party, which works to solve the problems of the poorer class.

As a class project, have students build a medieval castle using blocks or other suitable materials. Assign groups to various steps, such as measuring the circumference to verify how thick the supporting walls must be to bear the height and weight of the structure. Have another group decide where the various chambers—dining hall, bedrooms—and staircases should fit into the structure. Discuss how certain features of castles were designed to protect those living inside.

Help students to research a day in the life of an English child who worked in a clothing factory or mill during the Industrial Revolution. Very young boys and even girls were pressed into work as chimney sweeps in the 1800s. *Oliver Twist*, by Charles Dickens, gives a picture of forced child labor.

# Daily Life

Everyday life for an English family is much the same as that of a Western family. The parents and children eat a simple breakfast before leaving for work and school. Adults living in London frequently ride the *tube*, or underground subway, to the city and their places of work. Children ride their bicycles or walk to school. Public transportation is often used when a child's school is far away. English motorists drive on the left-hand side of the street. The steering wheels in English cars are on the right-hand side of the vehicle.

After school and work, families eat a meal together, either at home or at a local pub. They may stop at a fish and chips shop for a take-out dinner. In the evening after homework, they might watch TV or listen to the news on the BBC (British Broadcast Company). On weekends families may go to a movie theater, a sporting event, or visit relatives. If the weather is nice, many head to the seaside for a short get-away.

## School

School is compulsory, but free for students between five and 16 years old. Children from five to 11 attend primary schools and those from 11 to 16 years old attend secondary schools. Exams and achievement tests are given at regular intervals.

Children under age five often attend private nursery schools, and older students may choose to attend private schools that charge tuition fees.

The school day starts at 9 AM and ends at 4 PM. There are three sessions: Autumn, Spring, and Summer, with a vacation from July to September. Although students only have about six weeks of summer holiday, they have nearly a month off at Christmas, and a week break to mark each half-term and end-of-term.

Children move at their own pace through the school work. Science, English, art and drawing, and physical education are part of the regular curriculum. By the time they are 16, students should have some idea of their future careers.

After they are 16, some students continue in school for two more years to study for the university entrance. Government grants are open to all who need them because students are not allowed to work their way through college.

## Housing

Most of the English live in or near cities. Over 80% live in houses. The rest either rent or own apartments, which are called *flats*. In the suburbs are many attractive terrace houses, which combine the elements of a single dwelling and an apartment. Several families share a common wall; windows and doors face the front and back of the property. Many charming cottages, some hundreds of years old, have become new homes for families in the English countryside.

## Religion

The Church of England (also known as Anglican Church) has been the official church since the 1500s. The next largest is the Roman Catholic; other practiced religions include Methodist, Baptist, Congregational, Presbyterian, Quakers, Jewish, and Islam. Before the Reformation, England was Roman Catholic and under the jurisdiction of the pope. At the time of the Reformation of the 1500s, England left the Catholic Church and reformed as the Church of England. It is divided into two provinces, York and Canterbury, with 43 dioceses and 27,000,000 members. The reigning monarch appoints bishops and some clergy.

## Famous People from England

The Beatles, a music group from Liverpool, have been enormously popular since the 1960s. The band members (Paul McCartney, John Lennon, George Harrison, and Ringo Starr) are all well-known celebrities.

*The Beatles*

Sir Isaac Newton (1643-1727) was the inventor of modern physics, but he also worked in the fields of mathematics, astronomy, philosophy, alchemy, and theology. He also built the first reflecting telescope. Many of his theories and ideas are still widely used today. He is regarded as one of the most influential figures in world history.

David Beckham (1975-) is a football (soccer) star and global celebrity from England. Notorious for his bending corner kicks, Beckham holds the all-time appearance record for the England national team. He has captained several teams and led them to multiple championships. In 2007, Beckham announced that he would be leaving England to play professional soccer in America.

## In Your Classroom

Some students earn extra money by babysitting. In England many of the boys and girls deliver newspapers after school, following the same route each day. What other ways could the students earn money?

Ask students where they would like to spend their summer holiday if they were English students. Have them explain their choices.

Find a photograph or drawing of a terrace house. Have students draw a blueprint of one family's unit.

In London's Hyde Park, there is an open podium called Speaker's Corner where anyone who wishes may give a speech on any subject. Ask the students to think about a speech they would like to give.

# Language & Expressions

Here are some fun facts about verbal and nonverbal communication in England.

## English Proverbs and Sayings

Here are some English proverbs and sayings. What do you think they mean?

*Bob's your uncle.*

*Your eyes are bigger than your belly.*

*A stitch in time saves nine.*

*One man's meat is another man's poison.*

*The best advice is found on the pillow.*

*The cow that's first up is the cow that gets the dew.*

*A crown is no cure for the headache.*

*A good archer is not known by his arrows, but by his aim.*

## Body Language and Etiquette in England

Here are some examples of body language and etiquette in England.

*Queues, or lines, are common in England. If someone is there before you (at a street vendor, for instance), always let him or her go first.*

*When meeting someone for the first time, shake their right hand with your right hand.*

*Hugging and kissing is reserved for close friends and loved ones.*

*The English drink lots of tea. When sharing tea, you should not pour the tea right after it's done. Wait two or three minutes before pouring.*

*If you're eating peas, be sure to smash them with the reverse side of your fork before eating them.*

*Never eat off of your knife. This is considered impolite.*

*When invited to someone else's home, bring a small gift as thanks, like flowers or chocolates.*

*It is impolite for men to wear hats indoors in England.*

Name _____  Date _____

# The King's English

The English use many unique terms in everyday language. Learn some of these terms by matching each English term on the left to its translation on the right.

| | |
|---|---|
| BISCUIT | PANTS |
| BOBBY | BANDAGE |
| BOOT | FRENCH FRIES |
| CHEERS | COOKIE |
| CHIPS | YARD |
| TROUSERS | LINE |
| GARDEN | POLICE OFFICER |
| JUMPER | TRUCK |
| PLASTER | RAISINS |
| LIFT | GAS |
| LORRY | GOODBYE |
| PETROL | WRENCH |
| QUEUE | TRUNK |
| SPANNER | ELEVATOR |
| SULTANAS | SWEATER |

14                                                                 England - MP5129

# FOODS

England grows plenty of grains and fruit and raises cattle, sheep, and fowl. Fresh fish is available daily. Approximately eighty percent of England's food is produced locally. Other foods are traded from European countries. Grapes from Italy or cheeses from Holland or France are exchanged for English meats and other foods through the EEC (European Economic Community).

English school children generally eat a nourishing but light breakfast of cereal, milk, toast, fruit, and tea. Working people eat a large, hearty breakfast of sausage, bacon, mushrooms, tomatoes, beans, eggs, toast or fried bread, and tea.

Some English families serve their main meal at noon. Many students buy their lunches at school. The rest bring food from home—usually a sandwich, yogurt, fruit, potato chips, and milk. No candy is allowed in the lunch rooms.

On Sundays the whole family gathers for the noon meal, which is traditionally a joint of beef or lamb, roast potatoes with onions, and vegetables. Dessert is often pudding.

Afternoon tea, now an English tradition, was first served by the Duchess of Bedford in the 1840s. In addition to tea, scones with Devonshire cream, tiny cucumber sandwiches, crumpets (muffins), and strawberries are included. Most adults drink an average of five cups of tea during the day.

On Christmas the main dish is roast turkey, followed by the "Christmas pudding." This is a large steamed plum pudding with a sprig of holly on top and Christmas surprises hidden inside. Other traditional favorites are:

- *Stargazy pie*: tiny whole sardines, with their heads pointing up to the stars, line the rim of a pie plate. Breadcrumbs, milk, onion, and eggs, are poured into the plate and covered with pastry.
- *Bubble and Squeak*: fried potatoes with cabbage
- *Cottage pie*: beef covered with mashed potatoes
- *Toad-in-the-hole*: sausages baked in pancake batter

# Recipe: Yorkshire Batley Cake
## (also known as Courting Cake)

Plain breads, also known as cake, are English favorites. Here's a simple recipe simple enough for students to bake.

Ingredients:

    3/4 lb. plain flour
    3/4 oz. baking powder
    1/2 tbsp. salt
    6 oz. butter
    6 oz. sugar
    1 egg
    milk
    2 oz. jam (any flavor)
    1 beaten egg

Directions:

Sift the flour, baking powder, and salt; rub in the butter and add the sugar.

Mix with the egg and a small amount of milk.

Divide the batter in half and roll out into two round shapes each about 1/2 inch thick.

Spread jam on one round and top it with the other round. Pinch the sides together, brush the top with beaten egg.

Place round on a greased tray and bake for 30-40 minutes at 350° F.

# Holidays & Festivals

English holidays and festivals have ancient roots. Many of the celebrations have religious significance and are based on early rituals. Others mark historic events or the annual changes of seasons.

## Bank Holidays

Like many European countries, England celebrates several bank holidays per year, giving school children and workers an extra day off. All banks are closed on: New Year's Day, Good Friday, Easter Monday, Early May Bank Holiday, Spring Bank Holiday, Summer Bank Holiday, Christmas Day, and Boxing Day. Sometimes the government allows a special bank holiday in honor of a royal event, such as a birthday, wedding, or Queen Elizabeth's Golden Jubilee in 2002.

## Other Traditional Holidays

**Shrove Tuesday**
*The day before Lent begins*

The women who live in the town of Olney have an unusual contest. At noon they line up on one side of the town square. Each entrant has a frying pan holding one pancake. As they race across the square they try to flip the pancake three times before they reach the goal, the doors of Olney's Church.

**Mothering Sunday**
*Three weeks before Easter*

Children give gifts to their mothers.

**Holy Thursday**
*The Thursday before Easter*

The reigning English monarch distributes purses of money to show love for the poor.

**Easter Sunday**
*Two days after Good Friday*

In some towns, children go from house to house asking for treats. They try to get Easter eggs by singing, "Please give an egg or your hens will lay addled eggs and your cocks will lay stones." Good natured neighbors are always prepared with a supply of Easter eggs. Easter started from a pagan spring festival for the Anglo-Saxon goddess, Eostre. The Christian Easter celebrates Christ's resurrection.

**Guy Fawkes Day**
*November 5*

On November 5, 1605 Guy Fawkes led a group who tried to blow up King James I and Parliament to avenge its persecution of English Catholics. He stored barrels of gunpowder in a vault under the House of Lords and intended to ignite them as the King opened Parliament. An anonymous letter warned the government. Guy was captured and executed for his part in the plot. Today as a remembrance of the plot, neighborhood families build huge bonfires. Children swing a dummy of Guy back and forth and then throw it into the fire. Guy's "head" is a turnip, carved like a Halloween pumpkin and filled with firecrackers.

## Harvest Home Day
*Held at the conclusion of fall harvest*

At the end of the fall harvest families come to their church and lay sheaves of oats, pears, apples, and vegetables on the altar in thanksgiving for a successful harvest. There is no formal service, but some families kneel and say prayers of thanks.

## Christmas Day
*December 25*

Father Christmas visits homes early in the morning and leaves gifts. A special family dinner is served later in the day.

## Boxing Day
*December 26*

In wealthy families, servants were so busy cooking, serving dinner, and cleaning on Christmas Day that there was no special time for them. So on the day following Christmas, noblemen boxed gifts for their servants and distributed them in a simple ceremony of thanks. Gifts were also given to traders and minor public officials.

## Spring Festivals

Morris dancing is a type of ritual folk dancing usually performed on village greens or in a market square. It is accompanied by fiddle and accordion music. Other dances are performed year-round at local fairs and seasonal festivals.

Some celebrations of spring come from the simple child's game of Ring around the Rosy. Adults begin their celebrations by dancing around a tree. Later, a maypole is erected and decorated with flowers and ribbons for a May dance. Each dancer holds a long ribbon. Half of the dancers face right; the rest face left. As the music begins dancers weave their ribbons in and out as they dance around the maypole.

## In Your Classroom

Organize a Shrove Tuesday Pancake Race in the gymnasium or school yard. Divide the class into teams of about five and set *start* and *church door* marks. Use a stiff notebook and a plastic saucer for the skillet and pancake.

Compare England's Harvest Home Day to Thanksgiving Day. How are they similar? Different? What is the main idea behind both days?

Create a new holiday. Who or what would your new holiday honor? Would there be games or special food?

England - MP5129

# Creative Arts

## Music

England's earliest written music was for the Church, but secular music began to develop in the fifteenth century. Grand opera arrived far behind the performances in other European countries. Henry Purcell's opera *Dido and Aeneas* opened in 1689.

George Friedrich Handel, whose patron was King George I, composed operas and oratorios. The most popular were *Water Music* and *The Messiah*.

English audiences began to enjoy light opera in the 19th century. Sir William Gilbert and Sir Arthur Sullivan collaborated to produce fourteen exceptionally popular operettas in the late 1800s. *The Pirates of Penzance* was one of their most successful works.

In the early 1900s Benjamin Britten composed the opera *Peter Grimes*. In 1963 a group of young men from Liverpool, the Beatles, became pop stars almost overnight. In the later 1900s Andrew Lloyd Webber created several musicals, including *Jesus Christ Superstar*, *Cats*, and *The Phantom of the Opera*.

## Art

For almost 800 years, the major art studios of England were the monasteries. There the monks painstakingly copied texts of the Bible and *illuminated* them with elaborate and colorful painting. The *Lindisfarne Gospels* were completed in the sixth century. A later collection was the *Winchester Bible* with bolder figures and lettering. Religious painting faded when the Protestant Reformation began.

Portrait painting came into fashion during the reign of Queen Elizabeth I. Nicholas Hilliard created a miniature portrait of the Queen. King Charles I brought Anthony Van Dyke, a gifted portrait painter, from the European continent to England.

Thomas Gainsborough and Sir Joshua Reynolds were very successful portrait painters. William Hogarth portrayed action and drama in his work. George Stubbs became famous for his sports painting; much of his art featured horses.

In the Victorian era J. M. W. Turner and John Constable portrayed landscapes. Constable's work in particular was admired throughout Europe.

## Architecture

Early Roman missionaries first taught the English how to use materials at hand for building. They helped them build stone buildings. Many of England's lasting structures— cathedrals and castles—are still standing.

## Cathedrals

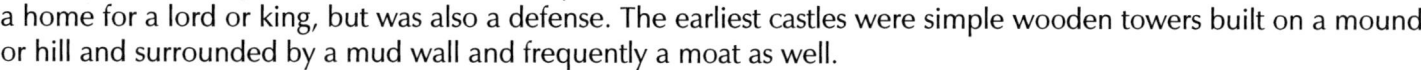
*Salisbury Cathedral*

England's stone cathedrals have beamed roofs, carved wooden choir stalls, stained glass windows, and wrought iron fixtures. Some of the most famous cathedrals are:

- *Canterbury Cathedral*: the historical center of the Church of England. It has distinctive round Norman arches.
- *Salisbury Cathedral*: has the highest spire in England, 404 feet (123m). It took 40 years to build.
- *Gloucester Cathedral*: a perpendicular Gothic structure
- *St. Paul's Cathedral*: a famous London landm

## Castles

In earlier days settlements and towns developed around monasteries. But by medieval days communities centered around castles and their lords. The word *castle* comes from a Latin noun meaning *fort*. A castle was not only a home for a lord or king, but was also a defense. The earliest castles were simple wooden towers built on a mound or hill and surrounded by a mud wall and frequently a moat as well.

Gradually, the wooden towers were replaced by larger stone structures and the walls were extended and strengthened. Additional buildings—a cook house, store rooms, stables, a church, and gatehouse—turned the castle grounds into a community.

William the Conqueror built the first castle at Dover soon after his 1066 defeat of the Saxons. Henry II expanded it in the late 1100s. Other interesting castles are Hurstmonceaux (hurst mon-sō) Castle in Sussex, the Stokesay Castle in Shropshire, and Windsor Castle, built as a royal castle in the eleventh century. It was rebuilt in the 1800s and is still the home of royalty.

In the countryside there are many handsome manor homes. The streets of Bath, a former spa for the wealthy, are lined with homes designed by 18th century architects. Other interesting structures are: Bank of England, which was founded in 1694 and has the same function as the U.S. Federal Reserve; Crystal Palace, a structure covering almost 20 acres, which housed the 1851 London Society's Exposition of Industry; the Tower of London, a group of buildings which served as an ancient fortress, a dark prison, and former royal residence; and Westminster Abbey in London, where most of the English rulers since William the Conquerer have been crowned.

Among the most influential architects: Christopher Wren, who rebuilt 50 churches after a London fire in 1616; Inigo Jones; and James Frazer Stirling, a modern designer.

## Literature

For over 1000 years English literature has been steadily developing and changing. No other country has equaled the quality and variety of English poetry, drama, novels, and essays. At times authors borrowed the form of a sonnet or novel, reshaped it, and invented new words and phrases. England has produced the largest range of modern literature.

The earliest of this work was developed from a mix of pagan Anglo-Saxon and Christian influences. Listed below is a selection of authors who represent each era.

| Author | Work | Category |
|---|---|---|
| **Anglo-Saxon** | | |
| Unknown | *Beowulf* | Epic poem |
| Bede | *Ecclesiastic History* | History |
| | | |
| **Middle English (1100-1299)** | | |
| Geoffrey Chaucer | *Canterbury Tales* | Verse |
| | | |
| **16th, 17th century** | | |
| William Shakespeare | *Hamlet* | Drama |
| John Bunyan | *Pilgrim's Progress* | Allegory |
| John Donne | "Death Be Not Proud" | Poetry |
| John Milton | *Paradise Lost* | Epic poem |
| | | |
| **18th century** | | |
| Daniel Defoe | *Robinson Crusoe* | Novel |
| Edward Gibbon | *Decline & Fall of the Roman Empire* | History |
| Samuel Johnson | *Dictionary of the English Language* | Lexicon |
| Henry Fielding | *Tom Jones* | Novel |
| Jonathan Swift | *Gulliver's Travels* | Novel |
| | | |
| **19th century—Early** | | |
| Lord Byron | "Childe Harold's Pilgrimage" | Poetry |
| Sir Walter Scott | *Waverley* | Hist. Romance |
| Jane Austen | *Pride and Prejudice* | Novel |
| William Wordsworth | "The Solitary Reaper" | Poetry |
| | | |
| **19th century—Late** | | |
| Charles Dickens | *Great Expectations* | Novel |
| George Eliot | *Middlemarch* | Novel |
| Emily Brontë | *Wuthering Heights* | Novel |
| Charlotte Brontë | *Jane Eyre* | Novel |
| Alfred, Lord Tennyson | "In Memoriam" | Poetry |
| Robert Louis Stevenson | *Treasure Island* | Adventure |
| | | |
| **20th century** | | |
| Agatha Christie | *Murder on the Orient Express* | Mystery |
| E. M. Forster | *A Room with a View* | Novel |
| George Orwell | *1984* | Novel |
| George Bernard Shaw | *Man and Superman* | Drama |
| Virginia Woolf | *To the Lighthouse* | Novel |
| D. H. Lawrence | *The Rainbow* | Novel |
| Evelyn Waugh | *A Handful of Dust* | Novel |
| J.R.R. Tolkein | *The Lord of the Rings* | Fantasy |
| C.S. Lewis | *The Chronicles of Narnia* | Fantasy |
| J.K. Rowling | The *Harry Potter* Series | Fantasy |

Name _____  Date _____

# Writer Write-Up

William Shakespeare; Charles Dickens; the Brontës – the list of great English writers is long and distinguished. Choose one of the writers from the list on page 21. Research their life and works and fill out the lines below.

**Writer**

_____

**Famous Works**

_____

_____

_____

**Biographical Information**

_____

_____

_____

_____

_____

_____

_____

_____

_____

_____

_____

_____

_____

_____

# Drama

Among the earliest known English dramas was *Everyman*, by an unknown sixteenth century playwright. Most of the early dramatic works in Elizabethan times were morality plays. Later works were greatly influenced by French and German dramatists.

Christopher Marlowe used blank verse, which he found worked well for dramatic expression. *Doctor Faustus* (c. 1588) was one of his early popular works.

William Shakespeare, poet, actor, theater manager, was perhaps the greatest playwright of all time. His tragedies, comedies, and histories continue to be performed by the Royal Shakespeare Company (RSC). *Hamlet* is one of his most powerful tragedies.

*William Shakespeare*

Ben Johnson wrote *masques* for the Court in the seventeenth century. In the late 1700s Oliver Goldsmith's *She Stoops to Conquer* and Richard Sheridan's *School for Scandal* charmed audiences.

In modern times George Bernard Shaw, Harold Pinter, Tom Stoppard, and Caryl Churchill have been among the most popular playwrights. The changes in subject and style continued to reflect the struggles, concerns, and joys of the audiences. The Royal Shakespearean Company tours the country and the National Theater performances are seen at Old Vic theater. The Royal Albert Hall also sponsors productions. Sir Lawrence Olivier, Sir John Gielgud, Noel Coward, and his wife Lynn Fontaine have been some of the bright lights on the English stage.

Much Like New York City's Broadway, London has its own theater district in the West End. Many famous musicals and other theatrical performances are held there. Additionally, Shakespeare's Globe Theatre was recently rebuilt on the south side of the Thames in London. The Globe was rebuilt near the spot of the original theater, and old-fashioned materials and building techniques were used to erect this great structure. In the spring, summer, and autumn, audiences come from all over the world to see Shakespeare's plays reenacted. The cheapest tickets are for spectators who wish to stand the in the center of the theater in front of the stage, just as the peasants did in Shakespearean times, while the nobility sat on cushions in the rounded stands.

Popular modern actors draw their own following. Among these are Ian McKellan, who has performed with both the Royal Shakespeare Company and the National Theater; also Alan Howard and Ben Kingsley.

## In Your Classroom

Play a recording of a lively Gilbert and Sullivan song. Ask students to compare it to Andrew Lloyd Webber's *Jesus Christ Superstar*. Ask students to name a favorite group of musicians. What type of music do they play, and how does their musical style compare to that of the Beatles?

Collect a variety of portraits, landscapes, and other paintings by English artists. Explain the different techniques used by various artists. Have students draw their own pictures, perhaps a modernistic version of a tree.

Divide the class into four groups. Have each group choose an era in literature. Ask them to report on the language and techniques used in that period or to choose an author and describe his or her work.

# Sports & Games

The English are enthusiastic sports fans and treat their athletes as national heroes. Young boys and girls practice their favorite sports with the hope of becoming perhaps a champion soccer goalie or a world-famous tennis star. There are many choices for fans and participants.

Association football is the most popular game in England, with over one and a half million players. Enthusiastic fans follow local games and the annual play-off competitions. Much like American baseball fans, young English fans collect cards of favorite football players. Association football has a long season—from August to the following May.

Rugby is similar to football. It was started at Rugby School in 1823 when a player picked up the soccer ball and ran with it. Unlike football, rugby players do not wear protective pads. The sport is extremely popular in many countries, particularly the Commonwealth nations such as Australia, New Zealand, South Africa, and of course England. It is gaining in popularity in America.

Cricket is also a very popular game. Its headquarters are at the Lord's Cricket Grounds in London, where the game has been played since 1814. The game, similar to American baseball, is played with two opposing teams using flat, wooden bats and a red leather ball. Wickets are the bases. The game is played against local and international teams. English teams play against Australian teams for an urn of ashes, which are supposedly from the bats that the English burned after their first defeat by Australia.

Some of the game's terms have been absorbed into daily language. When an action or term is offensive, it is described as *not cricket*. If things are getting difficult, it's a *sticky wicket*.

Tennis is a long-time favorite with players and spectators. The first Lawn Tennis Championship match was held at Wimbledon in 1877. Spectators at that first match numbered 200. Today Wimbledon seats over 10,000 fans and offers standing room for 3,500 more. Strawberries with cream are the special refreshment at Wimbledon. Members of the Royal Family have their own box and they award the prestigious Wimbledon trophies to the winners, who come from all over the world.

Polo has become more popular in recent years. It draws large crowds of spectators, who enjoy watching celebrities like Prince Charles play. The game requires several horses for each player, which makes it too expensive a game for the working class English person.

Horse racing and hunting with horses and hounds are exciting weekend activities. Other popular sports are lacrosse, field hockey, squash, rowing, car racing, and fishing.

# Recreation

## *Holidays (Vacations)*

During school vacations and three-day bank holidays many English choose to visit the beaches. Larger seaside resorts are at Blackpool, Bournemouth, Margate, and Brighton. There are lively, noisy carnivals, barrows filled with eels, cockles, piers, and bandstands. The pier becomes a grand promenade which stretches almost a mile out to sea. It is lined with arcades that sell water-wings, sand buckets, spades, and other beach items. At Brighton a favorite tourist attraction is its Royal Pavilion.

## *Gardening*

Gardening is recreation for many English men and women. For others it is a serious occupation which provides their families with vegetables, salads, and fruit for the dinner table. Nearly every English family, whether they live on a country farm, in a city home, or a tiny apartment, has a plot for growing vegetables or flowers. Roses are a particular favorite with nearly every gardener.

The most important date each year for the gardener is the annual May Chelsea Flower Show. It is sponsored by the Royal Horticulture Society and draws over 70,000 visitors and exhibitors for the five-day event.

# In Your Classroom

Ask students to describe how their family spends its summer holiday. Do they take a trip, or camp out, or visit a national park?

One English group, The Mudders, races sports cars down hills and across fields. How does this compare to other car races in the U.S.?

Discover several flowers that grow well in England. Plant window sill gardens in your classroom or have students plant them at home. Grow herbs in one and small flowers in another. Keep notes on the progress of the plants.

# Game – Pass the Parcel

This game is similar to musical chairs and is popular among English school children. It is often played at birthdays or other celebrations, but in this activity will be adapted for the classroom.

1. Wrap an item, such as a pencil case or other school supply, in newspaper or wrapping paper. Continue to wrap this package in layer after layer of paper until it is several times larger than it was originally.

2. Have the students sit in a circle.

3. Like you would in musical chairs, play a song from a CD or radio while the students are passing the parcel (recommendation: have an English folk song, etc. on the CD)

4. Stop the song at random. The student who is holding the package when the music stops must unwrap a layer of paper.

5. This continues until the last layer is unwrapped. This person is the winner and gets to keep the prize.

# France

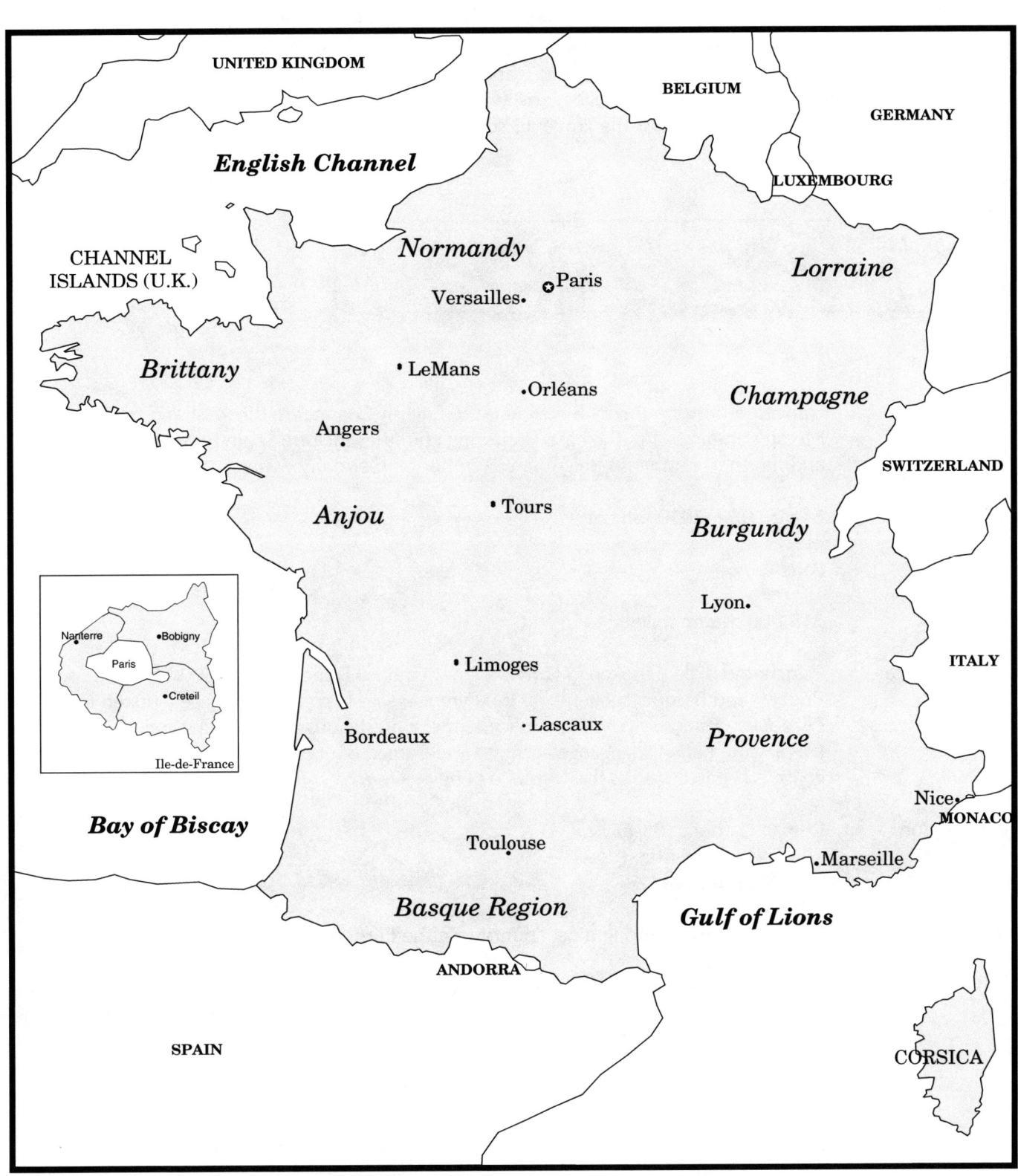

# Welcome to France!

France is the largest country in western Europe. In both manufacturing and trade, France is a world leader. Citizens are guaranteed free national health care and education. Population shifts from northern Africa and eastern Europe continue to affect French society and economy. Currently, France exports food and energy, as well as agricultural and manufactured goods, to countries in the European Union. France's culture and language have influenced the world for centuries. The natural beauty and richness of France is famous throughout the world. Tourism enhances the economy as people come to marvel at art collections, wander through towns of ancient to very modern architecture, indulge in fabulous meals, and view the gorgeous scenery.

## FAST FACTS

**Official Name:** France

**Location:** France borders the Bay of Biscay and the English Channel to the west and the Mediterranean Sea to the east. Bordering countries include Spain to the southwest; and (north to northeast) Belgium, Luxembourg, Germany, Switzerland, and Italy.

**Population:** 64,420,073 (2010 estimate)

**Capital City:** Paris

**Area:** 213,000 square miles

**Major Language:** French; the dialect spoken in Paris became standard French in the 1500s. Breton, spoken in Brittany, and Basque, spoken near the Pyrenees, are two other languages spoken in France. *L'Académie Française* (The French Academy), a prestigious academic institution, is in charge of keeping the national language accurate and purged of non–French words. The French language is highly prized as the "essence of being French."

**Major Religion:** Roman Catholic: 83-88%
　　Islam: 5-10%
　　Protestant: 2%

**Currency:** Euro; the euro is used in most countries in the European Union.

**Climate:** Most of France experiences moderately warm summers and mild, cool winters, with mild precipitation all year. In the south of France by the Mediterranean Sea, however, summers are hot and dry. The famous mistral winds— winds that blow across France from the Atlantic—blow cold and strong in the winter. On the Atlantic side, the weather is milder with much rain. Inland, the climate changes with the seasons.

**The Land:** Mediterranean areas, Pyrenees Mountains near Spain, Alps and Jura mountains near Switzerland, Central Highlands, Aquitanian Lowlands, Rhine River Valley and Vosges Mountains near Germany, Northeast Plateau near Belgium, northern plains, Brittany–Normandy Hills near the Atlantic coast, and Corsica, an island near Italy.

**Type of Government**: French Republic

**Flag**:

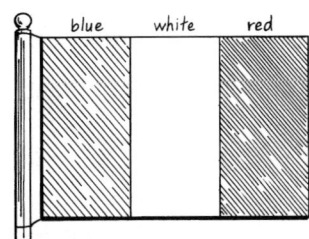

*Le Tricolore*, the French flag, is composed of three vertical panels of blue, white, and red. The flag originates from the French Revolution.

**National Flower**: Lily

**National Tree**: Yew

**Motto**: "Liberty, equality, fraternity"

## Natural Environment

In France, an amazing 90 percent of the land is fertile! The abundant and diverse plants and animals thriving on the land are important to French culture. Each region of France has food specialties harvested from the land. In Brittany and Normandy, apple ciders and cheeses are produced. Seafood is harvested from the North Atlantic and from the Mediterranean. Beef, poultry, pork, veal, and lamb are all raised carefully to suit the French palate; they are perfectly matched with fruits and vegetables grown in the Loire Valley. Farmers all over France take their work very seriously in this land where good and fresh food is considered vital. They grow enough to fill the nation's market baskets.

### *Plants and Animals*

Grape vines, mainly in the south and southeast of France, produce world-famous wines. Each region has its own special grapes and wines. Some famous wine regions are Bordeaux, Loire, Anjou, Burgundy, and Champagne. Wine is drunk with meals and is considered part of eating well. It is a vital part of France's economy and culture.

In the south of France, jasmine, geraniums, violets, roses, and bitter orange trees contribute to the ancient perfume industry. They create lavish fields of color. Herbs flourish with the flowers and are used to season foods. Herbs are essential in French cooking. They are inexpensive, interesting, and delicious. Some herbs important to the French are listed below:

ROSEMARY is a spiky small green bush with pale purple flowers. It is used to season lamb, is tasty in teas, and invigorating in baths. Put twigs in your hair, and you will remember important facts: rosemary is called the herb of remembrance.

TARRAGON has soft, green, thin leaves on a winding bush. It is delicious with fish and chicken. The French call it *Esdragon,* which means *little dragon,* because the roots of tarragon can take over a garden and the curly leaves look like escaping coils of smoke and fire.

LAVENDER is a tall, thin, flowering plant. Its purple flowers are used to scent soaps, perfumes, and sachets. Its smell and color are considered typical of southern France.

MINT includes spearmint, peppermint, lemon mint, and other varieties. It is fast-growing and useful to flavor drinks and sweets, to ward off mice, to soothe upset stomachs, and to keep rooms fresh smelling. Mint has been used for centuries in France.

ROSES, queens of flowers, are essential to the French perfume industry. Acres of petals are used to create tiny vials of scent. Roses have inspired stories like *Beauty and the Beast* and *Sleeping Beauty*. Rose hips are useful for making soothing teas.

Cookbooks and interior decoration books, ancient and contemporary, illustrate how important herbs are in French living.

Animals, birds, reptiles, and amphibians are admired all over France, and the French are famous for making all animals delicious to eat. Little creatures of the woods are cherished. *Hérisson* (hedgehog), *lapins* (rabbits), *grenouilles* (gren-oo-ee; frogs), and *escargots* (ess-car-gō; snails) are admired in sauces, as well as in stories. Turtle soup is a delicacy. Many kinds of birds live in France, too. The seacoasts and rich countryside provide good food and nesting places for the birds. The *merles* (blackbirds) sing sweetly as do nightingales and doves. Pheasants, geese, duck, chicken, and now, turkey are main agricultural products for the French market. Animals living all over France have found their way to the French dinner plate.

Additionally, as in all countries, animals are kept in the home as pets. In France, dogs outnumber cats as favorites. *Liberté, égalité, et fraternité* (Liberty, equality, and fraternity) is truly a revolutionary slogan—it seems to apply even to dogs! Dogs peek out of shopping baskets; dogs walk into stores; dogs sit patiently at sidewalk cafés. They follow their humans everywhere and are a part of the community. The French poodle comes in all sizes from miniature to giant. In France, animals are everywhere—in meals, in art, with families, in small apartments, at parks, in puppet shows, on sidewalks, and in the wild.

## UNESCO World Heritage Sites in France

France has a wealth of World Heritage Sites, including the capital city of Paris. Many cathedrals are on the list: Chartres, Amiens, and Bourges are just a few. Other well-known sites include the Palace of Versailles (home to the French royal families before the Revolution), Lyon, and Bordeaux.

**In Your Classroom**

Make a sachet. Simple sachets can be made using paper washing cloths, a stapler, and a variety of dried herbs and flowers. Have each student fold one paper washing cloth in half. The student should then fold the sides in and staple them closed to make a pocket. Students can select dried rose petals, rosemary leaves, mint leaves, or lavender flowers to put inside the pocket. (You may want to purchase these fresh and dry them in the classroom.) Then they can staple the top of the bag closed. Sachets can be placed in a clothes drawer or under a pillow. *Bonne nuit!* Good night! Sleep sweetly!

Plant a mint garden. Bring in mint cuttings and allow students to place them in water until roots grow. They can then plant the cuttings in pots or in a garden. They will love to watch the mint thrive! Pick leaves to steep for tea, to rub on a table for a fresh smell, or to dip in sugar syrup for elegant cake decorations.

Have students write and illustrate a story about a pet, real or imagined. They can include the French words for dog (*le chien*), cat (*le chat*), bird (*l'oiseau*), or fish (*le poisson*).

Name _____  Date _____

# Visitez la France! (Visit France!)

Try your hand at being a travel agent. In the space below, design a poster inviting people to visit France. Include a monument or feature (like the Eiffel Tower or Seine River) of the country in your poster.

# A History of France

France has a long, illustrious history which is a source of pride for the French people. History pervades the culture and its influence can be seen in France's architecture, urban planning, food, literature, and arts, as well as in its politics and economics. Although the old is highly respected, new ways and new styles are also admired.

## Early History

The area now known as France was settled over a period of centuries by many different peoples. The earliest settlers were the Gauls, a Celtic group who settled in the rich northern region. In later years, Norsemen (Vikings) raided in the north, most noticeably around Normandy, the northern coast of France. They occupied some areas and weakened the Gauls.

Led by Julius Caesar, the Romans defeated the Gauls (58 BCE -51 BCE) and added the territory to the Roman Empire. Roman law, Roman roads, and the Roman language of Latin formed the framework for much of modern France's infrastructure, judiciary system, and language. The popular modern cartoon character Asterix continues the "war" between Gauls and Romans.

After the collapse of the Roman Empire around 400 CE, barbaric Germanic tribes invaded Europe. The Franks inhabited the territory of France and gave France its name. In 486 CE, Clovis, King of the Franks, introduced Christianity to the region. He expanded France's territory and, after his death, his kingdom was divided among his three sons, as was the tradition.

In the 700s, the Moors from North Africa conquered Spain and attacked France, bringing Islam to southern Europe. Fighting in the name of Christianity, Charles the Hammer defeated these Arabs in the famous Battle of Tours, blocking their path through Europe. His son, Pepin the Short, became ruler in 751, and expanded the Frankish Kingdom. This was the beginning of the Carolingian Dynasty.

The most famous of all Frankish kings was Charlemagne (Charles the Great), son of Pepin the Short. He expanded France's borders to include most of western Europe, creating the largest empire since the Roman Empire. He was crowned Holy Roman Emperor by the pope in 800. During his reign, Charlemagne opened schools for clergy and teachers, set up regular courts whose judgments were based on common laws, improved farming techniques, and coined money. He gave large tracts of land to nobles, and in exchange, they supported him politically and militarily. The nobles also repaired and maintained bridges, roads, and defenses on their land. This type of arrangement is called *feudalism*.

During the Capetian Dynasty, which followed Charlemagne's death, the economy, as well as towns along major trade routes, began to thrive again. Craft workers joined together to form guilds and became a politically and economically powerful middle class in towns. Although some people moved to towns to look for jobs, the population remained largely rural. Agricultural techniques were too primitive to support a large population of non-agricultural workers. Slowly, France evolved from a loose union of powerful feudal states into a centralized monarchy. Norsemen again invaded France, and this time captured Normandy, as well as Anglo-Saxon England (1066). England was France's enemy, and now that the two were united, the stage was set for the intermittent battles of the 100 Years' War (1337-1453).

## The Growth of France

In 1328, Charles IV died without a male heir and the Capetian Dynasty ended. One of his cousins, Philip VI, took the throne, and thus began the Valois Dynasty. This dynasty endured the 100 Years' War, as France battled England to keep *fair France*. The saving grace for France was a young peasant girl who heard voices from God urging her to lead French soldiers against the English. With the armor, weapons, and horse given to her by a French prince, Joan of Arc drove the English out of France. When it was discovered she was female, Joan was captured and sold to England. The church burnt her at the stake as a witch. Despite this end, Joan of Arc became one of France's greatest heroes.

In the 1400s and 1500s, the Renaissance influenced and encouraged the creation of great art, literature, and architecture. France became a center for art, fashion, architecture, music, and theater. During this time, royalty, nobility, and the clergy gained immense wealth and power throughout France. However, civil war soon erupted. A well-educated German monk, Martin Luther, spoke out against the abuses of the Catholic Church. His ideas spread over Europe and ignited the Protestant Reformation. In France, Catholics and Protestants (known as Huguenots) fought bitterly, and again, France was war-torn.

Religious struggles continued until the leader of the Huguenots became King Henry IV, the King of France. Henry IV pledged to make France the greatest nation in Europe. He began by building new roads and bridges. His grandson, Louis XIV, known as the Sun King, continued his grandfather's vision of a great French nation. For royal glory, he had the largest and most elaborate palace in the world built in Versailles. He also established trading posts in India and North Africa to bring silks, spices, and exotic treasures to France, and he fought countries all over the globe for land. To support his extravagant ventures, he heavily taxed the common people who struggled to survive. They became increasingly dissatisfied.

## The French Revolution

*Napoleon Bonaparte, the greatest military genius of his time*

The 18th century brought revolutionary ideas and a bloody revolution. French thinkers, particularly *Les Philosophes,* inspired revolutionary thinkers in England's American Colonies. When the Colonies declared themselves to be an independent nation—the United States of America—a French general, the Marquis de LaFayette, went to help win their War of Independence. He then returned to France to aid his own people in their revolt against the upper classes.

In Paris, on July 14, 1789, angry mobs of the middle and lower classes stormed the Bastille, a royal prison, which was the beginning of the French Revolution. It was a Reign of Terror as the common people publicly beheaded tens of thousands of royalty, nobility, and clergy. The guillotine, an efficient beheading machine, became a tool for destroying the monarchy and building a democracy.

In 1799, Napoleon Bonaparte, a young general from Corsica, ended the Reign of Terror by taking control of France. By 1814, Napoleon had implemented a strong central government, a secular legal system, and an efficient military system in France. To build an empire, he conquered much of western and central Europe. Disastrous campaigns in Egypt and Russia, plus the growing power of France's neighbors led to his eventual downfall.

## Wartime in France

The 20th century brought the devastating invasions and battles of WWI and WWII to France. Both wars were heavily fought on French soil. The victorious French of WWI were quickly defeated in WWII by Germany. The Germans along with *des collaborateurs* (French citizens who sided with the Germans) governed France until the Allies freed Paris in 1944. General Charles de Gaulle successfully led *la Résistance* against the Germans and *les collaborateurs*.

After WWII, General de Gaulle became president of the French Republic and established France as an important force during the Cold War era. In the 1950s, the colonies in Indochina, which France had acquired a hundred years earlier, rebelled. Both Vietnam and Algeria fought for—and won—their independence. In spite of the damage caused by world wars and colonial struggles, France's economy continued to grow and the political system remained stable.

## Modern France

France is a leader in the European Union (European Common Market)—an organization created to remove barriers to the movement of goods, workers, capital, and services among members. The country has sought to improve EU unity, defense, and security. France continues to export goods to countries in the Union and around the world. Its main agricultural exports are fruits, grains, wines, cheeses, and perfumes. France also exports industrial products such as cars, nuclear power and machinery, and cultural products such as films, fashion, architecture, and literature. Current President Nicolas Sarkozy has worked hard to combat the global economic crisis of the early 21st century.

France's countryside, cityscapes, literature, art, and music are filled with images, memories, and artifacts from the grand history of the country. Throughout France, layers of history remind those in the present of the glory of France.

## In Your Classroom

Make a time line on shelving or computer paper. Mark important dates in French history with pictures and drawings.

Design posters describing French heroes like Charlemagne, Joan of Arc, the Sun King, the Marquis de LaFayette, Napoleon, and Charles de Gaulle.

Play Go Fish using superstars of French history. Divide the class into groups and have each group choose a superstar to study. After doing research, each group should write the four most important facts about the French superstar. Cut file folders into nine rectangles each, and have the class use them to create a set of Star Cards. They should write one fact on each card and illustrate it. Shuffle all of the cards and play Star Cards like Go Fish.

# Daily Life

## School

The typical day of a French child is heavily scheduled and includes several regular mealtimes. School, of course, dominates the week day. Schools meet daily, 9 AM-12 PM, then close for a lunch break from 12-2 PM. During this break, children can stay at school for lunch or return home to eat with their families. Either way, they eat a four- or five-course meal. Dismissal after lunch varies depending on the grade level. Wednesdays and Saturdays are half days. Wednesday afternoon is the time for extracurricular activities like soccer or gymnastics. Some schools still require uniforms, but in most schools, girls wear dresses and boys wear shorts. Children usually wear slippers or leather shoes inside the school. Sports shoes are expensive and are only used for outside games or organized sports. Younger children often wear smocks to protect their clothing. Children walk or ride public transportation to school. There is little parent involvement in the school room, and teacher–parent conferences are rare. Family and school have separate and equally important responsibilities so that the child will be properly educated to be a competent French adult.

The national education system, headed by *le Ministre de l'Éducation,* designs curriculum, educates teachers, and handles school finances all over France. In addition to public schools, there are many private and religious schools. From age two through 18, education is free. Children attend *l'école maternelle* (elementary school) from ages six through 12, then they attend *le collège* (middle school) and later *le lyceé* (high school). Students choose either a vocational or pre–baccalaureat (college preparatory) high school. The *bac* is so difficult to earn that often only two-thirds of students taking the final examination for the degree pass. There are over 75 public universities in France, plus many more private ones. The *Sorbonne* in Paris has been the seat of French intellectual thought since it was founded in 1253. Today it is well regarded throughout the world. The big schools are even more selective than other universities. The educational system in France is standardized with the express goal of preparing competent and highly literate citizens for France. As members of the European Union, French people are valued as well-educated employees.

## Family Life

*Les grandes vacances,* or vacation time, offers French children and their families time to explore their beautiful country, as well as to travel to other places. Schools close for several two- to three-week blocks in fall, winter, and spring. Adults are allowed five weeks a year paid holiday plus time off for national holidays like Bastille Day. Families often go away from home for a month at a time, especially during the summer. Summer vacation is spent at the beach, in the mountains, in the country, or travelling throughout Europe. Second and third foreign languages are encouraged at French schools and children use the languages regularly.

French families are very close and spend a lot of time together. Children are considered to be an important part of the extended and nuclear family. Families eat together daily, and on weekends, big meals provide the center of activity for the extended family. On a typical Sunday, families shop for and prepare a full meal. Meals can last three hours or more. The meal begins with an *apéritif* and *hors-d'oeuvre* (or-derv; pre-dinner drink and appetizer). Then the *entrée* (main course) is served, followed by the *plat principal* (meat or fish course). Next comes the *salade* (salad course), *fromage* (cheese course), *dessert* (pastry or fruit course), and *digestif* (after-dinner drink). After the meal, the family goes out for a walk in the park, around the local castle, or just in the neighborhood. Later, the whole family watches TV or videos, or plays video games. Holidays mean even more cooking and eating and celebrating with family.

## Urban France

Most French people live in cities and towns. Few still live on farms. Appliances and room space are small and energy efficient. The French can choose ultra-modern or quite ancient houses or apartments. People are less transient in France than in the United States. Rural roots are important, and many families return to the countryside for the holidays. Paris remains the hub of the country, as it has been for centuries, but each city and village maintains its character and a reputation that is proudly shown.

The transportation system is swift and efficient. The TGV *(Train à Grande Vitesse)*—a very high speed train which connects different parts of France—is the world's fastest train. It rides so smoothly that while riding it one can read, nap, and even write without a problem. Buses, cars, and bicycles share the roads. The *Métro*, or subway, makes moving around Paris quick and cheap. Parking is not easy to find anywhere in France because many narrow streets remain from the days before automobiles. On rivers and canals, barges still move slowly, carrying vacationers or cargo. At ports like Marseille, ships bring in huge loads of imported raw materials. Fishing villages on each coast are filled with luxury boats, as well as working boats. Now that the Chunnel—a tunnel that crosses under the English Channel—is open, people can travel by bus or car between France and the United Kingdom. There is also a train that runs through the Chunnel, making it possible to travel between Paris and London in just over two hours! Walking remains a constant means of transportation in France for both work and pleasure.

## Famous People from France

*Joan of Arc, Maid of Orléans*

Joan of Arc (1412-1431) was born a peasant in eastern France. After witnessing divine visions, Joan joined the French army and led it to many victories during the Hundred Years' War. She was captured, tried (for heresy), and executed by the English at the age of 19. She was later declared innocent, and was made a saint by the Catholic Church. She is considered one of France's national heroes.

Claude Monet (1840-1926) is one of history's great artists, and the founder of French Impressionism. He produced a great amount of art during his life, including icons like *Impression, Sunrise* and *Water Lilies*. His paintings continue to be popular – *Water Lilies* recently sold for more than 70 million dollars!

Claude-Achille Debussy (1862-1918) was a renowned composer. His works include the three *Nocturnes*, twelve *Préludes*, and two *Études*. In 1903, he was made *Chevalier de la Légion d'honneur* (Knight of the Legion of Honor), France's highest honor.

Napoléon Bonaparte (1769-1821) was a military and political figure, eventually made Emperor of the French in 1804. He achieved the position after staging a coup in 1799, seizing control of France. He expanded French territory through military campaigns across Europe, but was eventually defeated and exiled in 1814. He managed to escape exile and recapture control of France. He was defeated again in 1815 at the Battle of Waterloo, and spent the remainder of his life in captivity.

Louis Braille (1809-1852), blinded at the age of three, was the inventor of Braille, a system of reading and writing by touch. It is still used today, and has been adapted to nearly every language. Braille was also an intellectual and a musician, playing the cello and organ across France.

Gerard Depardieu (1948-) is a well-respected French actor. He has been nominated for and won multiple awards, including César, Golden Globe, and Academy Awards. Some of his films include *Cyrano de Bergerac*, *The Last Metro*, and *Green Card*. He also co-owns a successful winery in France.

# Language & Expressions

French is spoken worldwide by millions of people. It has been an international language of diplomacy for centuries. Former French colonies in Africa and Asia continue to speak French, as do French Canadians and some Swiss. In Europe and the Americas, many people speak French as a second language. In France, citizens are dedicated to their own language. The French Academy is an organization of intellectuals that exists to keep the language pure and correct. Although they discourage people from using English words, several favorites such as *le week end*, *le pique-nique*, and *le homework* are used. French language study is the core of the school's curriculum. Throughout France, it is considered very important to speak, write, and read French properly, elegantly, and articulately. Politeness is important in language, as well as in manners. Using *madame* or *monsieur* in saying hello, answering a question, or making a request is considered proper. Foreigners are often chagrined when their French is corrected by bus conductors, bread sellers, and friends. Speaking well is considered the mark of a French person.

French is a phonetic language structured much like English. The alphabet is the same although pronounced differently. Nouns have gender, indicated by the masculine *le* and the feminine *la*, and adjectives and possessives reflect the gender. Most verbs follow regular conjugations. French is based on Latin. Some say it is only Latin spoken with the prevalent French cold stopping up the nose and resulting in a twang!

French pronunciation is fun and easy!

| | | |
|---|---|---|
| **a** is like fAther | **è** or **ê** is like sEt | **é** is like the A in cAke |
| **o** is like mOth | **i** is like E in Eat | **oi** is pronounced WA |
| **au** or **eaux** is like O in Open | **r** should be rolled | **qu** sounds like a K |
| **ç** is soft as in Cider | **ch** is like sh | |

A final **e** is silent. Final consonants are also silent, except for a final **c**, **r**, **f**, or **l**.
(Remember the consonants of CaReFuL!)

## Common Words

| | | | |
|---|---|---|---|
| *les enfants* | children | *le chat* | cat |
| *le garçon* | boy | *la table* | table |
| *la fille* | girl | *la chaise* | chair |
| *l'ami* | friend who is a boy | *le crayon* | pencil |
| *l'amie* | friend who is a girl | *la cantíne* | cafeteria |
| *le père* | father | *la sale de classe* | classroom |
| *la mère* | mother | *l'ordinateur* | computer |
| *la soeur* | sister | *la maîtresse* | teacher |
| *le frère* | brother | *le professeur* | teacher |
| *le bébé* | baby | *l'école* | school |
| *le chien* | dog | *la toilette* or *W.C.* | bathroom |

## Numbers

| | | | |
|---|---|---|---|
| *un* | 1 | *six* | 6 |
| *deux* | 2 | *sept* | 7 |
| *trios* | 3 | *huit* | 8 |
| *quatre* | 4 | *neuf* | 9 |
| *cinq* | 5 | *dix* | 10 |

## Colors

| | |
|---|---|
| *rouge* | red |
| *bleu* or *bleue* | blue |
| *vert* or *verte* | green |
| *jaune* | yellow |
| *noir* or *noire* | black |
| *blanc* or *blanche* | white |

## Famous French Proverbs

Here are some famous French proverbs. What do you think they mean?

*To a valiant heart, nothing is impossible.*

*The tree often hides the forest.*

*Other times, other customs.*

*With ifs and buts, one would put Paris in a bottle.*

*It's the empty barrels that make the most noise.*

*Hit the iron while it is hot.*

*One shouldn't put the finger between the tree and bark.*

*You need to break the shell to have the almond.*

## Body Language and Etiquette in France

Here are some examples of body language and etiquette you'll find in France.

*If possible, don't introduce yourself to a stranger in France. The French prefer a third party to introduce new people to them.*

*When leaving, do not wave – this is considered impolite. Shake hands instead.*

*You should 'air kiss' a friend – first, on the left; then on the right.*

*The French are comfortable standing close to one another.*

When shopping in France, do not touch fruits of vegetables unless you intend to buy them.

Always hold your fork in the left hand and your knife in the right hand.

Don't place eating utensils on your plate until you're finished eating – this is a signal to remove your dishes.

'Small talk' on a bus or train is not encouraged in France. Passengers keep mostly to themselves.

## Know before You Go

Here are some common phrases you'll use in France. Refer to the pronunciation guide on page 38 for help.

### Expressions

| | |
|---|---|
| *Bonjour, Madame / Monsieur* | Hello |
| *Au revoir, Madame / Monsieur* | Good–bye |
| *Merci* | Thank you |
| *S'il vous plait* | Please |
| *Comment vous appellez–vous?* | What is your name? |
| *Je m'appelle ____.* | My name is ____. |
| *Quel âge avez–vous?* | How old are you? |
| *J'ai ____ ans.* | I am ____ years old. |
| *C'est magnifique!* | It's magnificent! |
| *C'est dommage* | Too bad |

# FOODS

Food in France is *magnifique* (magnificent). The taste and appearance of food and the act of eating are both very important to the French. Purchasing food can be as elaborate a process as the preparation of the meal itself. In big cities and in small villages, outdoor markets are held weekly. Local farmers bring cheese, pâté, fresh meat, sausages, fruits, vegetables, shell fish, and fresh breads from their farms in the countryside. At these *marché*, one can wander the town square munching on fresh bread and cheese. Throughout the week, the French shop daily at local specialty shops for the freshest produce: *la boucherie* (butcher shop), *la boulangerie* (bakery), *le marchand de légumes* (green grocer) *la poissonnerie* (fishmonger), *la charcuterie* (delicatessen) and *la patisserie* (pastry shop). Shopping is also a social activity during which patrons and merchants can share local news. Only recently have large supermarkets opened in France. These *supermarchés* are not likely to become as popular as the traditional specialty shops. A market basket or string bag is an attractive necessity for regular shopping duties. Children bring home the bread for lunch or pick up a fancy cake for the Sunday meal. Meals involve everyone in the shopping, preparing, and of course, eating.

Mealtimes in France are not taken lightly. The day begins with breakfast—*le petit déjeuner*. Children usually have a large cup of cocoa in which to dip their morning baguette. They may eat cereal and toast, and drink orange juice. The bread for the meal is usually picked up from the bakery in the morning. After breakfast, children leave for school. About 10:00 AM, they stop for a *goûter*, literally a *taste* or snack. They might eat cookies, fruit, small sandwiches, or a chocolate bar before going back to work. At noon, many children go home for lunch. *Le déjeuner* is a family meal which begins with soup, continues with a meat or fish dish, and finishes with a dessert. After the meal, children return to school. Along with many adults across the nation, they stop their work between 3:30 and 4:30 PM for another snack. Chocolate-filled pastries (*pain au chocolat*), a piece of fruit, or a big chunk of baguette satisfies until dinner. On their way home, children may purchase the evening's bread. Later in the evening, the family gathers for *dîner*, often a light meal in three courses. Before going to bed, children enjoy one more snack of bread, fruit, or chocolate.

## In Your Classroom

Set up a market. Make signs for French specialty stores: *boucherie, pâtisserie, boulangerie, charcuterie, poissonnerie,* and *marchand de légumes*. Students can then go shopping and practice math using some simple French sentences.

| | |
|---|---|
| *Combien de francs pour_____?* | How much money for____? |
| *Merci, madame/monsieur.* | Thank you, madame/sir. |
| *Au revoir, madame/monsieur.* | Goodbye, madame/sir. |

# Recipes – Sample French Food

Simple French recipes will extend students' taste of France! You may want to research some of the many excellent French cookbooks available for popular *ragouts*, *quiches*, and *potages*. Bring in a collection of cookbooks for your Explore France! area. Students will notice how decorative the dishes are. Assist students in converting recipes to the English system. Plan an outdoor picnic or formal dinner, complete with hand–lettered menus, to celebrate your flair for fabulous French foods. *Bon appétit!* Eat well!

### Baguettes
Purchase long sourdough loaves or make your own from frozen breads. Serve hot. You may want to include toppings such as cheese, butter, or jam.

### Les Fromages (Cheeses)
France is famous for its cheeses. Some say there is a different cheese for each day of the year, but there are probably more than 365 kinds of cheese available in France. Purchase a variety of cheeses to sample in the classroom. You may want to look for *chèvre* (goat's cheese), *Camembert* and *Brie* (round creamy cheeses), and blue cheeses (in varying degrees of pungency). Hard cheeses, soft cheeses, sweet cheeses, and salty cheeses are all part of daily life in France. All these cheeses go very well with the national treasure of French bread.

### Crêpes
Prepare a thin pancake batter. Cook in a crêpe pan. Flip and roll with jelly, butter, or powdered sugar. An easy favorite!

### Langues de Chats (Cat's Tongues)
Cream together 1/2 cup butter with 1/2 cup white sugar. Add 1 egg, 1/2 teaspoon vanilla or almond extract, or lemon rind. Beat in 3/4 cup flour into mixture. Drop cookies onto a greased cookie sheet and bake at 375°F for about 6 minutes. These delicate buttery cookies will have slightly browned edges.

### Meringues
Separate 5 egg whites and beat until frothy. Add a pinch of cream of tartar (optional) and 1/2 teaspoon almond or vanilla extract. Slowly add about l cup sugar until the batter is stiff and shiny. (Depending on the humidity, more or less sugar is required to make the egg whites stiff. Use less rather than more.) Add food coloring or sugar sprinkles. Drop into little mounds on an ungreased cookie sheet. Bake at 250°F for about an hour. Serve *á la mode* (with ice cream or fruit) or eat plain. Enjoy these elegant, inexpensive, and fun French treats!

### Tarte aux Pommes (Apple Tarts)
Prepare a crust by creaming 3/4 cup butter with 1/3 cup sugar. Add 1 egg, 2 cups flour, and 1/2 teaspoon salt. Press dough into a pie pan. Chill for several hours. Peel and slice 10 apples. Sprinkle with sugar and lemon juice. Arrange apple slices in circles in the crust. Bake at 350°F until apples are slightly soft and crust is golden brown.

### Galette des Rois (Cake of Kings)
Double the recipe for Cat's Tongues and bake 2 large pie–shaped cookies. Cool. Spread one cookie with sweetened almond paste. Tuck a *fève* (tiny porcelain figure, raisin, or bean) somewhere in the paste. Then place the second cookie on top of the first. Cut and serve. Whoever gets the *fève* should be crowned king or queen of the party.

### Pain au Chocolat (Bread with Chocolate)
Buy croissants, fresh or frozen. Insert chocolate chips, and heat until chocolate is melted. Or take a baguette, and spread melted chocolate on it. Enjoy as a snack!

# Holidays & Festivals

In France, festivals give families and communities the opportunity to celebrate historic events, and religious and cultural traditions. Elaborate foods and decorations are prepared, and traditional games are played.

### Feast of the Epiphany
*January 6*

This day is a Christian holiday celebrating the arrival of the Three Wise Men to Bethlehem to visit the infant Jesus. *La Galette des Rois* (The Cake of Kings) is eaten and *Tirez le Roi!* (Grab the King!) is played. Epiphany continues the feasting of Christmas. People eat sweets and exchange gifts.

### Mardi Gras (Fat Tuesday)
*February or March*

This holiday traditionally heralded the Christian fasting season of Lent. The French make crêpes and cakes to deliciously and usefully finish up the flour, butter, eggs and other fat ingredients in the house. People dress in elaborate costumes, wear masks, and parade through the streets.

### Poisson d'Avril (April Fish Day)
*April 1*

This is a fun festival like April Fool's Day. On this day, the French must beware of silly announcements in the newspapers, on TV, or from friends. People eat chocolates shaped like fish.

### May Day
*May 1*

This is a special day that traditionally honors Mary, mother of Jesus. Children sell or give lily of the valley flowers to others. Many people eat chocolates, cakes, and cookies shaped like lilies of the valley.

### Bastille Day
*July 14*

July 14 celebrates the fall of the Bastille in 1789, which began the French Revolution. It is a day when the French glory in the past, fly the flag, sing the national anthem, shoot fireworks, and march in parades.

### Saint Nicholas' Eve
*December 5*

During the night, small presents and candies are sometimes left for good boys and girls by Saint Nicholas, the patron saint of children.

**Noël (Christmas)**
*December 25*

December 25 is a Christian holiday. On December 24, Christmas Eve, the French solemnly commemorate the birth of Jesus by going to church for a Midnight Mass. Late in the night, adults share a feast. While children sleep, *Père Noël* (Father Christmas) visits and brings toys and presents. On Christmas Day, the family gathers together for another splendid feast. Between December 25 and January 6, the French visit friends and family throughout the country. As usual for France, bakeries and *chocolatiers* are filled with exquisite, seasonal specialties.

In every town and village, people celebrate local holidays. Local holidays are devoted to a patron saint, commemorate a military victory, or celebrate a legend. On the special day, streets close, merchants offer sales, and people gather to watch local legends acted out on stage or in a parade. Children participate in the performances. Through the festivities, they learn about their heritage and have a great time with family and friends.

**In Your Classroom**

For the Epiphany, play the game, Grab the King! To prepare for the game, outline a pizza round (or other circle) on poster paper. You will need a circle for every eight children. On copier or construction paper, outline and cut out the same number of circles. Then cut these into eight pie-shaped pieces, and distribute them so that the children can decorate them. Locate dice marked with dots, numbers, colors, or shapes (one die for each group of eight), and have children include these markings on their pie pieces. Collect the pieces and lay them on top of the poster–paper circles. Mark one piece on each circle as the *fève*. The *fève* is the winning piece of cake. Whoever receives it should be crowned as king or queen for the day. To play the game, give each group of eight children one game set (poster paper circle, eight pieces, one die). They should take turns rolling the die and serving themselves the piece of cake indicated. The child who pulls the *fève* wins. He or she is crowned king or queen and should be awarded special privileges all day. The king or queen will have *bonne chance*, or good luck, all year.

Explain the origins of *Poisson d'Avril* (April Fool's Day): In the 600s, the calendar that people used began on April 1—that was the first day of the new year. But there were not enough days on the calendar to match the solar year, so dates were mixed up. Pope Gregory changed the calendar to fix it. On the new calendar, the first day of the new year was January 1. Some people forgot this, and they would celebrate the new year on April 1—April Fools' Day. They were like fish out of water! Make April Fish to hang in your windows. Have students draw a simple fish shape on large construction paper. (You may want to provide a pattern for them to trace.) They can then decorate the fish with gentle watercolors or flashy acrylics. Remind students to add eyes, gills, scales, and fins. Cut out the fish and hang them on the bulletin board or in the window. Make a spring pond scene. Alternatively, fasten string to the head and let students fly their fish—fish out of water make quite a splash!

To celebrate Mardi Gras, make crêpes or cakes (see *Foods*). Have a family night to wear masks, display French projects, and eat French foods. Mardi Gras is celebrated in many countries around the world. Help students discover the Mardi Gras traditions in your community. Ask them to discover how the holiday is celebrated in Spain, Brazil, and other countries. They might be able to find pictures at the library of carnival games, floats, and costumes.

Help your class make their own Mardi Gras masks. Cut file folders to fit over the eyes and top of the head, and cut out eye holes (or provide inexpensive eye masks). Tape craft sticks to the backs of the masks. Ask children to decide what kind of creatures their carnival masks will represent. Will they be of real or imaginary animals? Then provide them with staplers, glue, scissors, and masking tape, as well as construction paper, markers, feathers, sequins, glitter, and other decorating materials. When the masks are complete, have a parade with them.

On May Day, have children make lily of the valley cards. Show children pictures of lilies of the valley. Then give each child a piece of green construction paper to fold into a card. They can use the center fold of the card as the flower stalk and glue cotton balls onto the card as bells. You may want to splash a little lily of the valley cologne on the cotton balls.

Make flower cookies using the Cat's Tongue recipe (see page 42). Decorate the cookies with candied rose petals or violets, or sprinkle them with colored sugars.

For Bastille Day, play a recording of the French national anthem, "La Marseillaise." Let children use construction paper to make tiny *tricolores* (French flags). They could glue these to toothpick flag poles. Serve cheese or meat sandwiches on baguettes. Read aloud French books like the Madeline (by Ludwig Bemelmans) or Babar (by Jean and Laurent de Brunhoff) books. Show videos like the *Red Balloon, Asterix,* or *Charles Perrault's Fairy Tales.* Discuss the beginning of the French Revolution in 1789, and compare it to the American Revolution.

For Noël, help children discover Christmas customs around the world. Provide materials for them to design and make cards illustrating the customs.

Art is part of daily life in France. Knowing how to appreciate many different forms of art is important. Children are taught at school and by example. Art fills the culture from cooking to home decorating, from fine arts to gardening. School field trips, as well as Sunday afternoon family walks, are directed toward knowing about and appreciating different aspects of French creative arts.

## Early Art

The earliest known art created in France is seen in prehistoric cave paintings. The first paintings were discovered in Lascaux, when a boy and his dog fell into a cave. Careful archaeological research revealed delicate scenes painted on cave walls more than thirty thousand years ago. Paintings and drawings of hundreds of horses, as well as reindeer, bison, and other wild animals were found in the Lascaux cave and later in other caves in France. Many archaeologists think they were drawn for magic or religious ceremonies, or to symbolize the animals early people hunted.

Thousands of years later, the Romans inhabited France (58 BCE -400 CE). They built temples, amphitheaters, civic buildings, and roads in France. Their style, now known as the classical style, can still be seen in many places in France. The style is characterized by tall, heavy columns and rounded stone arches.

## Art of the Medieval Period

*Notre Dame*

After the collapse of the Roman Empire, there was a period of several hundred years (early Medieval Period) when little art was created. Then Charles the Great built his empire and attempted to revive Roman civilization. He encouraged architects, painters, writers, and other artists. Catholicism was spreading across France, and many new cathedrals and castles were built. At first they were built of thick and heavy stone, and as a result, these buildings were very dark inside. Eventually, technology advanced and a Gothic style developed. Buttresses and pointed arches allowed architects to design thinner walls. They built taller and taller build-

MP5129 - France

ings, and included more windows to bring lots of light into their cathedrals. Splendid stained glass windows, often showing religious images, were created for these cathedrals.

During the Medieval Period, many manuscripts, namely the Bible and other prayer books, were copied in beautiful handwriting and were illustrated with beautifully colored pictures. Literature of this time consisted mostly of romantic poetry set to music. Nobles would often hire troubadours to sing and entertain the people living in the castle. Some troubadours wandered from place to place entertaining anyone who would listen. Epic poems about lovers and knights were also common.

Tapestries, or woven pictures, also developed as an art form during this time. They were needed to cover cold, drafty castle walls. The Normandy Bayeux tapestry depicting the 1066 invasion of England by the Norman Duke, William the Conqueror, and the splendid Apocalypse tapestry of Angers demonstrate how tapestries became functional works of art that recorded history. Today, tapestries are still made in France, but usually to cover less grandiose objects, such as purses, belts, and small walls.

From Medieval times to the present, French handiwork has been admired. Kings and queens, nobles and common people all dressed to fit their occupations and to decorate their rooms. Elegant designs and intricate stitches continue to make French clothing, furniture, and accessories famous and desirable. Paris is one of the world's centers for high fashion.

## Revolutionary Art

France has been a cradle for the fine arts, too. Art movements and artists found inspiration and support in France. People came from around the world to paint, sculpt, design, study, and admire art in all forms. During the Renaissance in the 16$^{th}$ and 17$^{th}$ centuries, artists, musicians, dramatists, writers, and scholars were drawn to the royal court. Under royal and aristocratic patronage, the arts flourished. Music of Lully and Rameau and their followers were encouraged. Writers and philosophers such as Voltaire, Rousseau, and Diderot inspired readers and incited discussion. Racine, Corneille, and Molière, three famous dramatists, broadened the French language with their stories, and mirrored an increasingly stressed society.

Many genres of art originated in France. Art of the Renaissance, highly influenced by the Italians, depicted mostly religious scenes and portraits of aristocrats and royalty. However, with the French Revolution came new thinking and new styles. As the clergy and royalty and aristocracy lost power, they no longer sponsored artists. As a result, artists began to experiment more, choosing new subjects—often common people in scenes of everyday life— new techniques, and new ways of representation.

Art became studies in color, shadow, light, line, and pattern, rather than the beautified, idealized portraits and religious scenes of earlier art. Realism, surrealism, cubism, and impressionism are words we have come to associate with 19$^{th}$ and 20$^{th}$ century art.

The late 19$^{th}$ century and early 20$^{th}$ century saw a flowering of art. Artists flocked to France to participate in what is now called the Impressionist period. Artists such as Degas, Toulouse Lautrec, Monet, Van Gogh, Renoir, Picasso, and Matisse continued to experiment and stretch imagination and technique through the 20$^{th}$ century: Van Gogh's strong lines and bright oil colors created a powerful impression of the south of France. Monet's garden provided a whole career for him. Although Monet was a prolific painter, the works he is most famous for are the huge canvases depicting his garden at Giverny. He chose to paint the same scenes over and over, each time at a different time of day, thus illustrating the essential ingredient of light, as well as form. Matisse was involved in many of the 20$^{th}$ century art movements. His cutouts came toward the end of his life and make a strong contrast to the impressionist philosophy. Picasso created in a variety of media. His paintings, drawings, sculptures, costumes, and collages contribute to the richness of 20$^{th}$ century art. One of the more intriguing styles he experimented with was cubism.

Picasso took figures and broke them at different angles to create nontraditional forms of representation.

In the 20th century, France has continued to lead the world in the arts. French culture teaches, practices, and highly values the artistic view of life. From castles to cakes, much of French art is *frou frou*. Castles are decorated elaborately and cakes glory in swirls and arcs of candied fruit or wisps of chocolate curls. Contemporary movements have produced utilitarian buildings, like the *Gare Montparnasse* (train station) and *Centre Pompidou* (museum), which glory in their structural points. The *Louvre,* a world famous art museum in Paris, pairs a Renaissance palace with a late 20th century glass pyramid. In the Paris subway, people ride the swift, sleek, metallic Metro trains and use the Metro's 19th century art–nouveau decorative gates. Maintaining and preserving the old, while constantly reinventing how people use and decorate space is a way of life in France. Creative art movements from ancient days to the present have shaped France's history and still impact the whole world.

**In Your Classroom**

Have students use sidewalk chalk to draw scenes from their everyday life. Compare the drawings with cave paintings.

Have students research and illustrate fashions from various time periods. Create a *History of French Fashions* book.

In the fashion industry, dolls have been fitted with tiny versions of the latest fashions. Use Barbie dolls and create your own miniature fashion show.

Display works by various artists that worked in France. Let students copy the styles. They could use markers to imitate Van Gogh, watercolors for Monet, and objects made of construction paper that are cut and scrambled to resemble Picasso.

Listen to recordings of medieval church music and Renaissance court music, as well as to the music of Lully, Rameau, and Debussy.

Name _____  Date _____

# Everyone's a Critic

France has produced some fantastic artists. Look back at the information on French art. Then do some research of your own. Find three pieces of French art that you admire (or dislike). In the spaces below, explain your opinion of the work. What do you like/dislike? What are your favorite/least favorite elements? What do you think the piece of art is about? Write what you feel!

France - MP5129

# Sports & Games

French children spend a lot of time playing in parks. Even in the cities, there are many green areas with trees, carousels, sand pits for games, slides, and fountains. For example, Luxembourg Gardens in Paris has splendid statues, wide ponds for sailing boats, sandy paths for people, dogs, and ponies to walk on, and spaces for picnics, reading, intense discussions, and impromptu concerts. Parks surround castles, office buildings, and churches. They are in the midst of industrial areas and block housing. Every weekend after dinner, families take walks to digest and to be together.

Bicycling is a way of transportation for many people. A light two–wheel bicycle is easier to park than a big four–wheel car. Bike racing is a serious sport. People in bicycle clubs practice all year long for *Le Tour de France,* an international bike race which takes place in July. Children collect souvenirs of their favorite riders and teams, and winners are instant heroes.

Soccer, known in France as *football,* is the favorite national sport. It is played year round, at school, in parks, and on formal teams. Swimming, tennis, basketball, and other team programs are popular, too. *Boules*, a game of lawn bowling played in the park, and *pelota*, a game similar to handball, are common in some areas. Fitness is now considered to be an important health goal for adults and children alike.

Children's games seem the same the world over. Children fill recess and free time with jump rope (*sauter à la corde*), jacks (*osselets*), hopscotch (*la marelle*), and hide and seek (*cache-cache*), as well as with tag and many witty word games.

# Germany

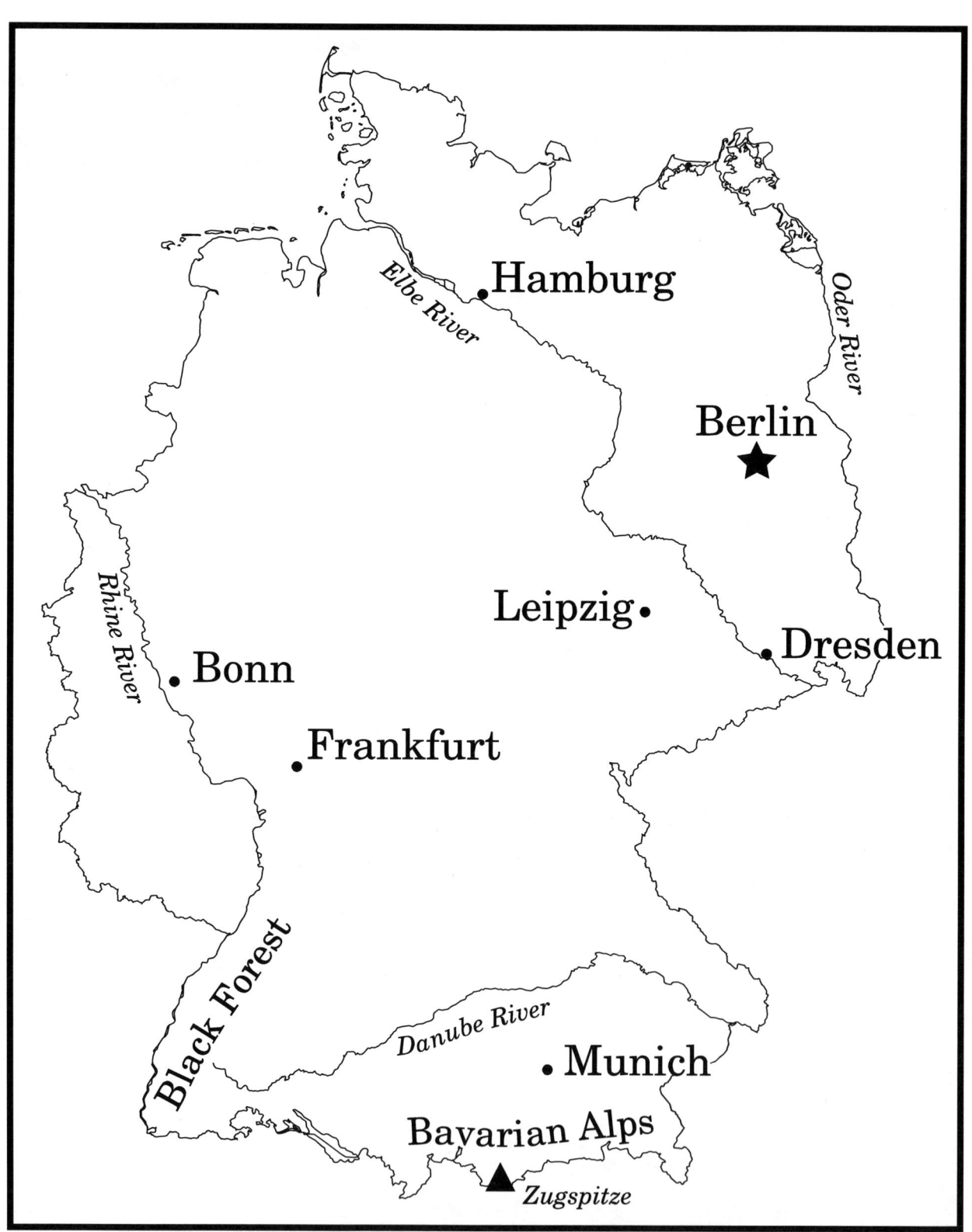

# Welcome to Germany!

After World War II, Germany was divided into two countries—West Germany and East Germany. Even Berlin, the capital city, was divided by a wall, further emphasizing the separateness of these two nations. This division forced the West German government to create a provisional capital in the city of Bonn. Many neighborhoods and families were split apart when the wall was built. East Germany was a political satellite of the Soviet Union and West Germany was an ally of the United States. Then on October 3, 1990, East and West Germany were formally reunited. The German government enacted a law on March 10, 1994, to return the seat of government officially to Berlin—a process that took some time. The reunification of Germany has been the cause of much rejoicing for its people.

| | |
|---|---|
| **Official Name:** | Federal Republic of Germany |
| **Location:** | Situated between the Netherlands and Poland, Germany borders the Baltic and North Seas. |
| **Population:** | 82,329,758 (2010 estimate) |
| **Capital City:** | Berlin |
| **Area:** | 137,778 square miles; Germany is somewhat smaller than the state of Montana. |
| **Major Language:** | German; the national language of Germany is High German, though a number of German dialects are also spoken in different parts of the country. Many people also speak English. |
| **Major Religion:** | Protestant: 34%<br>Roman Catholic: 34%<br>Islamic: 3.7% |
| **Currency:** | Euro; the euro is used in most countries in the European Union. |
| **Climate:** | Germany features a temperate climate, with cool, cloudy, and wet summers and winters. |
| **The Land:** | The Bavarian Alps rise in the south, with uplands in the center and lowlands in the north. |
| **Type of Government:** | Federal Republic |
| **Flag:** |  The flag of Germany features three horizontal bands of (top to bottom) black, red, and gold. These colors can be traced to the standard of the Holy Roman Emperor. |

MP5129 - Germany

**Coat of Arms:**  The German coat of arms depicts a black eagle, with red beak and talons, on a gold background. Like the flag, these colors recall the Holy Roman Emperor's standard.

**National Animal:** Black Eagle

**National Tree:** Oak

## Natural Environment

There are several different landscapes in Germany. The Northern Lowlands are sandy plains that were formed by glaciers. The Central Uplands have large rock masses and mountain ranges that are old and worn down by erosion. These mountain ranges, which include the Ore, the Harz, the Thuringian Forest, the Taunus, and the Rhineland Slate, are heavily wooded. Trees found in this area include pine, beech, spruce, and oak. The southern hill country and the Black Forest are popular with tourists. Some people say the Black Forest was given its name because of the dark green color of its pine trees; others believe it earned its name due to the density of the trees that allowed very little light into the forest. A small section of the Alps, known as the Bavarian Alps, stretches into Germany. One of the Alps' highest peaks is located there. It is called the Zugspitze and is 9,721 feet high.

The climate in Germany is moderate even though the country is far north. One reason for the mild temperatures is the North Atlantic Drift, an ocean current that warms western winds in the winter and cools them in the summer. Temperatures vary by region. Winter temperatures may range from 21° to 34° F, while summer temperatures may reach anywhere from 61° to 70° F. It rains frequently in Germany.

Germany has many rivers, including the Danube, the Rhine, the Elbe, and the Oder. Rivers are used for recreation, as well as for transportation and industry.

The area around the Rhine provides the best farmland in Germany. Farmers in this area primarily grow berries, fruit trees, and grapes for wine. Wheat, rye, potatoes, and sugar beets are grown in other areas of Germany.

Wildlife native to Germany includes deer, wild boar, bears, wolves, foxes, otters, badgers, wildcats, sea eagles, and white storks. Most of these animals can only be found deep in the forest. White storks may be seen nesting on chimneys of houses in more rural areas. Herring, mackerel, and cod abound in coastal waters.

Because Germany is an industrialized nation, pollution is a concern for many people. Although laws now prevent the dumping of chemicals into rivers, many rivers have already become polluted, causing many fish to die. Many of the trees in Germany, especially in the famous Black Forest, are diseased or dead due to acid rain and other pollutants. These concerns have led to the organization of a new political party called the Green Alternative.

Some areas of what was formerly East Germany were heavily industrialized and had no controls on pollution in place. These areas are now severely damaged. It will be extremely expensive to repair the damage in these areas, if it can be repaired at all.

# UNESCO World Heritage Sites in Germany

There are more than 30 World Heritage Sites in Germany. Many of them are cathedrals, including Aachen, Speyer, and Cologne Cathedrals. Wartburg Castle is a well-preserved structure dating to Feudal Europe. Museum Island sits on an island in the Spree River, in Berlin. The complex is home to five internationally renowned museums.

## In Your Classroom

Make a German flag. Use construction paper or paints. Use the flag on a bulletin board as a centerpiece for a display of pictures and information about Germany.

Trace or copy a map of Germany. Remember to trace all of Germany—not just the East or the West. Show students the border along which Germany was once divided. Be sure they realize Berlin was also divided between East and West.

Discuss different types of pollution and the effects each has on nature. What are some ways to control pollution? How can each child contribute to help keeping the environment clean?

# A History of Germany

Germany was inhabited by several different tribes for many years. These tribes were controlled by the Roman Empire for a time. They eventually overthrew the Romans and created hundreds of constantly changing, small kingdoms.

Karl der Grosse, or Charlemagne, incorporated Germany as part of his empire. In 800 CE, he was crowned emperor by the Pope. He encouraged people in his empire to learn to read and write, sponsored artists and musicians, and formed a central government and court system. All of this lasted until his death, at which time his empire was divided into three separate kingdoms.

Most of the area that is present-day Germany was ruled by Louis the German, one of Charlemagne's grandsons. He was not as strong a leader as his grandfather had been, and eventually local dukes and counts grew to have more power than the kings in Germany.

In 1517, a Catholic priest named Martin Luther protested many of the practices of the Catholic Church. His protest began the Protestant Reformation, which led to many wars. The worst of these wars was the Thirty Years' War, which lasted from 1618 to 1648 and involved some of the countries along Germany's border. The Treaty of Westphalia ended the Thirty Years' War. It created a Germany that was comprised of a series of small states and city-states, each of which had its own system of government and religion.

Prussia soon emerged as the strongest of the states. It was ruled by Frederick the Great from 1740 to 1786. Frederick created laws against torture and religious discrimination, and he encouraged freedom of the press.

In the early 1800s, Germans fought Napoleon and his French armies as they tried to expand French territory. Many areas of Germany were ruled by the French for a time. After Napoleon was defeated, the Congress of Vienna met and created thirty-nine German states.

In 1871, Otto von Bismarck, the chancellor of Prussia, united Germany. King Wilhelm I was crowned *kaiser* (or emperor) of Germany, and all the states were united into one kingdom. This made Prussia the center of much political and economic power.

When Wilhelm II became kaiser, Bismarck was removed from his position as chancellor due to Wilhelm's desire for more power. People in neighboring countries were concerned, because they believed Germany had too much power already. During this period, countries in Europe frequently made and broke treaties and alliances in an effort to prevent one country from becoming too powerful.

On June 28, 1914, Archduke Franz Ferdinand, heir to the Austrian throne, and his wife were assassinated while in Bosnia-Herzegovina. Due to the various alliances of countries in Europe at that time, this event led to World War I.

World War I lasted four years, and when it was over, Germany had lost a large part of its population. Many cities lay in ruins, and a great deal of the countryside had been destroyed as well. As a result of the Treaty of Versailles, signed in 1919, Germany was forced to accept responsibility for the war and was required to pay large sums of money to countries it had opposed. This led to a weakened and poorly organized German government. Inflation spun out of control; the cost of an item could increase over the course of one day. German currency had no real value, and Germany suffered a severe economic depression.

Adolf Hitler and the Nazi party used the Germans' anger over the war debt and their desire to stop apologizing for the war to rise to power. Hitler maintained his power by jailing and executing people who disagreed with his policies. He believed in a master race of German people, called the Aryan race. He told the German people that the Jews were responsible for many of the hardships the Germans were experiencing. He instituted laws that prevented Jews, as well as others who did not fit within his master race, from owning property, working in certain jobs, and attending schools. Many Jews, Slavs, and Gypsies, among others, were sent to concentration camps where they were forced to do hard labor and where millions were tortured and killed. Under Hitler's leadership, Germany began World War II with the invasion of Poland in September of 1939. Once again, allies in Europe joined together in a war to protect their borders and governments.

## Two Germanys

World War II ended in 1945, and Germany was divided into four zones. One was controlled by the former Soviet Union, and the other three by Great Britain, France, and the United States. Berlin was also divided into four zones. The Soviets wanted Germany to be a socialist state, but the British, French, and Americans wanted Germany to be a democracy.

During 1948 and 1949, the Soviets tried to seal off Berlin from the other German zones by closing all roads to the city from the western part of Germany. To combat this, allied forces flew supplies into Berlin. This operation was called the Berlin Airlift. In 1949, Germany was officially divided into two countries—East Germany and West Germany— because no agreement could be reached as to how the country should be governed.

In 1961, the Soviets and the East German government erected the Berlin Wall to block East German access to the west. The wall divided families and friends. It also prevented some people from getting to their jobs.

Germany remained divided for 45 years. The governments of East Germany and West Germany were very different. West Germans were allowed much freedom politically, economically, and socially. East Germans, on the other hand, followed policies and laws dictated by the Soviet Union, many of which strictly limited personal freedoms.

# German Reunification

In May of 1989, Hungarians dismantled the barbed wire fences and guard posts that separated them from Austria. East Germans could now go to Hungary and from there get to West Germany for the first time in many years. These East Germans were considered refugees and thus entitled to West German citizenship and other benefits. More and more East Germans gathered in Hungary, where they were allowed to go into Austria and from there to West Germany. In time, East Germans could get to West Germany by going to Czechoslovakia and taking special trains from there.

The Berlin Wall was destroyed on November 9, 1989. On October 3, 1990, the two Germanys were reunited into one under the chancellorship of Helmut Kohl. There were many problems to solve as the two countries continued to merge. It was a very costly transformation. However, most Germans feel it was worth the effort and expense to be able to enjoy a unified Germany once again.

# Modern Germany

Germany entered the 21st century as a unified nation. A founding country of the European Union, Germany has played a large role in the organization's continued development. Germany has also been involved in international issues, sending troops to join the U.S.-led military campaign in Afghanistan in 2001. In 2005, the country welcomed its first female chancellor, Angela Merkel. The country has been affected by the recent global economic crisis; the government continues to work diligently to solve Germany's problems, and continues to be an important influence in Europe and throughout the world.

# In Your Classroom

Show students maps of Germany at different periods in its history, from the times of Charlemagne, Bismarck, post-World War I and II, and after the German reunification. These maps may be found in books, atlases, and encyclopedias.

Gather some newspaper and magazine articles as well as photographs of some of the events leading up to the reunification of Germany and of the celebrations afterward. Share with students. Older students may help by visiting libraries or asking parents if they have any pertinent articles or photographs that they may have saved.

# Daily Life

## Clothing

In southern Germany, many people still wear traditional clothing. Some men wear *lederhosen*, short overalls made out leather, and alpine hats, while some women wear *dirndls*, full-skirted dresses with fitted bodices. Most Germans wear clothes that are very similar to those worn in North America.

## School

School begins at 8:00 AM and ends by 12:30 or 1:00 PM. Since German children's school days are much shorter than in most countries, they have much more homework assigned to them. Children may go to kindergarten when they are three years old. Most children begin *Grundschule*, or elementary school, when they are six.

After four to six years of schooling, children and their parents decide which kind of secondary school they will attend. A *Hauptschule* is a secondary school that readies students for apprenticeships in the manual trades. A *Realschule* prepares students to start office or manual trade apprenticeships. Classes at a Gymnasium prepare students to go on to a university. Students today can also attend a *Gesamtschule*, a new type of school designed to integrate kids who might normally go to *Hauptschule*, *Realschule*, or Gymnasium. The *Gesamtschule* is similar to a high school.

Classrooms in Germany are more formal than those in other countries. German students are very courteous to their teachers. When a teacher enters a classroom, students stand to greet him or her. Students usually say, "*Guten Morgen, Herr Lehrer* (or *Frau Lehrer*)." Teachers often call older students by their last names instead of their first names.

All students study some of the same subjects no matter what kind of school they attend. They have classes in German language and literature, at least one foreign language, history, art, music, math, and science. Germans value education and learning very highly. There are many adult education classes in Germany that teach about specific jobs as well as many other subjects in which people might have an interest.

## After-School Activities and Sports

In Germany, the main meal of the day is usually served at lunchtime, so German children go home to eat with their families. After eating, the children do their homework and then play with friends or watch television.

German children like to go to sports clubs to play after school and on weekends. At the clubs, they swim and play soccer, handball, table tennis, and other games. During their free time, many German families enjoy walking and biking. Many people also like to ski in the winter.

German schools do not have sports programs. People who want to play a sport join an organization. The soccer organization is very popular. It has over four million members, including children, teenagers, adults, and professional players. Many people are soccer fans and go to the games played by professional teams.

## Housing

The majority of Germans live in apartments, though many people have houses. Most German families have fewer than three children. As a result, apartments and houses are built for small families. Rooms are small, and the furniture is small or built into the apartment walls. Many German children have their own rooms, but children of the same sex may share a bedroom. People sleep under duvets (comforters made of feathers and down), called feather beds. On sunny days, the duvets are hung over window sills so they can freshen in the air. Because yards are small or not available, most German children belong to athletic clubs.

Though most Germans live in cities, many still love to garden. Many German homes and apartments are decorated by window boxes. Some Germans who live in apartments buy or lease small gardens near their cities. They work in these gardens during their leisure time and grow flowers and vegetables. Some of the gardens have enough space for a small house so the owners may stay for a weekend.

## Famous People from Germany

Johannes Gutenberg (1398-1468) invented movable type and the printing press. His innovations led to historical and cultural events such as the Renaissance, the Reformation, and the Scientific Revolution. His invention of the printing press is often considered the most important event of the modern period.

Nicolaus Copernicus (1473-1543) was an astronomer during the Renaissance. He was the first person to suggest that the Sun, not Earth, was the center of the universe. His discovery is often described as the beginning of modern astronomy and a spark for the Scientific Revolution.

Ludwig van Beethoven (1770-1827) was a German composer and pianist, and is arguably history's greatest musician. Despite hearing difficulties that eventually lead to his being totally deaf, Beethoven produced some of the world's best-known musical works: *Sonata Number 14 (the Moonlight Sonata)*, *Für Elise*, and his *Ninth Symphony* are just a few.

The Brothers Grimm, Jacob (1785-1863) and Wilhelm (1786-1859), were responsible for the well-known *Grimm's Fairy Tales*. The brothers were academics; they set out to collect folk tales and fairy tales, gathering a list of stories, many of which are still told today: *Hansel and Gretel*, *Cinderella*, *Little Red Riding Hood*, and *Sleeping Beauty* among them.

Albert Einstein (1879-1955) is one of the best known scientists and intellectuals of all time. He is often called the father of modern physics. He is especially known for his theory of relativity. Einstein won the Nobel Prize in Physics in 1921.

## In Your Classroom

Make window boxes to decorate the windows of your classroom. Use half-gallon milk cartons to make the window boxes. Cut out one side, rinse well, fill with soil, and add flower seeds. Let children examine seeds to see that each type of flower has a different kind of seed. Children may make charts to show which seeds sprout first and grow fastest. Keep some gardening books in the classroom for reference.

Help students organize the information they have learned about Germany by making a mural of a typical German day. Have them make a list of things they want to include in the mural. Let your students refer to books about Germany in your book area for ideas of what to include. Objects for the mural may be drawn, painted, cut out, or glued together. Be imaginative!

Shake each child's hand, and encourage children to shake the hands of classmates when they arrive at school in the morning. Have children greet teachers and the principal when they enter the classroom in the typical way that German students do, by standing and saying, "Guten Tag, Frau _____ (or Herr _____)."

Name _____  Date _____

# Your Own Fairy Tale

The Brothers Grimm collected and wrote some of history's most timeless stories. Head to the library or check out the Internet for one or two of their tales (don't worry, most aren't long). After you've read the Brothers Grimm, try your hand at writing a fairy tale on the lines below.

TITLE: _____

# Language & Expressions

English and Dutch are related to German—all three languages are considered Germanic languages. There are many dialects spoken in the different regions of Germany. Someone from northern Germany might have difficulty communicating with someone from southern Germany if each person speaks in his or her local dialect. All Germans learn to speak *High German*. It is the language taught in school, used in books and magazines, and spoken in films and on television.

## Pronunciation

German is spoken crisply with each word pronounced clearly. Pronunciation rules are reasonably consistent:

> Say **v** for **w**.
> Say **i** as in *bite* for **ei**.
> Say **e** as in *feet* for **ie**.
> Say **a** as in *bait* for **e**.
> Say **oo** as in *boot* for **u**.
> Say **k** for **ch**.
> Say **a** as in *father* for **a**.
> Say **oy** as in *boy* for **eu**.
> Say **ou** as in *round* for **au**.
> Say **s** as in *hiss* for **ß**.

## Famous German Proverbs

Here are some famous German proverbs. What do you think they mean?

*Old foxes go with difficulty into the trap.*

*Old bread isn't hard; no bread, that is hard.*

*There is sunshine after every rainfall.*

*From damage, one becomes intelligent.*

*Better one-eyed than blind.*

*The bone doesn't come to the dog; the dog goes to the bone.*

*First think, then steer.*

*Sweep the ground in front of your own door.*

## Body Language and Etiquette in Germany

Here are some examples of body language and etiquette you'll find in Germany.

*Always greet shopkeepers when you enter a store; be sure to thank them upon leaving.*

*When greeting a friend in Germany, shake hands and look them in the eyes.*

*Germans are extremely punctual. Don't be even a few minutes late to any appointment.*

*When invited to a friend's home, be sure to bring flowers. This is a traditional gift.*

*Before you eat lunch in Germany, say "Mahlzeit." This is a common custom.*

*Never telephone a German after 10 PM unless you have permission from him or her.*

*Germans are very respectful when it comes to noise. Don't be loud before 9 AM or after 10 PM.*

*Close friends greet one another with a kiss on both the left and right cheeks.*

## Know before You Go

### Numbers 1-10

| | |
|---|---|
| one | eins |
| two | zwei |
| three | drei |
| four | vier |
| five | fünf |
| six | sechs |
| seven | sieben |
| eight | acht |
| nine | neun |
| ten | zehn |

### Commonly Used Expressions

| | |
|---|---|
| I wish you a good appetite | *Guten Appetit!* |
| Good health | *Gesundheit!* |
| Everything is in order | *Alles in Ordnung.* |
| Good day / Hello | *Guten Tag.* |
| Goodbye | *Auf Wiedersehen.* |
| Thank you | *Danke.* |
| It is nice to see you | *Es freut mich, Sie zu sehen.* |

Name _____  Date _____

# Sprechen Sie Deutsch?
## (Do You Speak German?)

Now that you know a little something about the German language, let's see if you can translate it. Draw a line from the English word on the left to its German translation on the right.

|  |  |
|---|---|
| red | die Kinder |
| book | weiß |
| blue | rot |
| yellow | schwarz |
| children | die Schule |
| black | blau |
| green | gelb |
| school | das Buch |
| white | grün |

# Foods

Germans generally eat breakfast early in the morning. Breakfast usually consists of rolls, cheese, cold cuts, jam, and butter. Later in the morning, Germans eat a second breakfast of a small sandwich. The main meal is usually eaten at midday. The evening meal is often sandwiches or sausages eaten with cheese and salad. People in Germany like to have coffee in the afternoon, whether at home or at a *kaffeehaus* (coffeehouse). They usually eat a piece of torte or some sort of *kuchen* (cake) along with the coffee.

## Recipes

Here are some popular German foods known around the world, along with recipes detailing how to make them.

### *Apple Strudel*

Apple strudel is a popular dessert in Germany. It is served warm with whipped cream. The pastry in the strudel is made by stretching the dough until it is paper thin. The recipe below uses phyllo dough instead of making the pastry from scratch.

    4 medium apples, peeled and sliced very thin
    1/8 cup raisins
    1/4 cup sugar
    1/4 cup blanched almonds
    1/2 teaspoon ground cinnamon
    1/4 teaspoon ground cloves
    6 sheets of thawed phyllo pastry
    1 stick of butter, melted
    1/4 cup fine dry bread crumbs

Combine the first six ingredients. Place one sheet of phyllo on a damp towel, and brush lightly with butter. Layer five more sheets of phyllo, one at a time, brushing each with butter. Sprinkle bread crumbs over the top layer. Spread the apple mixture over the phyllo, leaving a two-inch border all around. Fold all edges over two inches. Starting at one end of the long side, roll, using jelly roll method. Place seam side down on a lightly greased cookie sheet. Brush with butter. Bake at 375° F for 30 minutes. Cool on a wire rack. Slice and serve with whipped cream.

### *Hot Potato Salad*

    6 boiled potatoes, sliced
    4 strips of bacon, crumbled
    1 dill pickle, chopped
    1 small onion, chopped
    3 celery stalks, chopped
    1/4 cup water
    1/2 cup vinegar
    1/2 teaspoon sugar
    1/2 teaspoon salt
    1/4 teaspoon paprika

Sauté onion and celery until golden. Heat the last five ingredients to boiling. Mix all the ingredients together and serve hot. This salad is also good when cold.

### *Potato Pancakes*

    4 large potatoes, peeled and shredded (2 1/2 cups when shredded)
    1 onion, grated
    2 tablespoons flour
    2 large eggs
    1/8 teaspoon pepper
    1/8 teaspoon salt
    vegetable oil

Mix potatoes, onion, and flour together in a large bowl. In a smaller bowl, combine the eggs with the salt and pepper, and beat with a fork. Then add the egg mixture to the potato mixture. Stir until blended.

To fry the pancakes, pour a bit of oil into a skillet and heat over medium to medium-high heat. Put a tablespoonful of the potato mixture into the skillet and flatten with a spoon. When the edges brown, turn pancake over. Cook the other side until its edges brown. Remove pancake from skillet and drain on a paper towel. Continue this process until all the potato mixture has been used. You can cook several pancakes in the skillet at one time. For a sweet and tasty treat, serve with applesauce, or for a hearty meal, serve with cooked sausage.

### *Sandwiches*

German sandwiches are usually served open-faced and are eaten with a knife and fork. Make German-style sandwiches using dark rye bread or a dense wheat bread. Butter the bread and spread a German-style mustard on each slice. Add corned beef or ham and Swiss or Gouda cheese.

*Marzipan*

Germans enjoy *marzipan*, a colorful and artistically crafted candy. Most candy stores and coffeehouses have beautiful marzipan candies for sale. Marzipan is often shaped and colored to look like fruit or animals. At holiday times, marzipan is made with holiday themes.

Marzipan can be purchased in rolls. Made with crushed almonds or almond paste, its texture is similar to bread dough. Children will enjoy shaping marzipan into fruits or animals. They can then paint their candy creations with diluted vegetable coloring.

**In Your Classroom**

Prepare and serve a typical German evening meal for the children's lunch. Children may make German-style sandwiches. Apples, pears, and grapes may be washed and placed in bowls. Apple strudel or marzipan could be made for dessert. Ask students to try eating like a European, keeping the fork in the left hand and the knife in the right.

# Holidays & Festivals

### Fasching or Karneval

*Fasching* is a pre-Lenten celebration similar to Mardi Gras in New Orleans. It is also a festival which welcomes spring and celebrates the end of winter. In some areas of Germany, people—especially children—dress in costumes just as children in the United States do for Halloween. They participate in parades and have parties at school. In the Black Forest, people dress in costumes and wooden masks. They frighten winter spirits away with loud noises.

### Easter
*April or May*

At Easter time, Germans decorate eggs by painting them with geometric or floral designs and pictures. Some eggs are dyed, and the dye is scraped away to form a design. Usually the eggs are pierced at each end and the contents are blown out. Other eggs are left intact. The contents dry up after several months. After the eggs have been decorated, they are hung on an egg tree. The tree is made by putting flowering branches in a vase.

The Easter rabbit hides eggs for children to find on Easter morning. The eggs are usually hidden outside. Children in different parts of Germany prepare for the Easter rabbit's visit in various ways. Some children make rabbit gardens using grasses and decorations, others make moss nests, and still others have baskets in which they place the eggs they find. Later in the day, children play games with their eggs. They may roll them, have relay races, or have egg-eating contests.

### May Day
*May 1*

Like many European countries, Germany celebrates May Day as a sign of spring. The day involves bonfires, parties, and maypole dancing. The night before May Day, boys deliver treats wrapped in colorful streamers in the front yard of a girl they admire.

### St. Martin's Day
*November 11*

On November 11, children celebrate St. Martin's Day. Children make paper lanterns which they carry in a procession led by St. Martin on horseback. St. Martin pantomimes tearing his cloak to share it with a beggar. There are fireworks after the procession, and children receive candy and fruit in small sacks. At some schools, a campfire is built. Children sing and listen to the story of St. Martin, and they share a large loaf of bread shaped like the saint.

## St. Nicholas Day
*December 5*

Another special holiday for children in Germany is St. Nicholas Day. On December 5, St. Nicholas and his servant Ruprecht visit German children. St. Nicholas looks like a Catholic bishop and was the historical figure on which Santa Claus was modeled. Ruprecht is dressed in a dark hooded robe, and his face is covered. St. Nicholas and Ruprecht bring gifts in person to some children. Other children leave their shoes outside their front doors or on a window sill on the evening before St. Nicholas Day. Ruprecht leaves sticks and coal in naughty children's shoes. Good children receive small toys, candies, and a bundle of gilt sticks to remind them to be good. Many stores in Germany sell Ruprecht dolls made from prunes and toothpicks.

## Christmas
*December 25*

The Christmas season in Germany begins in November. Many cities and towns have a special Christmas market that sells decorations, gifts, and holiday foods. This is called a *Christkindlmarkt*. The largest one is in the city of Nuremberg.

Christmas trees are an important part of Christmas celebrations. A German legend tells of Martin Luther decorating a small fir tree with candles on Christmas Eve to show his family how beautiful the woods were at night. Many German families decorate their trees on Christmas Eve instead of earlier in the Christmas season. Handmade ornaments, small gifts, cookies, and candies, as well as candles or electric lights decorate many German Christmas trees.

On Christmas Eve, many families open gifts, attend Midnight Mass, and come home to a festive supper. Christmas itself is a quiet day spent with the family. The day after Christmas is a holiday traditionally spent visiting friends.

## In Your Classroom

Try making a Ruprecht doll in your classroom. Place two prunes lengthwise on a toothpick to create a body. An additional prune may be speared on a separate toothpick and placed on the body to create a head. Arms and legs may be formed by spearing prunes with toothpicks and placing them on the body. Raisins or other bits of dried fruit may be used for facial features, hands, and feet.

Children may make masks using large paper bags, pre-cut heavy paper, or poster board. Let them decorate their masks with feathers, buttons, sequins, yarn, and markers.

Younger children may decorate wooden or hard-boiled eggs with markers. Older children may use paint and small paintbrushes to decorate the eggs. Allow children to display their eggs in a basket, moss nest, or rabbit garden.

Students may make paper lanterns out of lunch sacks. They may cut designs out of the sacks, and then color them. Attach each decorated sack to a stick with a short piece of string. Children may have their own procession on the playground. Have students use bread dough to form a large St. Martin to bake and share, or have them bake individual St. Martin-shaped breads that they may take home.

Children may make ornaments from self-hardening clay. The ornaments can be painted or colored with markers when they have dried. Create a market in your classroom using tables and desks as stalls. Children may take turns buying and selling items. Items for sale may include fruits, cookies, juice, and small ornaments or toys.

# Creative Arts

### Fairy Tales

Germany is famous for its fairy tales collected by the Brothers Grimm. Fairy tales are a part of Germany's cultural heritage, and they are loved by children all over the world.

### Puppets

Many wooden toys and puppets are made and enjoyed in Germany. Marionettes are puppets moved by strings attached to the puppet from a T-bar handle. Lifelike movements are created by tilting the T-bar and by lifting individual strings. Marionette shows were a popular form of entertainment in Germany's royal courts and remain popular with Germans today.

### Music

Germany has a rich musical history. Much of the classical music we enjoy and study today was composed by German musicians. These musicians include Johann Sebastian Bach, George Frideric Handel, Ludwig van Beethoven, and Richard Wagner.

Folk songs also hold a very important place in German culture. Many are very well known and are often sung by people when they are celebrating and having fun.

### Art

Three of Germany's greatest artists were Albrecht Dürer, Hans Holbein the Younger, and Paul Klee. Dürer and Holbein were contemporaries in the sixteenth century. Klee was an artist of the early twentieth century.

Albrecht Dürer was a painter and printmaker best known for the woodcuts and engravings he created to make his prints. His woodcuts were more detailed and graceful than others created at that time.

Hans Holbein the Younger was a great portraitist who painted the images of many famous people of his time.

Paul Klee was part of the Expressionist movement in Germany (though not born there) and was influenced by primitive art, drawings made by young children, and Cubism.

MP5129 - Germany

# Architecture

*Castles*

During the Middle Ages, many kingdoms in Germany were weak, and fighting was a frequent occurrence as various people tried to gain power and land. Castles were built for protection. Many castles were built throughout Europe between CE 1050 and 1350.

The earliest castles were built of wood. Each one had a tower and outbuildings that were protected by a strong wooden fence. In the eleventh century, stone was used in place of wood. Stone would not burn and was even harder to break through than wood. Stone walls were built to replace wooden fences. In time, castles became larger. Their towers were rounded, and an extra wall was added to help defend the tower.

Castles were built in places that would be easy to defend. Many were built on steep hillsides or atop rocky cliffs. In areas that were flat, great mounds were made of rocks and earth, and the castles were built on these.

One of the castles built on the banks of the Rhine was the Marksburg Castle, the only castle to escape capture during the Thirty Years' War. It still stands today in Braubach, Germany.

## Inventors, Inventions, and Scientists

Over 400 years ago, Johannes Gutenberg invented a printing press with moveable type. The Chinese had invented printing with moveable type long before that, but because their language was so complex and involved so many individual characters, the printing method did not develop in China. Printing as we know it today was invented by Gutenberg. Because of his invention, books no longer had to be copied by hand. They became more readily available and allowed more people to share ideas.

Gabriel Fahrenheit invented a system of measuring heat and cold. Fahrenheit degrees have been used since the 1700s.

Gottlieb Daimler, Karl Benz, Rudolf Diesel, and Felix Wankel were inventors of the internal combustion engines which led to the cars and trucks we drive today.

Bicycles, x-ray machines, electric trains, and pocket watches were all invented by Germans. Albert Einstein was a physicist who won a Nobel prize for his discoveries. He left Germany to escape Nazi persecution.

Wernher von Braun also left Germany to escape the Nazis. He was a rocket engineer and was involved in the development of the U.S. space program.

# In Your Classroom

Share some of the famous Grimm fairy tales with your students. Have students write their own fairy tales and share them with the rest of the class. Younger children may dictate their stories to the teacher and draw pictures to accompany them. Make a mural out of construction paper illustrating the students' favorite fairy tale characters.

Read *The Jolly Postman*, a book written by Janet and Allan Ahlberg (see the Additional Resources section on page 180). This book includes letters written to fairy tale characters from other fairy-tale characters. Children may then write their own letters to one of their favorite fairy-tale characters. Older children may want to write as though they were fairy tale characters themselves.

Some of the fairy tales enjoyed by the class may be reenacted by making simple marionettes or finger and hand puppets to represent fairy tale characters. Divide children into small groups to create puppet shows of these fairy tales.

Introduce children to some of Germany's famous composers by playing selections of their music. Include Bach's *Brandenburg Concertos*, Handel's *Water Music*, and Beethoven's *Eroica*. Tell children the story of *Die Meistersinger von Nürnberg* (The Mastersingers of Nuremberg) by Wagner and play the "Heavenly Morning" aria. Read *Behind the Golden Curtain* by E. Lee Spruyt to introduce the Hansel and Gretel opera composed by Engelbert Humperdinck. This book tells about the behind-the-scenes preparations involved in the Metropolitan Opera House's production of *Hansel and Gretel*. Show students a video of this opera as performed by the Metropolitan Opera, if possible.

Use prints, posters, and postcards to introduce children to the works of these and other German artists. Some libraries may have prints or posters that can be borrowed. Museum shops will carry postcards of the works of various artists. Encourage students to discuss similarities and differences in the works of the artists.

Take children to visit a printing press at a print shop or newspaper publishing company. Set up a print shop in your classroom with rubber stamps and ink pads. Children may use these to create their own books, cards, and posters.

Use a thermometer with Fahrenheit degrees to measure the temperature outdoors every day at the same time. Make a graph of the temperatures.

Display some pictures of early automobiles, bicycles, x-ray machines, and pocket watches. Discuss the concept of an invention. It is an idea that someone comes up with to fill a need or a desire for something. Have students list ideas for inventions of things they might need or enjoy having. Give them a chance to be inventors by having them draw and/or write (or tell) about their inventions. Older children might actually be able to create simple inventions. Display the children's work in the classroom or school library.

Display photographs showing the progression from early rockets to the shuttles used by the space program today. Add some books to the class library about rockets and space.

Build a model of a rocket as a class project. Make a mural of the solar system. Have each child make a page of a book for the class about a question they have about rockets or space, or make a book about what each child would like to visit in space.

Make a model of a castle. Include a gatehouse, drawbridge, towers, and a moat. See the Additional Resources section on page 180 for books about castles and how to create them.

# Sports & Games

*Football*

Soccer, known as football in Europe, is by far Germany's leading team sport. There are an incredible number of teams kicking the ball around in Germany. The highest league is *Bundesliga*; it's also one of the best-attended sport leagues in the world, which shows just how popular soccer is. The German national teams (both men and women) have won multiple FIFA World Cups and European Football Championships.

*Winter Sports*

Winter sports might not be as popular as soccer, but Germany really excels at them. Ice hockey is by far the most popular, but German athletes also participate in the bobsled, luge, and skeleton. These are sports that involve teams hurling down tracks of ice in or on vehicles on large skates. German teams regularly dominate these extreme winter sports.

*Motorsports*

Germany has a strong presence in motorsports around the world. Many racecars that fly around tracks at incredible speeds are manufactured in Germany. Michael Schumacher, a racer in the Formula One series, has won more driver championships than any other driver, and is known around the world for his driving ability.

*Germany at the Olympics*

Germany has had much success at the Olympics. They rank in the top ten of the all-time medal count. As mentioned above, Germans are particularly talented when it comes to winter sports. In the 2006 Winter Olympic Games in Turin, Germany won the most gold medals; they also won the most total medals. The country has hosted the Summer Games twice and the Winter Games once.

## Children's Games

Children in Germany play many games with their friends during school recess or while at each others' homes. Below are some games that you can play with the children in your classroom.

*One, Two, Three, Who Has the Ball?*

Children stand in a row with their hands behind their backs. One child is **It**. The child who is It stands several feet away from the other children with his or her back to them. One of the children in the row holds a small ball in his or her hand. The children chant, "ONE, TWO, THREE, WHO HAS THE BALL?" It walks towards the child that he or she thinks has the ball. If It is correct, then he or she is It again. If It is incorrect, the child with the ball runs to a base. It must tag the child before he or she reaches the base to remain It. If the child with the ball reaches the base before being tagged, then he or she becomes It. The object of the game is to remain It.

### Change, Change, Little Tree

This game is typically played in a wooded area. If there are no trees around, circles may be drawn on the ground to represent trees, or other objects may be used as bases. Each child stands beside a tree, or a base called a tree. The child who is **It** stands in the middle of all the children and calls, "CHANGE, CHANGE, LITTLE TREE." All the children must run to a new tree or base while It tries to tag a child. If It tags someone, the child who is tagged becomes the new It. If It does not tag anyone, then he or she remains It for the next round.

### All Birds Fly High

Children sit in a circle and clap their hands on their knees. One child or the teacher acts as the leader and says, "ALL BIRDS LIFT HANDS." The children lift their hands and then resume clapping. The leader then says, "ALL MOSQUITOES LIFT HANDS." The children lift their hands and then resume clapping. The leader may then say, "ALL TABLESPOONS LIFT HANDS." The children should continue clapping, but should not lift their hands after the leader's phrase. Each time the leader's phrase includes an animal or object that flies (such as a kite, bee, butterfly, or helicopter), the children lift their hands and then resume clapping. If the phrase does not include an animal or object that flies (such as a dog, pencil, or child), the children should keep clapping and not lift their hands. Other categories—e.g., farm animals, colors, nouns, verbs, number pairs that equal ten, or words beginning with various letters of the alphabet—may be used with this game to reinforce concepts being learned by the students.

### Little Bird Say Peep

Children sit on chairs in a circle. The child who is **It** stands blindfolded in the middle of the circle. All the children quietly change chairs. The teacher takes It to a child in the circle, and the two children hold hands. All the children chant, "LITTLE BIRD SAY PEEP." The child holding It's hand says "PEEP." It tries to guess who the child is. If It guesses the child's name correctly, he or she remains It. If It is wrong, the child holding his or her hand becomes It. The object of the game is to remain It.

MP5129 - Germany

# Iceland

# Welcome to Iceland!

Iceland, the second largest island in Europe after Great Britain, is located in the North Atlantic Ocean. The country has a unique landscape due to its active volcanoes, glaciers, and fields of sand. The people are proud of their Norse (ancient Scandinavian) culture and heritage. Their hard work has helped them to become one of the most developed, wealthiest nations in the world. Like other Nordic countries, the people of Iceland benefit from a universal welfare program that provides health care and post-secondary education for all citizens.

## Fast Facts

**Official Name:** The Republic of Iceland (Ísland or Lýðveldið (leeth-vel-dith) Ísland)

**Location:** Situated between the North Atlantic Ocean and the Greenland Sea, Iceland sits northwest of the United Kingdom.

**Population:** 306,694 (2010 estimate)

**Capital City:** Reykjavik (rik-ja-vik)

**Area:** 39,769 square miles

**Major Language:** Icelandic; this language descended from Old Norse. English is also widely spoken.

**Major Religions:** Lutheran Church of Iceland: 80.7%
Roman Catholic: 2.5%

**Currency:** Icelandic *króna* (written as kr.); their most frequently used notes are the 500, 1000, and 5000 krónur. Coins come in denominations of 1, 5, 10, 50, and 100 krónur. During the economic crisis in 2008, the króna's value plummeted, causing the Icelandic government to rethink their currency options, such as adopting the euro and joining the EU.

**Climate:** The coastline of Iceland is sub-polar oceanic, experiencing milder temperatures than the interior of the country. The coastal climate is similar to that of the Alaskan peninsula and remains ice-free throughout the winter. Iceland's interior is quite cold; most of its glaciers are located in this region.

**The Land:** The majority of the island is plateaus, broken by mountains and ice fields. The coastline features many bays and fiords.

**Type of Government:** Constitutional Republic; the republic is governed by an Alþingi (Althing), which is a parliamentary democracy. The president of Iceland is the head of state. The prime minister is the head of government.

**Flag:**  The flag of Iceland is deep blue with a horizontal white cross, and a bright red cross inside the white cross. The colors represent the three elements of Iceland: the blue of the Atlantic Ocean, the white snow, and the fiery red volcanoes.

**Coat of Arms:**  The coat of arms features a shield with the silver and fiery red crosses and blue field of the flag. The shield is surrounded by the four protectors of Iceland: the bull, the eagle, the dragon, and the rock giant, each protecting a different region of the country.

**National Flower:**  Mountain Avens

## Natural Environment

Iceland is located just outside the Arctic Circle atop the Mid-Atlantic Ridge. The Mid-Atlantic Ridge is an area where the ocean crust spreads and reforms. The island was formed by 150-200 volcanoes, 30 of which are still active today. The island of Surtsey, just off the coast of southern Iceland, was formed by volcanic activity in the 1960s. Today it is a nature reserve where scientists can study geology and research.

Because of this and the extreme weather conditions, only one fourth of the island can support vegetation of any kind. The rest of the country is covered in glaciers, waterfalls, lakes, geysers, cirques, and fjords (a valley carved by glacial movement). Deforestation has destroyed many of the few trees that were there, and much of the available grass is used for livestock grazing. The Icelandic sheep and horse, as well as goats, cattle, and chickens, live and graze in this area. Iceland's wild animals include the Arctic Fox, mink, mice, rats, rabbits, reindeer, as well as the occasional polar bear. Iceland is home to rare birds such as the skuas, kittiwakes, and endangered puffins.

Fishing is an important industry in Iceland, responsible for over half of the country's exports. Another important industry is commercial whaling and scientific whale hunts. Iceland is known for its hot springs, many of which provide home-heating, aid the greenhouse industry and attract tourists. Because of its milder temperatures, most Icelanders live along the coast.

## In Your Classroom

Draw a map of Iceland. Label the major cities and color the different geographical regions. Color the inner glaciers blue and the coastline green.

Locate Iceland on a map and note its location in relation to Europe and North America. Compare its size to the United Kingdom. Trace the Viking's route from Norway and the Irish path from Ireland.

Using construction paper, tape, scissors and paint, have the students make an Icelandic flag to hang in the classroom. Remind the students what the colors symbolize.

# A History of Iceland

Iceland has a Nordic and Celtic origin. The island was discovered by Irish explorers around 800 CE. Vikings from Norway began to settle the country during the late 9th century. In 930, they established an Althing—a representative governing body. Iceland's Althing is the oldest parliamentary body in the world.

Norwegians gained control of the country in 1263 and in 1381 made it a part of the Norwegian-Danish state. Under their rule, Iceland became one of the poorest countries in Europe. The harsh climate, infertile soil, and volcanic eruptions made it a difficult place to live. Nearly half of Iceland's population died during the Black Death in 1402-1404 and in 1494-1495.

Around the middle of the 16th century, like many other European countries, Iceland left the Catholic Church and became Protestant, specifically Lutheran. In the 17th and 18th century, the country suffered many hardships including pirate attacks, a smallpox epidemic, a disastrous volcanic eruption, and famine.

In 1814, following the Napoleonic Wars, the Norwegian-Danish state was broken into two separate nations. Iceland belonged to Denmark, but increasingly difficult conditions forced many Icelanders to migrate to the New World. The 19th century was not all bad, however. Inventions such as the steamship and the transatlantic cable improved communication and transportation, making Iceland less isolated from the rest of the world. These developments helped inspire an Icelandic independence movement. This movement was led by Jón Sigurðsson. (sig-erth-son) In 1874, the country was granted a constitution and limited home rule.

In 1918, the Act of Union was signed, granting Iceland full self-government under the Danish crown. After 25 years, either country had the right to dissolve the union. During World War II, the Germans overtook Denmark while British and U.S. troops protected Iceland from invasion. The Act of Union expired in 1943, and Icelanders voted on the issue of independence. Iceland declared its independence on June 17, 1944. Sveinn Björnsson (byorn-son) was the first president. Iceland became a member of NATO in 1949.

During the 1960s and 70s, Iceland and England became involved in *cod wars* over fishing rights in the waters of the north Atlantic. The country elected its first female president and head of state in 1980. She was reelected in 1984.

After Iceland gained independence, it experienced much economic growth. In 1994, the country joined the European Economic Area. Following the turn of the century, Iceland grew into a global financial powerhouse; however, the global financial crisis of 2008 had an especially dramatically negative impact on the country's economy. This resulted in a sharp increase in migrations. The government now faces the challenge of bringing people back to Iceland.

# Daily Life

Icelanders are reserved and confident people who are proud of their tradition and heritage. The country's isolation and Nordic roots give it the unique character it has today. To preserve their language, Icelanders continue to use native words for foreign products. For instance, they call a computer a *tölva*, which combines the ancient Icelandic terms for *number* and *seer*.

In Iceland, social class does not vary much; no one is particularly wealthy and no one is particularly impoverished. The country uses renewable resources to provide practically all of its electricity, and over 70% of its total energy. By 2050, Iceland plans to be energy-independent.

On average, Icelanders live longer than most people in the world. Iceland is a progressive country and its citizens value self-sufficiency and independence. Like other Scandinavian countries, it is known for its liberal attitude toward women; many Icelandic women hold high positions in the government and prominent positions in society.

## Living in Iceland

Most of the larger settlements in Iceland are found along the coastline, including the capital of Reykjavík and its outlying towns. This is due to the fact that the island's interior, called the Highlands of Iceland, is largely inhabitable. The majority of Iceland's population lives in the cities and towns.

Most people get around Iceland in automobiles, even though most of the roads throughout the country are unpaved. The main road is called Route One, or Ring Road, because it loops the island's outer edge, connecting all of the settled parts of Iceland. Many of the unpaved roads are found in the country's rough, mountainous interior.

## School

Children begin their education at nursery school, called *leikskóli*. This level of schooling is not required, but the curriculum helps prepare children for the transition to regular schooling, called *grunnskóli*. *Grunnskóli* is primary and lower secondary education (roughly six to 16 years of age), and is required by law. The school year lasts nine months, beginning in August or September and ending in May or June.

The next step is upper secondary education, *framhaldsskóli*. These institutions are known as gymnasia in English. This highest level of education is not required, and can only be accessed upon completion of the required *grunnskóli*. The University of Iceland in the capital of Reykjavík is the largest such school.

## Famous People from Iceland

Leif Ericson (approximately 970-1020) was a Norse explorer and son of the famous Eric the Red. Leif is believed to be the first European to discover the land that is America. He made this discovery some 500 years before Christopher Columbus did so. In America, October 9 is Leif Ericson day.

Halldór Kiljan Laxness (1902-1998) was an Icelandic novelist. Some of his books include *Independent People*, *Iceland's Bell*, and *The Atom Station*. He won the Nobel Prize in Literature in 1955.

Björk Guðmundsdóttir (1965- ), better known simply as Björk, is a singer and songwriter from Icleand. A talented musician, she works in a number of genres. She is known for her flashy, eccentric costumes and music videos. She is also an actress. She has been nominated for multiple awards for both her music and acting.

# Language & Expressions

Icelandic is the official language of Iceland, but English is widely spoken as a second language. Danish is also spoken, as well as other Scandinavian languages. The Icelandic alphabet is somewhat different than the English one. Like other Scandinavian languages, it combines the Latin alphabet with Runic characters (Ðð, Þþ, and Ææ and Öö).

## Icelandic Alphabet

The Icelandic alphabet has 32 letters. The letters that do not have listed pronunciations are pronounced the same as they are in the regular Latin alphabet.

| Letter | Pronunciation | Letter | Pronunciation |
|---|---|---|---|
| A | ah | N | |
| Á | ow | O | o (as in *song*) |
| B | | Ó | ō |
| D | | P | |
| Ð | th | R | er |
| E | eh | S | |
| É | yea (as in *yeah*) | T | |
| F | | U | uh |
| G | | Ú | oo (as in *foot*) |
| H | | V | |
| I | i (as in *simple*) | X | |
| Í | ee | Y | i (as in *simple*) |
| J | | Ý | ee |
| K | | Þ | th |
| L | | Æ | ī |
| M | | Ö | u (as in *further*) |

Instead of using family names like other European countries and America, Icelanders use patronymics. This means their first names are followed with a patronymic. For instance if your name is Karl and your father's name is Lars, you would be called Karl Larsson, or *Karl, Lars' son*. Because of this, Icelandic telephone directories list people by their first name rather than their last name.

## Famous Icelandic Proverbs

Here are some famous proverbs from Iceland. What do you think they mean?

*Blind is a man without a book.*

*You will reach your destination even though you travel slowly.*

*Money makes monkeys of men.*

*A bad rower blames the oar.*

*A burnt child keeps away from fire.*

*It often takes little force to move great masses.*

*It is better to stand on your own feet than someone else's.*

## Body Language and Etiquette in Iceland

Greet people with a firm handshake and eye contact in Iceland. Do the same when leaving.

Generally, surnames (mister, miss, etc.) are not used in Iceland. Once you know someone's first name, feel free to use it.

Icelanders might seem unfriendly at first glance, but this is not the case! Excessive smiling and cheerfulness are not common greetings.

Tipping (at restaurants, in taxis, etc.) is never required in Iceland. Service fees are added to bills.

Always remove your shoes before entering someone else's home.

# Know before You Go

Here are some common phrases you will use in Iceland, along with numbers one through ten. The spellings and pronunciations are also included.

| **English** | **Icelandic** | **Pronunciation** |
|---|---|---|
| Hello | Góðan dag | go-an dog |
| How are you? | Hvað segir þú? | hvash-ā thoo? |
| What's your name? | Hvað heitir þú? | hvī-tay thoo? |
| Good morning. | Góðan daginn. | go-an dog-in. |
| Good night. | Góða nótt. | go-an not. |
| Do you speak Icelandic? | Talar þú íslensku? | tall-er thoo eez-lensh-ku? |
| Thank you. | Takk | tok |
| | | |
| one | einn | een |
| two | tveir | tveer |
| three | þrír | threer |
| four | fjórir | fyor-eer |
| five | fimm | fim |
| six | sex | sex |
| seven | sjö | syoo |
| eight | átta | ah-ta |
| nine | níu | nee-yuh |
| ten | tíu | tee-uh |

# In Your Classroom

Have the students write their names using the Icelandic alphabet. Have them also use patronymics to refer to themselves the rest of the day and to label all of their class work.

MP5129 - Iceland

# Foods

Icelandic cuisine revolves around the fishing industry and most of their traditional dishes involve fish of various sorts. The more common varieties are haddock, plaice, halibut, herring and shrimp. *Hákarl* (Icelandic for *shark*) is rotten shark meat, known for its pungent flavor and smell. Eating this unique dish is said to give strength.

Icelanders have eaten sheep meat for centuries. Horse meat is often served salted and boiled. Iceland also produces quality beef as a result of its cold weather. A wide variety of birds are hunted and eaten, as well. Reindeer meat is a special treat reserved for rare occasions.

Many of the country's fruits and vegetables are imported as a result of poor growing conditions. Greenhouses produce cabbage, rutabaga, and turnips. Tomatoes and cucumbers are grown indoors. Berries are also grown in Iceland, one of the only fruits native to the island.

Due to Iceland's history, breads and pastries often feature Danish origins and influences. *Snúður* (snu-thur), cinnamon rolls, are popular, as are coconut-glazed chocolate cakes called *skúffukaka*. Layer cakes are common, filled with jam, icing, or fruit preserves. Rye breads are often eaten. *Kleina* are delicious fried buns shaped into knots.

## Icelandic Feasts

*Porramatur* (thor-a-ma-tour) is a sampling of uniquely traditional Icelandic foods, most of which are cured in lactic acid. It's very popular with older generations of Icelanders – but it might make you lose your appetite! *Hákarl* (rotten shark meat) is often included. Other possible additions include: seal flippers, sheep heads, blood pudding, and head cheese. Traditional rye bread rounds out this 'special' feast.

If *Porramatur* doesn't make your stomach growl, an Icelandic Christmas feast might be more to your liking. Served on Christmas Eve, these dinners feature smoked lamb, salted pork rib, and various types of game (usually birds). The main course is usually served with a mushroom sauce, along with potatoes, peas, beetroot, cabbage, and jam. Dessert is rice pudding with raisins, cinnamon, and sugar.

Family events (birthdays, weddings, etc.) are occasions to eat well, and Iceland embraces this idea. Coffee is served to guests, who enjoy *brauðterta* (browth-tear-ta), layers of white bread filled with fillings of salmon, shrimp, and mayonnaise. The meal is sweetened with sponge cake topped with fruit, whipped cream, marzipan, and meringue.

## In Your Classroom

*Skyr* is a famous Icelandic dessert made with skim milk and fresh bilberries. *Skyr* is not complicated to make, but needs to be made in a proper kitchen, not a classroom. You can access recipes for it at http://www.skyr.is/Recipes/ and distribute them to the students. Or, prepare *Skyr* the night before and bring it into the classroom for the students to try.

# Holidays & Festivals

**Sprengidagur**
*Tuesday before Lent*

Also called Bursting Day, this holiday is meant to prepare Icelanders for the Lenten season. The day is all about eating. Salted meat and peas are common dishes. You're supposed to eat until you feel about to burst, so you'd better come hungry!

**Öskudagur (Ash Wednesday)**
*First Day of Lent*

Lent begins with church and family get-togethers. The ashes are gathered into small bags and given to children. Children are encouraged to secretly pin the ash bags on others as a prank. This day also features children's parades. There is much singing and begging for treats from local shops.

**Sumardargurinn Fyrsti (First Day of Summer)**
*June*

This festival marks the transition from spring to summer. This holiday was a big deal in the past, when Iceland only had two seasons – summer and winter. Icelanders still celebrate the day with parades and sporting events.

**Sjómannadagur (Seamen's Day)**
*June*

The Sjómannadagur is a celebration that pays tribute to Iceland's seafaring past. A variety of special activities take place. Parades take place throughout the country. Swimming and rowing races are held. There are even competitions in tug-of-war and sea rescue.

**Icelandic Republic Day**
*June 17*

This specific day was chosen to celebrate Iceland's independence because it is the birthday of Jón Sigurðsson, the leader of the independence movement in 19th century. Reykjavik is the center of the largest celebrations. There are parades, performances of street theatre, and dancing. In more rural parts of the country, picnics are common.

**Verslunarmannahelgi (Labor Day Weekend)**
*First Week of August*

Icelanders use this summer weekend to celebrate and appreciate the outdoors. The idea is to be outside as much as possible. Many Icelanders will pack up and head for the country to camp or picnic. Many organized events, including music festivals, are held outdoors, as well.

**Reykjavík Arts Festival**
*August*

Iceland's capital features many unique cultural destinations. On this night in August, churches, cafés, galleries, museums, restaurants, and stores stay open late into the night. Concerts, exhibitions, and various performances are held. Icelandic food and drinks are served. The evening concludes with a spectacular fireworks display.

# Creative Arts

Because so much of the island is uninhabited, the unknown regions are clouded in mystery. Through the years, Icelandic fairytales and legends about elves have passed from one generation to the next. Many people in Iceland claim to still believe in elves.

Over the years, Iceland's rich cultural history has been preserved through art and writing. The saga, a historical tale of adventure, is an Icelandic form of writing that dates back to the Middle Ages and has significantly contributed to the literary world. Sacred verses, hymns, and rhyming epic poems called *rímur* are also part of Iceland's literary tradition.

Iceland is known for its hand-made crafts, such as knitwear. Icelandic architecture is similar to that of other Scandinavian countries. Because of the scarcity of trees available on the island, many houses are covered with grass and turf.

The island's distinct landscape has served as an inspiration for artists over the years. Þórarinn Þorláksson, an Icelandic painter who studied in Denmark, is credited with being the forerunner of contemporary Icelandic painting. During this time, several other Icelanders studied painting in Denmark and began to follow in his footsteps. In recent years, painting has become especially popular on the island. Many attribute this increase in interest to the work of Einar Hákonarson, an expressionistic painter from Iceland known for painting figures.

Traditional Icelandic music has religious themes. The *rímur* is also an Icelandic music tradition, as well as a literary one. Folk music, pop, electronic music, and medieval influences are present in modern Icelandic music. Several bands from the island have become famous worldwide, such as Björk, Sigur Rós, and The Sugarcubes.

## In Your Classroom

Discuss the legend of elves with the students. See which students believe they are real and which ones do not. Have them write stories about elves.

Hold an Arts Festival in the classroom. Have students create masterpieces, whether paintings, models, embroidery, or photography, to put on display. Be as creative as possible and remember that *art* is a relative term!

Have the students collaborate to write a saga about history. Discuss important facts and dates to include, but remember that a saga's purpose is a historical tale of adventure, not necessarily a history *lesson*. Writing a creative narrative is half of the fun. Once the saga is finished, read it aloud as a class.

# Sports & Games

Many sports are popular in Iceland. The Icelandic people are generally very healthy, and enjoy physical pursuits. Football (soccer), basketball, volleyball, tennis, and swimming are some common sports played around the country.

Team handball is one of the most popular national sports. The national team is one of the highest-ranked teams in the world. They won the silver medal at the 2010 Summer Olympics in Beijing, China.

Other sports that are especially popular in Iceland include chess, shooting, and ice or rock climbing. A number of chess Grandmasters were born in Iceland. Rifle shooting has been around since the 19th century, and was especially popular during the years when Icelanders hungered for independence.

Iceland has produced some of the strongest men in the world. The country is known internationally for its dominance in strength and powerlifting competitions. An Icelander has won the World's Strongest Man competition eight times, along with several top-three finishers. *Glíma*, a form of wrestling that is thought to have originated during medieval times, is another Icelandic sport focusing on strength.

# Ireland

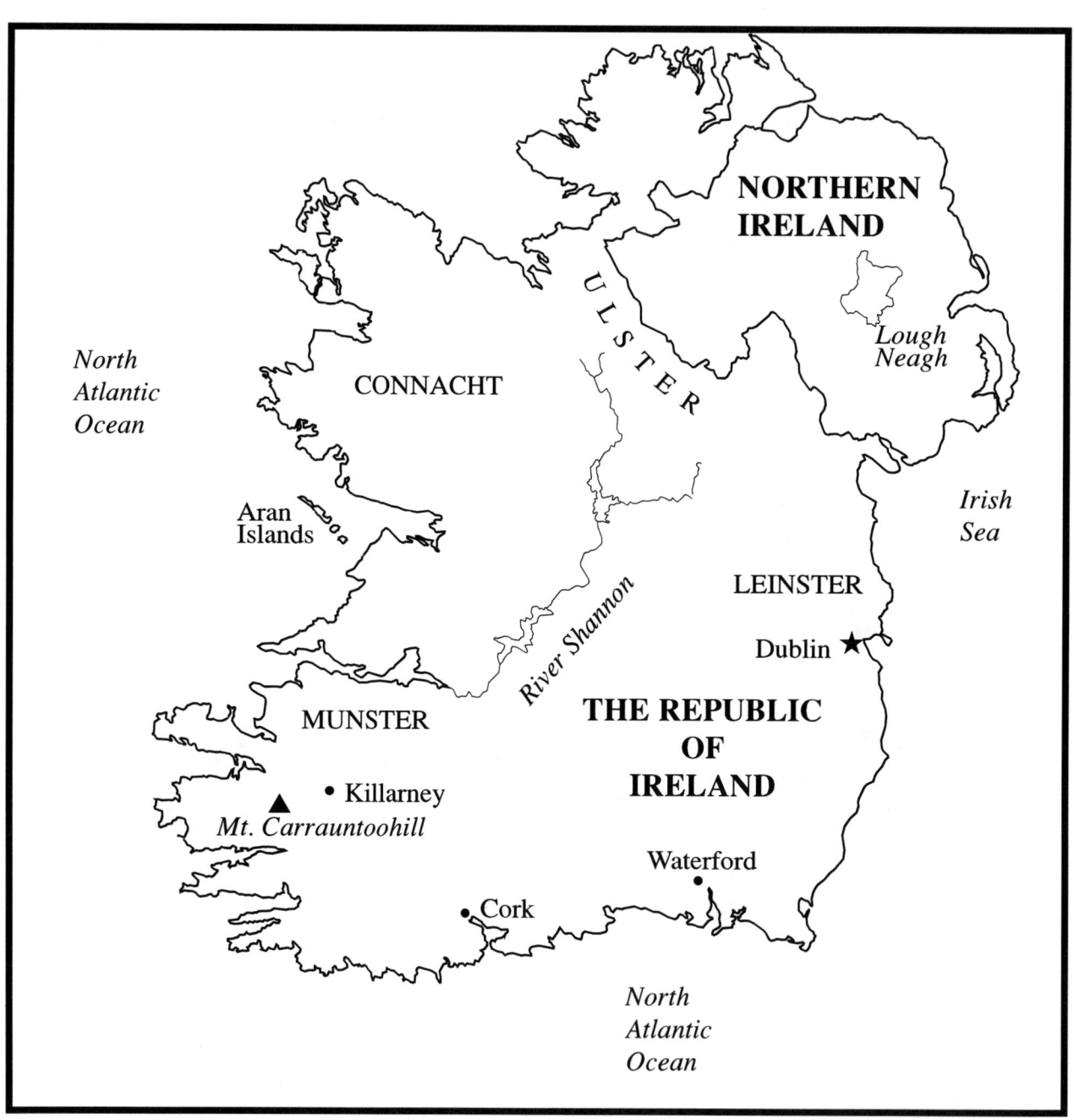

# Welcome to Ireland!

The earliest known inhabitants of Ireland came from the European continent at the end of the Ice Age, about eight thousand years ago. The search for food led these early people along Europe's western coast to Scotland. From there, they crossed an ice bridge on foot or sailed over open water in primitive boats to the northeast coast of Ireland. At first, they lived a nomadic life, killing animals and catching fish for food. Gradually they learned how to plant and grow food, and they established communities.

A large number of Ireland's people continue to tend the earth today. Although it comprises only a small part of Europe, Ireland has given the world an abundance of fine literature, poetry, scholars, music, and art. The Republic of Ireland, which is independent, consists of 26 counties and covers 85 percent of the island. Northern Ireland, which is governed by the United Kingdom, consists of six counties. Four ancient provinces are still recognized: Ulster, Connacht, Leinster, and Munster.

| | |
|---|---|
| **Official Name:** | Ireland |
| **Location:** | Ireland is an island located off the west coast of Great Britain, in the North Atlantic Ocean. One-sixth of the island belongs to Great Britain – this part of the island is called Northern Ireland. |
| **Population:** | 4,203,200 (2010 estimate) |
| **Capital City:** | Dublin |
| **Area:** | 27,136 square miles |
| **Major Languages:** | English is widely spoken. Irish, or Gaelic, is the official language of the country, and is still spoken, especially along the west coast. |
| **Major Religion:** | Roman Catholic: 87.4% |
| **Currency:** | Euro; the euro is used in most countries in the European Union. |
| **Climate:** | Ireland has a temperate maritime climate. This results in mild winters and cool summers. The sky over Ireland is overcast nearly half the time. |
| **The Land:** | Sea cliffs on the west coast give way to low mountains and hills. The interior of the island is mostly rolling or flat plains. |
| **Type of Government:** | Republic; Parliamentary Democracy |

**Flag:** 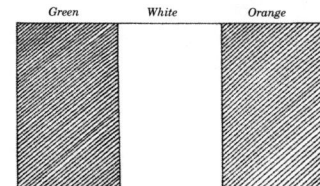 The flag of Ireland has three vertical bands. The left band is green, which symbolizes the Celts and modern Catholics. The right band is orange, which symbolizes the English King William of Orange and modern Protestants. The central band is white, which symbolizes peace between Catholics and Protestants.

**Coat of Arms:**  The coat of arms features a silver-stringed golden harp on a field of St. Patrick's blue. The harp is a Gaelic Harp, and has been Ireland's heraldic emblem for a long time.

**National Flower:** Shamrock

**Motto:** "Sworn to be free"

## Natural Environment

The Republic of Ireland covers the bulk of a large island off the northwest coast of Europe. The island is a fragment that became detached from mainland Europe many centuries ago. Most of the Republic is surrounded by water. It is bordered on the south, west, and northwest by the Atlantic Ocean. To the east is the Irish Sea, which lies between Ireland and Great Britain. There are many small islands off the coast. The most famous of these are the Aran Islands to the west.

On land, there are three major regions: the central plain, the mountains, and the coast. Because of the dozens of shades of green seen in the lush fields and on mist-covered mountains, Ireland is often called *the Emerald Isle*.

The central plain covers layers of glacial drift, limestone, and rock. This has created rich, fertile soil where wheat, barley, oats, potatoes, sugar beets, and turnips are grown. North of this are thousands of acres of wet, spongy ground that forms peat bogs. Peat, cut into bricks and dried, is an important source of fuel for Irish farmers.

Among the abundant wild and cultivated flowers in Ireland are primroses, gorse, heather, bluebells, daisies, foxglove, roses, peonies, irises, clematis, and delphiniums. Trees include oak, yew, beech, horse chestnut, sycamore, blackthorn (wild plum), and crab apple.

While all trees are appreciated, the thorn tree is the most respected. In Irish folklore, it is the magic tree. Trouble will most certainly follow anyone who kills or mutilates a thorn tree. In modern times, construction workers built roads around ancient thorn trees rather than dig up the trees.

After the glaciers melted, many clear, beautiful lakes and rivers remained. Lough (pronounced lock; Lake) Neagh is the largest lake in Ireland. It covers 153 square miles. The Lakes of Killarney are famous landmarks. The River Shannon flows 230 miles from northwestern Ireland to the Atlantic Ocean. Other important rivers are the River Liffey and the River Lee.

Surrounding the central plain are huge rock cliffs and an irregular series of mountain ranges. The highest point is Carrauntoohill in the mountains of Kerry. Its peak is 3414 feet high.

One of the country's most impressive rock formations is known as the *Giants' Causeway*. As lava erupted and then cooled, strange basalt columns formed. Legends describe these rock formations as stepping stones for giants when they walked along the coast and across the sea to Scotland.

Beyond the mountains lies the coastal area. It is characterized by numerous bays cut deeply into the 3500 miles of coastline, which support the country's important fishing industry.

*Animals*

At one time, wolves, brown bears, lynx and Irish elk—huge deer with 13-foot antlers—were among the species of Irish wildlife. Today there remain the red deer, foxes, badgers, squirrels, and hares. Domestic animals include cows, goats, chickens, and both thoroughbred and working horses. The Irish Wolfhound is the tallest dog. It has been used for hunting in Ireland for over two thousand years.

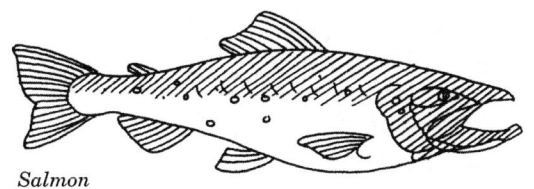
*Salmon*

*Newt*

*Irish Wolfhound*

Numerous lovely songbirds nest in the trees and in the fields. A variety of beautiful sea birds, both native and migratory, populate the coasts.

Among Ireland's 32 species of fish are herring, cod, lobster, mackerel, and salmon.

There are no snakes in Ireland. In fact, the only reptile on the island is the small viviparous lizard. The newt and the grass frog are the only two native amphibians.

## In Your Classroom

Show students a large map of Europe and help them locate Ireland. Ask them to compare its size to other European countries, such as Germany and France.

Show students a map of the United States. Locate the state of Maine, which is about the same size as Ireland. Help them draw conclusions about the differences between an island and a larger country.

Point out that Ireland was once part of the European continent. Make a copy of a map of Europe for each child. Ask students to cut out the country of Ireland (the Republic of Ireland and Northern Ireland together) and then to try to fit Ireland's coastline into the coastline of Great Britain. Explain how the underwater plates shifted, causing part of the land to become detached.

# A History of Ireland

Although an island, Ireland is close to mainland Europe and has experienced a number of invasions from the continent. Many of the invaders enriched Irish history and culture. Others reduced its population to poverty and starvation.

## Early Ireland

The earliest of the Irish people came from the European mainland. They lived during the Stone Age around 6000 BCE. Though they were nomadic at first, they began to form permanent settlements by 4000 BCE. Tools, knives, and other weapons were made from nearby supplies of stone. The area was heavily forested at this time, and many of the dwellings were made of wood. They also built stone burial chambers, many of which are still standing.

Most of these tombs were more impressive than the homes. Passage graves are the simplest tombs, having one or two chambers. A corridor lined with heavy stones leads to a central chamber. Ornaments discovered in the chambers indicate a belief in afterlife. Intricate spirals, triangles, zigzag lines, and representations of the sun are carved on the walls. Gallery graves are similar to passage graves but are more elongated and have no corridor.

Dolmen—stone tables—or portal tombs have a large chamber formed by five or six huge vertical stones with an enormous, sloping stone roof. Early natives thought the dolmens were burial sites of the giants.

During the Bronze Age in about 2000 BCE, the Irish made stronger weapons than they had before, creating them from the local supply of hard bronze metal. Farming and building methods improved. The Irish built many hill forts for protection. Their sacrifices and early religious celebrations were held within large circles of stone. *Menhirs*, or long stones, served as tombstones and were the predecessors of the Christian high crosses.

The Iron Age began in Ireland around 400 BCE, when the Celts of western Europe invaded the island. They brought iron weapons, stronger than the local bronze weapons, and they subdued the Irish inhabitants. The Celts were well organized. They divided the country into small kingdoms, each ruled by a minor chief or king. A high king created laws, encouraged music, and built roads. The Celts had no written language, so storytellers were highly respected. Although little is known of burial customs in this age, ring forts were the characteristic fortification. Farms and huts were enclosed by a high circular rampart. Some had underground passageways that connected the dwellings. These were used to store supplies and provide refuge.

## Christian Ireland and Invasions

In the fifth century CE, St. Patrick, a priest and former slave, brought Christianity to Ireland. He established monasteries and taught the people to read. The monks developed a written language. While most of Europe suffered a cultural decline during the Dark Ages, literature, learning, and art thrived in Ireland. The famous illuminated manuscript, the *Book of Kells*, and the Celtic crosses were created during this era.

*St. Patrick*

At the end of the eighth century CE, many Vikings, fierce fighters and good sailors, left their overcrowded Scandinavian homeland and began invasions of Ireland. The Vikings killed people and destroyed farms, stole valuable manuscripts from monasteries, and built strong forts, which became the sites for major cities like Dublin and Cork.

Of all the lands in western Europe, Ireland was the only one to escape an invasion by the Romans, who generally set up a system of central government.

So although the Irish had many minor kings, there was no single leader. Then, in 1002, Brian Boru unified the country and became the high king. In 1014 Brian Boru's army defeated the Vikings and ended their rule. For 150 years there was peace and prosperity in Ireland.

Then several small Irish kingdoms began fighting each other. In the 1160s, one of the kings, Dermot, asked Norman-born King Henry II of England to help him regain control of Ireland. Henry offered his Norman soldiers to Dermot in return for a share of the conquered land. Dermot led a successful invasion, but he died in 1170. After Henry II visited these new lands in 1171, the Norman soldiers declared him Lord of Ireland. Gradually the new lord's territory began to shrink as Normans intermarried with Irish and built homes. English territory was finally reduced to a small stretch of land around the city of Dublin. It was known as the Pale.

## English Control

Henry VIII, his daughter Mary, and then Elizabeth I continued to send armies and English settlers into Ireland. The Irish lost battle after battle and, by 1700, were reduced to slavery. The Irish, who had once owned 95 percent of the land, now held only five percent. They could not vote, own property, hold public office, or become teachers or lawyers. *Hedge schools*, secret spots where the Irish could teach their children, became common. For the millions of Irish who had no land, no food, and no political power, survival was a daily struggle.

Then, in 1845, the potato crop was destroyed by blight (plant disease.) About 750,000 Irish starved to death and hundreds of thousands emigrated to other countries. Within five years, the Irish population plummeted from eight million to five million. Although most of the Irish sailed for America, others emigrated to Canada, South America, Australia, the West Indies, New Zealand, Nova Scotia, and Britain. At Ellis Island in 1992, a life–size bronze statue of Annie Moore, a 15-year-old girl from County Cork, was dedicated. In 1892, Annie brought her two young brothers across the ocean on the *S.S. Nevada* to join their parents in New York. She was the first immigrant to go through the Ellis Island facility.

## Partition

In 1858, a new drive for freedom began. Irish Catholics wanted to be free from England. Protestants preferred to stay under English rule. In the 1870s, a movement called Home Rule began. Although a bill was enacted in 1914, it was suspended until the end of World War I. Frustration over the delay in Home Rule led to the 1916 Easter Rising. After several meetings, confrontations, and compromises, a settlement was finally reached. The British Parliament passed a law to divide the country. The larger area became the Irish Free State in 1921. In 1948, the Free State voted to end its association with England and, in 1949, became the Republic of Ireland. In 1955, Ireland joined NATO.

# Modern Ireland

Since becoming an independent republic, Ireland has continued to expand its influence on the world at large. In 1973, the country joined the European Economic Community. They signed the Treaty on European Union in 1991. Since then, Ireland has played its part in European politics and business.

The young country has not been without its problems, however. Religious violence between Ireland and British-controlled Northern Ireland strained tensions between Ireland and England. Attacks and deaths were common in the latter part of the 20th century. In the 1990s, the two countries began working together to stem the tide of violence. In 1998, the Good Friday Agreement settled many issues, and tensions lessened greatly as a result.

Economic problems have plagued Ireland since the 1980s. Like most European countries, they have been hit hard by the recent financial crisis. The government works hard to combat these and other problems. Ireland maintains their unique and proud culture while becoming increasingly involved in European and global affairs.

## In Your Classroom

Ask students to examine the hut structure of early Ireland and compare it to an early Native American home. Discuss similarities such as weapons, lifestyles, and so on.

Compare the writings on Celtic crosses to Egyptian hieroglyphics.

Discuss the Dark Ages in European history. Point out the artistic and literary achievements in Ireland in contrast to the intellectual and cultural decline suffered throughout the rest of Europe.

Name _____   Date _____

# Mapping out History

Use the map of Ireland to record some of the country's historic locations.

1. Ireland is divided into two separate regions, the Republic of Ireland, which makes up a majority of the island, and Northern Ireland, a part of Great Britain. Trace the division between the Republic of Ireland and Northern Ireland with a thick line. Label each region.
2. The capital of Ireland is Dublin, and it is found on the eastern coast. Locate and label the city.
3. Belfast is the capital of Northern Ireland, and it is also found on the eastern coast. Find and label it on the map.
4. Ireland is bordered by the North Atlantic Ocean on its west coast, and the Irish Sea on its east coast. Label these bodies of water and shade them blue.
5. Ireland was plagued with Viking invasions for much of its history. The Vikings established many settlements that have become large Irish cities, including Dublin. Cork, Limerick, and Waterford were all once Viking settlements. Cork is the southernmost city on the map. Waterford is east of Cork, but it is not a coastal city. Limerick is north of Cork and southwest of Dublin. Locate and label these cities on your map.
6. In 1169, the first Norman forces arrived in Ireland. They captured the city of Wexford and went on to control the Irish region of Leinster. Label Wexford, which is east of Waterford.
7. The geography of Ireland is characterized by a ring of coastal mountains, and an interior of lush plains. Label the coastal mountains of Ireland with ∆s and shade them brown. Shade the interior green to symbolize the plains.

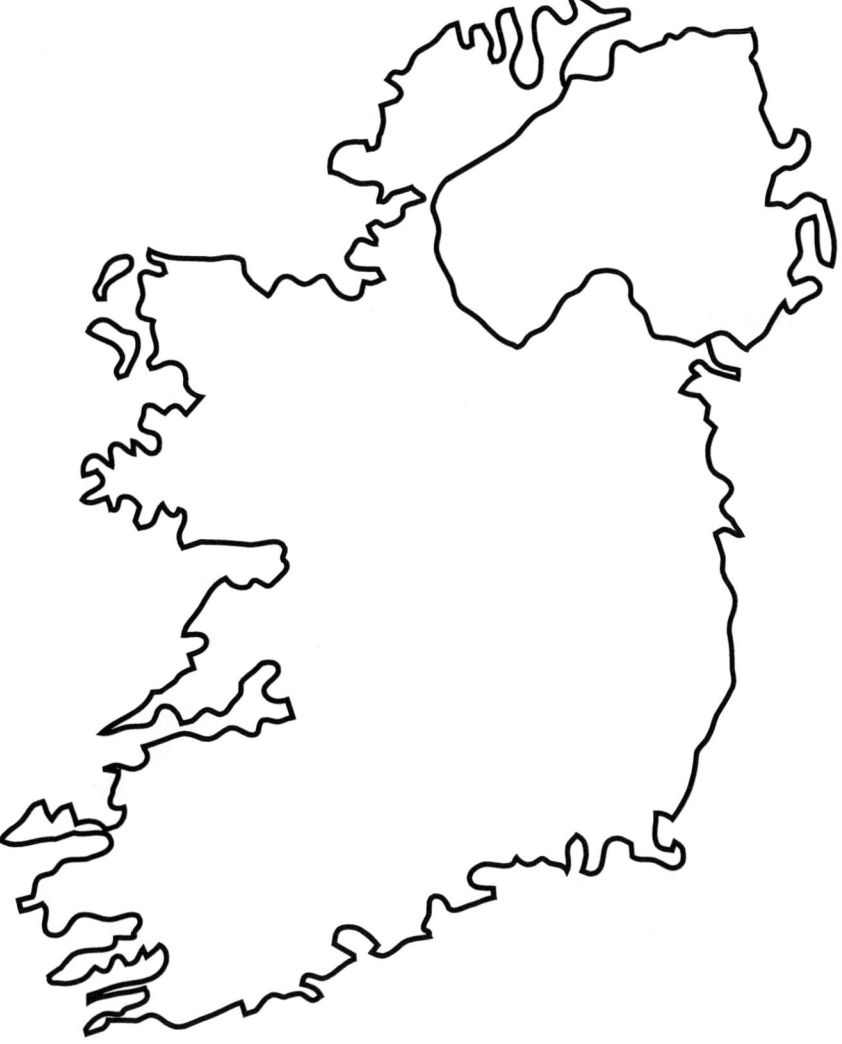

MP5129 - Ireland

93

# Daily Life

The daily life of a family living on an Irish farm is familiar and unhurried. The same pattern has been followed for years and much of the work is determined by the seasons. Much of Ireland is farmland. The people who live on these lands plow and plant fields, milk cows, and feed their livestock. Housewives cook, churn butter, and care for the children. Many rural families live in small stone or clay cottages, heated by peat or turf fires. Some roofs are still thatched with hay. Families enjoy each other's company and make room for grandparents and other relatives.

Life in Irish cities is similar to life in other European metropolitan areas. Some people in Ireland own homes, while many others live in apartments. Regular office hours are kept and office workers, clerks, and salespeople ride buses or walk to work. On the way to their offices, they might stop to admire the work of a sidewalk artist or to buy a piece of fruit at an outdoor produce stand. Fresh fish is also available at outdoor stands. It was in Dublin that Molly Malone, the subject of the ballad "Cockles and Mussels," sold her fish. A life-size statue of Molly and her barrow stands in Grafton Street in Dublin.

School is mandatory for children from six to 15 years old. Irish students attend primary schools similar to grade schools in other countries. They study reading, writing, math, music, art, and crafts. When they are 12 years old, Irish students attend the second level of school, which is similar to high school. They can either take a course of general studies or they can learn specific skills to help them become workers in certain industries, such as manufacturing.

## Famous People from Ireland

Ireland has produced many of history's great artists in several fields. Here are a few examples:

Jonathan Swift (1667-1745) was an Irish writer. Two of his most famous works are *Gulliver's Travels* and *A Modest Proposal*.

Bram Stoker (1847-1912) was an Irish author best known for his gothic novel *Dracula*. This story laid the foundation for seemingly countless spin-offs and inspirations. The vampire continues to be extremely popular in modern entertainment.

Oscar Wilde (1854-1900) was an Irish playwright, poet, and author. His most famous play, *The Importance of Being Earnest*, is still performed today.

Annie Moore (1877-1924) was the first immigrant to be processed at Ellis Island in New York City. Ellis Island has become an iconic American landmark; Annie will always be remembered as the first person to enter America through its gates.

Many of the finest actors and actresses were born in Ireland. Daniel Day-Lewis and Peter O'Toole have won Academy Awards for their work; Maureen O'Hara is famous for her portrayal of Esmeralda in *The Hunchback of Notre Dame*; Pierce Brosnan played the part of James Bond in several films; Brendan Gleeson has starred in famous films like *Braveheart* and the *Harry Potter* movies – the list is too long to finish here!

## In Your Classroom

Point out how Irish farmers use materials at hand to build their homes. Help students list items like rocks, hay, and so on, which are used by the farmers.

Discuss the differences between the Irish school systems and your school system.

Ask students what subjects they might wish to add to their curriculum.

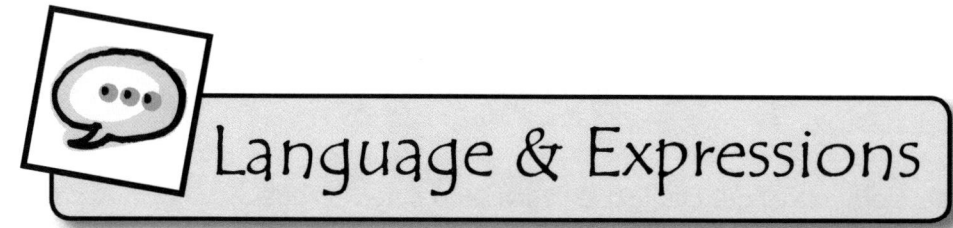

# Language & Expressions

Irish is a Celtic language first used by early scholars. It is closely related to the Scottish, Gaelic, and Manx languages. Irish, which sounds quite different from English, is spoken mainly in the west of Ireland.

| Roman | Irish | Roman | Irish | Roman | Irish |
|---|---|---|---|---|---|
| a | A | g | S | o | o |
| b | b | h | h | p | p |
| c | c | i | i | r | R |
| d | d | l | L | s | S |
| e | e | m | m | t | τ |
| f | F | n | n | u | u |

Many Irish names begin with **Mc**, **Mac**, or **O'**. **Mc** or **Mac** means *son of* or *descendent of*. **O'** means *grandson or descendent of*. For example, **McDonald** means *son of Donald*. **O'Connor** means *descendent of Connor*. If your last name does not start one of these ways already, write it using **Mc**, **Mac**, or **O'**:

_____

The people of Ireland have many descriptive everyday phrases and words. The Irish language has a number of words similar to ancient Celtic in both spelling and meaning. Among these phrases are:

*Slainte* – Here's to your good health. (a toast)
*Erin go bragh* – Ireland forever. (a patriotic phrase)
*Cead mile failte* – A hundred thousand welcomes. (a greeting)

In the English language, there are these phrases:

*It's a soft day.* – raining gently
*fall of the table* – dinner scraps saved for pets or livestock
*keening* – weeping or mourning for the dead
*pampootie* – a rawhide shoe without a heel, which is worn on the Aran Islands for climbing over rocks and out of boats
*praitie* – potato
*The top of the morning to you.* – a greeting
*And the rest of the day to yourself.* – the reply to that greeting

The Irish language has no words for *yes* and *no*. When a question is asked, the answer contains the verb from the question. For example:

Question: Is he going to town?
Answer: He is. OR He is not.

Name _____  Date _____

## Famous Irish Proverbs

Here are some famous Irish proverbs. What do you think they mean?

*One beetle recognizes another.*

*It is one after another that the castles are built.*

*The nest is enough for a wren.*

*A friend's eye is a good mirror.*

*There's no hearth like your own hearth.*

## Body Language and Etiquette in Ireland

Here are some examples of body language and etiquette that you'll find in Ireland.

*The Irish don't like to be too close when conversing. Keep at least an arm's length apart.*

*Public displays of affection (hugging, kissing, etc.) aren't common in Ireland.*

*Be very careful with the "peace" sign in Ireland. When reversed (palm towards you), this is considered a very rude gesture.*

*The Irish have a relaxed sense of time. If you are a few minutes late for an appointment, it's unlikely there will be a problem.*

*If an Irish acquaintance offers you a drink, be sure to accept. Declining a drink is considered offensive.*

## In Your Classroom

Ask students to circle the Irish letters that are different from English ones.

Ask students to write their first and last names using Irish letters.

# Foods

In the years after the great famines of the 1840s, Irish people ate very simple foods and were careful to waste nothing. Potatoes and bread continue to be staples in the daily diet. As the population prospered, more variety in foods was introduced. Much of it was grown on family farms. In general, Irish meals are simple, nourishing, and plentiful. However, on special occasions, Irish food can be as elegant as French cuisine.

Irish food can be broken down into two categories: traditional and modern. Traditional Irish food uses a lot of potatoes. Here are a couple of examples of traditional Irish meals:

*Irish Stew*—a stew loaded with lamb or mutton, potatoes, onions, and parsley
*Irish Breakfast*—a fried or grilled dish served with bacon, eggs, sausage, black and white pudding, fried tomatoes and fried potatoes

Modern Irish dishes still use lots of potatoes, but have adopted some different ingredients as well. Seafood has become very popular, particularly shellfish, which are found all along the coast and are of very high quality. Oysters are also eaten, as well as fish, particularly salmon and cod. Bread is a staple in modern Irish cooking.

**Breakfast foods**

Stir-about—a porridge made from oat or corn meal stirred into boiling water or milk
Eggs—fried or boiled
Irish soda bread
Griddle cakes
Sausage
Buttermilk
Honey

**Noon meal (often the main meal of the day)**

Soup—nettle, onion, or other
Irish stew, mutton, or lamb
Potatoes—boiled, mashed, or baked
Vegetables from the fields—carrots, onions, cabbage
Apple cake—made from fruit stored in special apple houses

**Supper or Tea**

Sandwich or cold plate
Cold salmon or fish

**High tea (flexible time, generally late afternoon)**

Jam and scones—quick bread or small pastries like biscuits
Blueberry tarts
Cheese
Herring
Crab cakes
Fruit cake

Tea is served at all meals. The kettle is always ready to heat when visitors call. The Irish brew strong tea and add sugar, honey, or cream. Traveling tea vans with many kinds of tea visit the country cottages to let people select their favorite blends.

# Recipes – Enjoy Irish Cuisine!

Here are a few recipes that will give your students a sampling of the Irish diet. Try them out in your classroom!

### Baked Potatoes

Wash and scrub one baking potato for every two students. Bake in an oven at 375°F for 45 minutes or until the potato is soft. While the potatoes are baking, help students assemble various toppings, such as margarine, parsley, onion flakes, shredded cheese, chives, salt, and pepper. Slice the cooked potatoes in two and serve a half to each student. Let students add their favorite toppings.

### Irish Soda Bread

Preheat the oven to 375°F. Put 2 cups of sifted white flour, 3/4 teaspoon of baking soda, 1/2 teaspoon of salt, and 3 teaspoons of sugar into a large bowl. With a pastry blender or knife, cut 6 tablespoons of shortening into the flour mixture. Add 1 cup of regular or golden raisins and 2/3 cup of buttermilk. Knead the dough four or five times (*it should not be dry*), and shape it into a round loaf. Place in a greased pan. Slash a deep cross on the top to prevent cracking. Bake 45 to 50 minutes or until done. Bread should sound hollow when tapped. Allow to cool. Serve in wedges with orange marmalade.

### Baked Custard

Beat two eggs together with 2 tablespoons of sugar. Scald 2 1/2 cups of milk and pour into egg mixture while beating. Pour into individual ovenproof custard cups and bake in a pan of water in 350°F oven until the center is firm. Remove from oven. Cool slightly. Have students sprinkle 1 teaspoon of brown sugar on each custard. Place under broiler until sugar begins to bubble. Cool. Makes four large or six small servings.

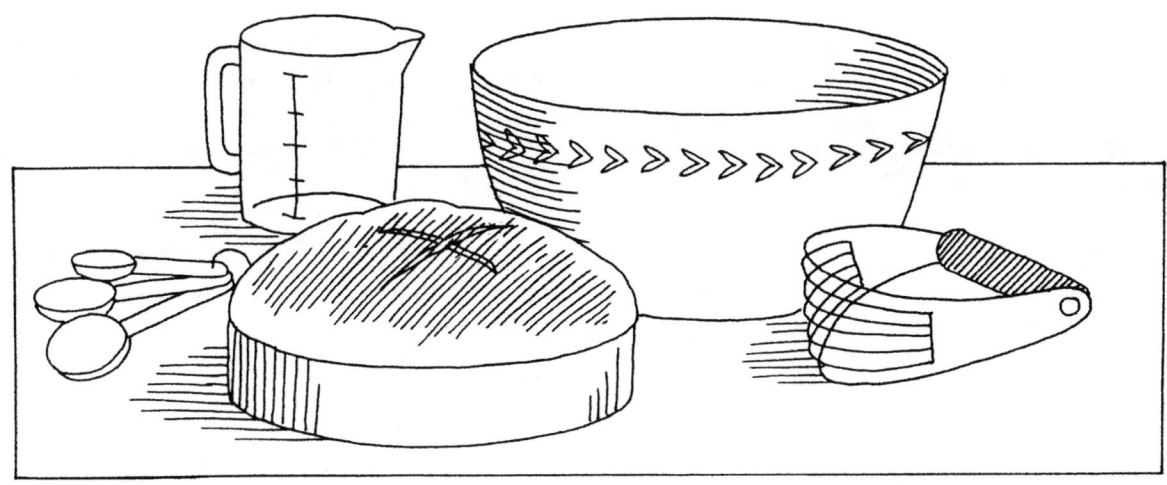

# Holidays & Festivals

New Year's Day—January 1
St. Patrick's Day—March 17
Good Friday—Friday before Easter
Easter—first Sunday after the first full moon on or after March 21
Easter Monday—Monday after Easter
Bank Holiday—First Monday in June
Bank Holiday—First Monday in August
Christmas Day—December 25
St. Stephen's Day—December 26

*Céile*—Regular and impromptu gatherings at which food is served and Irish dancers and musicians entertain
*Feis*—An all-day competition for step dancing and other traditional Irish arts

### Saint Patrick's Day
*March 17*

Easily Ireland's most important and celebrated holiday, Saint Patrick's Day is a celebration of Saint Patrick, patron saint of Ireland. It is the national holiday of Ireland, but has become extremely popular in the rest of the world. The Irish celebrate by dressing in green clothes. Irish food and drink is consumed, and large celebrations are held all over the country. A five-day festival is held in Dublin, including a giant parade through the city streets.

### Easter Monday
*Monday after Easter Sunday*

Monday is a Christian holiday that is celebrated in many countries, including Ireland. Families and friends gather together to celebrate their faith. Sometimes egg-rolling competitions take place. When celebrating Easter Monday, it might be wise to wear a raincoat. One popular tradition is dousing friends and family with blessed water.

### Labour Day
*First Monday of May*

This holiday celebrates Irish workers and their contributions to the country. It is also sometimes called May Day, a festival that involves singing, dancing, and the decoration of homes with egg shells and flowers.

### Samhain (Celtic New Year)
*October 31*

This festival began thousands of years ago as a day to celebrate the end of the harvest. The Irish lit large fires and prayed to the gods that the sun would return after the winter and allow their crops to grow again. People dressed in costumes to protect themselves from any bad luck. Today, Samhain is more commonly known as Halloween. Irish children dress in costumes and carry lanterns from house to house, asking for treats.

**Christmas**
*December 25*

The Irish celebrate Christmas much like the rest of the world. The insides of homes are decorated with live Christmas trees. After Midnight Mass, children go to bed and wait for Santa to arrive with gifts. Gifts are placed in children's rooms in large sacks. Families and friends gather to celebrate the season.

**Saint Stephen's Day**
*December 26*

A holiday celebrating the life of Saint Stephen, this day is full of tradition in Ireland. It is also known as Wren's Day. Groups of people carry a wren (sometimes a fake one, sometimes an actual live bird) to different houses, singing and dancing, asking for money. Families and friends visit one another as well.

**In Your Classroom**

Discuss the St. Patrick's Day parades held in the United States.

The shamrock is closely associated with St. Patrick, who used its three leaves on one stem to teach about the Trinity. If available, bring shamrock plants to the classroom and let the students examine them.

## Literature

Storytelling has always been an important facet of Irish life. In its earliest days before there was a written language, storytelling was considered so vital that the Celts assigned it a god, Ogma. The storyteller, or *séanchai* (sén á ke), was expected to be a knowledgeable historian as well as a skilled speaker. A traveling *séanchai* was welcomed warmly and entertained in each community.

Among the earliest of literary heroes was Cuchulainn, a mighty warrior and the son of a god. His deeds are thought to have influenced the development of the legends of King Arthur. Finn MacCool was the hero of epic tales which celebrated the splendors of third–century Irish kings. Myths and fairy tales are associated with every county on the island. There were *leprechauns*, fairy folk, *banshees* who foretold death, and the *pooka*, who appeared in the form of a black horse.

Among the modern storytellers is William Butler Yeats, considered the finest poet of his time, who also founded Dublin's Abbey Theater with Lady Gregory. Other important Irish writers are James Joyce, Brendan Behan, Oscar Wilde, Samuel Beckett, Sean O'Casey, George Russell (also known as Æ), Liam O'Flaherty, Bram Stoker, Jonathan Swift, Padraic Colum, J. M. Synge, George Bernard Shaw, and Frank O'Connor.

## Art and Architecture

Ireland's most famous work of art is the *Book of Kells*, a manuscript illustrated by monks around CE 800. The book contains Christian gospel writings, meticulously copied by Irish monks and "illuminated" by beautiful designs in glowing colors. Of special interest are the ornate capital letters in the text. Grotesque or amusing creatures were often seen in medieval art. The Kells manuscript is on display at Trinity College in Dublin. Each day, a page is turned. It is frequently called the most beautiful book ever recorded.

Celtic crosses, many of which are still intact, are found around the Irish countryside. They are made of stone and covered with carved symbols and figures that tell a story. The magnificent crosses are often called *storybooks in stone*.

Round towers, sentinels of the past, dot the landscape. These served as lookouts as well as small fortresses. The entrance to a tower was well above 12 feet. It required a ladder, which could be pulled up to make the tower secure.

Castles are found on the coast as well as inland. Some are in ruins; others are still habitable. Using the plentiful stone from fields, early Irish built some giant fortresses. Later castles were built by "planters," people sent from England to settle in Ireland.

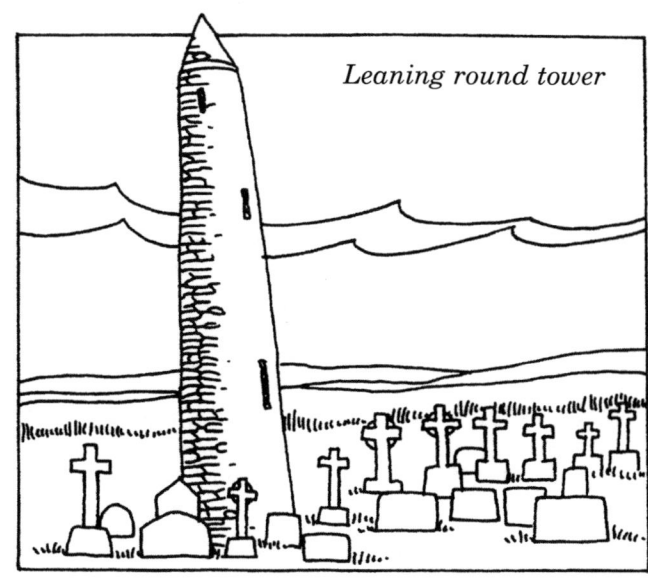
*Leaning round tower*

One of the most impregnable of these castles was Carrick Kildavnet Castle, which was owned by Grace O'Malley (*Gráinne Ní Mháille*), a sixteenth-century pirate queen. Her castle was strategically placed on Clare Island off the coast of County Mayo. She outlived two husbands, and with a band of two hundred men and three galley ships, she collected tolls from passing ships. For forty years, she enjoyed harassing Queen Elizabeth's fleet.

*Carrick Kildavnet Castle*

Blarney Castle, a fifteenth-century structure, is more accessible and draws many visitors each year. Visitors climb the tower of Blarney Castle to kiss the blarney stone embedded there. Blarney's legend claims that those who kiss the stone will be fine speakers.

## Jewelry and Fabric

Two famous ancient pieces in gold and silver are the Tara Brooch and the Ardagh Chalice. Waterford crystal, blown and hand-cut, is still produced in Ireland today. Delicate Beleek china is popular around the world.

Knitted and woven materials are produced both by hand and by loom. The popular fishermen sweaters are associated with knitters on the Aran Islands. Each family has its own stitch—moss, leaf, ivy—which helped to identify drowned sailors.

Weaving flax into linen cloth was once a cottage industry, and the work was done by women in their homes. Today it is manufactured commercially by machines. Irish lace, either handmade or sewn by machine, is prized for its intricate and delicate designs.

## Music and Dance

Impromptu gatherings in Irish homes and pubs nearly always lead to music. In general, Irish music and dancing is exuberant and joyful. However, many of its songs are sentimental and sad, often reflecting the expatriate's longing for home. Irish ballads sung by local singers have become popular.

Traditional folk dances like jigs, reels, and step dancing have complicated patterns. Young dance students must spend time practicing. Only accomplished dancers earn the right to wear the beautifully embroidered traditional dance costumes. *Fire and ice* is a phrase used to describe contrasts in Irish matters. In step dancing, the application of *fire and ice* is that the performer's head, neck, back, and arms do not move (like ice), while the feet move so rapidly that they are almost a blur (like fire).

The Irish harp, the national symbol, is an ancient instrument, once played in the courts of high kings. Other popular instruments are the fiddle, guitar, flute, penny whistle, accordion (cor–deen), bagpipes, and the bodhran (bow–rahn), which is a small drum made from goatskin.

John Charles Thomas was a famous Irish tenor who was exceptionally popular in the United States during the early 1900s. In the late 1900s, Irish instrumental groups such as The Chieftains and U2 became equally popular. Roger Whittaker, a modern traveling musician, also sings many Irish ballads.

## In Your Classroom

Have students listen to a tape of traditional Irish music. Help them to identify the different instruments.

Make miniature bodhrans by stretching muslin over clean, empy tuna or fruit cans. The bodhran usually has a symbol painted on the goatskin. Have the students draw or paint a design on the muslin.

Name _____   Date _____

# Write a Limerick

The limerick is a very old form of poetry popularized by the Irish in the 18th century. Limericks were originally written or spoken to describe the adventures of Irish people, and took their name from one such poem, "Will You Come Up to Limerick?" Limerick is a town in Ireland.

There are five lines in a limerick. The first, second, and fifth lines all rhyme, and contain eight syllables. The third and fourth lines rhyme also, and are made up of five syllables each. Read the sample limerick below.

> There once was a young man named Stan,
> Who fancied himself a sports fan,
> He went to the games,
> Knew the players' names,
> His job was being Hot Dog Man!

Limericks are often silly poems meant to make readers laugh. It's also very common for the poems to begin with "There once was a...," but they certainly don't have to.

Now it's your turn. Keeping in mind the rules listed above, try writing your own limerick. It can be about anything you want. Try writing one about yourself, or maybe one about your best friend. Share your limericks with your classmates and teachers.

_____
_____
_____
_____
_____
_____
_____
_____
_____
_____

# Sports & Games

The game of *hurling*, over three thousand years old, is the most popular sport in Ireland. It is the fastest of all stick and ball games. The modern game is played by two teams on a field about the same size as a U.S. soccer field. Each of the fifteen players carries a broad, curved stick similar to a hockey stick. Players pass a small leather ball to teammates and move it toward the goal. The game lasts sixty minutes and is won by the team with the most goals. A straight shot into the goal counts for three points. A shot over the crossbar is counted as one point. A tournament is held each year between the top teams.

Thoroughbred horse racing is also exciting and popular. The Irish National Stud is located near Dublin in an area called the Curragh. The Curragh is a large, drained bog with ideal ground for raising and training champion horses. The annual Irish Derby is held nearby. Many other racing and jumping events are held throughout the year.

Football (soccer) is very popular in Ireland, and is played at all levels. There are two professional football organizations: Gaelic Football and Association Football.

Rugby was played in Ireland in the 18th century, and is still extremely popular today. Rugby is a team contact sport that has some similarities to American football. A ball is run up and down the field. Defenders attempt to stop the ball carrier. Points are scored by grounding the ball in the opponent's in-goal area, much like a touchdown. You can also score points by kicking goals.

Other sports are road bowling, golf, fishing, boxing, sailing, and tennis. Irish children also create their own simpler games. Most of these include running and/or the use of a ball.

**In Your Classroom**

The Rover game reflects the close bond between Irish children and the countryside. There may be any number of players.

**The Rover**
The grouse and the hare
And the badger and the bear
And the bird in the old willow tree
And the pretty little rabbit
Who lives among the cabbit*
They all have a home but ME.
(*cabbage)

1. One player is chosen as the Rover and stands in the middle of the play area.
2. The other players each choose a home. An indoor home can be a chair or corner of the room, and so on. An outdoor home can be a tree, a rock, and so on.
3. The game begins as the players chant or sing *The Rover*. When they reach the word ME, all of the players leave their home and exchange it for another.

During the exchange, the Rover tries to reach one of the homes. The player left without a home becomes the next Rover and the game continues.

Another ancient Irish game is road bowling. Players roll metal balls along a road or other suitable surface for two or three miles. Experts can roll the ball 500 or 600 feet with each turn. The one who finishes with the least number of rolls is the winner. Frequently, the contest covered the road between two towns. An adaptation of road bowling could be played in the classroom, gym, or playground. Use a tennis ball or handball, and mark off the road that will be used. Mark a goal line. Although teams are not part of the original game, students could be divided into teams for easier participation.

# Italy

# Welcome to Italy!

Italy's geographic location in the Mediterranean Sea has brought explorers, warriors, and travelers through Italy on their way to Europe, Africa, and the Far East. These groups all helped create a rich cultural history for ancient Italy. Modern Italy was formed as a single nation only in 1861. In 1946, Italy, or *Italia*, became a democratic republic.

## FAST FACTS

**Official Name:** *Repubblica Italiana* (Italian Republic)

**Location:** Situated in southern Europe, Italy is a peninsula that reaches into the central Mediterranean Sea.

**Population:** 58,126,212 (2010 estimate)

**Capital City:** Rome

**Area:** 116,320 square miles

**Major Language:** Italian

**Major Religion:** Roman Catholic: 90%

**Currency:** Euro; the euro is used in most countries in the European Union.

**Climate:** The climate is mostly Mediterranean, with mild winters and hot, dry summers.

**The Land:** Italy is largely composed of rugged mountains. There are also plains and coastal lowlands.

**Type of Government:** Republic

**Flag:** 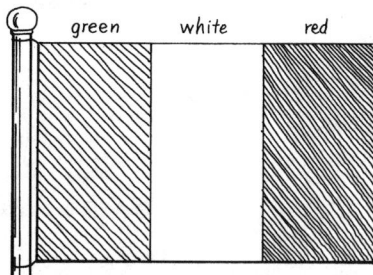 The flag presents three equal vertical bands of, left to right, green, white, and red. The flag is similar to the French flag, and the colors come from the colors of Milan.

**Coat of Arms:**  A five-pointed star sits in front of a 5-spoked cogwheel and between an olive and an oak branch bound together by a red ribbon reading *Repubblica Italiana*.

**National Tree:** Elm

**National Animal:** Italian wolf

## Natural Environment

Italy, a peninsula in southern Europe, is easy to find on a map because of its boot-like shape. Approximately the size of Arizona, Italy juts out into the Mediterranean Sea and almost reaches the coast of North Africa. Other smaller seas making up the coast line are the Adriatic, Ionian, Tyrrhenian, and Ligurian seas. With water surrounding three sides of the land, Italy has an enormous coastline (6,000 miles). This helps support large shipping and fishing industries and provides miles of sandy beaches for recreation.

In addition to the peninsula, Italy's national territory includes two large islands, Sardinia and Sicily; the offshore islands of Capri, Elba, and Ischia; plus several smaller islands.

Northern Italy borders France, Switzerland, Austria, and Slovenia. The Alps, the largest mountain range in Europe, stretch across the northern border of Italy. Another mountain range, the Apennines, runs down the center of Italy. Between the Alps and the Apennines is a fertile farming area known as the Northern Plain.

The Po River flows from the Alps east to the Adriatic Sea. Other rivers include the Adige, Tiber, and Arno rivers. The largest lakes in Italy are in the Alps: Lake Garda, Lake Maggiore, and Lake Como.

*Mount Vesuvius, an active volcano*

Mount Vesuvius, near Naples, and Mount Etna in Sicily are active volcanoes. In 79 CE, Mt. Vesuvius was blown apart by a tremendous volcanic eruption which buried the ancient Roman cities, Pompeii and Herculaneum. Since then, Mt. Vesuvius has erupted 18 times; the last eruption was in 1944. Mt. Etna is 10,703 feet above sea level, the highest of Europe's active volcanoes. It last erupted in 1979. Other volcanoes in Italy include Stromboli and Vulcino.

## UNESCO World Heritage Sites in Italy

Italy is full of World Heritage Sites. In fact, it has ranked on or near the top in total number of sites. The beautiful canal-packed city of Venice is one site. Others include: the buried ruins of Pompeii (a village destroyed by a volcanic eruption); the town of Assisi; and parts of the cities of Pisa, Florence, and Naples.

**In Your Classroom**

Show the students a large map of Italy. Help them find famous cities, mountains, and islands. Then ask them to find and trace the Po River by themselves.

Point out the island of Elba where Napoleon was confined. Ask them to discover Napoleon's fate.

Have students research volcanoes and then draw a cross-section of an erupting volcano. If they are interested, tell them more about the ruins of Pompeii. They can also make a model volcano. Have students shape small pinch pots from clay. Next, they can pour a small amount of vinegar into the pot, and add a pinch of baking powder. Enjoy the eruption!

Have the students look up the word *sirocco* in the dictionary and then discover how it affects Italy. Ask them to find out where the wind comes from, how long it lasts, and why it is so hot.

As a class project, have students use clay or plaster to make a relief map of Italy; let them discover Italy's shape and interesting placement of mountain ranges. Discuss how the mountains have affected Italy as a nation.

# A History of Italy

## Early History

**Prehistory:** Nomadic tribes from central Europe crossed the mountains surrounding northern Italy and began to move south and west. The tribes were mostly hunters seeking game and fish. Gradually, the hunters were replaced by agricultural settlers, who were pleased with the fertile land and the many streams and rivers of northern Italy.

**Around 800 BCE:** Greeks settled the island of Sicily and planted grapes and olive groves. Etruscans began developing the area of the Po River valley and the western coast of Italy. As the Etruscans expanded their territory, many city-states, including Rome, were established.

**500 BCE–200 BCE:** Citizens of Rome began expanding throughout the peninsula and edged out the Etruscans. As Rome's strength and power grew, it came to the attention of Carthaginian General Hannibal. Hannibal planned a surprise attack on Rome. After capturing the city Saguntum in Spain, Hannibal moved up the Rhône River and into France. With a line of elephants—the first used in battle— Hannibal and his troops crossed the Alps to invade Rome. The troops captured a few small settlements, but in the end were unsuccessful. They returned to Carthage where the Romans defeated them.

**200 BCE–400 CE:** The Roman Empire grew and passed from one emperor to another with mixed results. The divisions between the ruling classes who lived in luxury and the masses who struggled to survive led to frequent civil wars. Under Constantine, Christians gained freedom of worship; Christianity eventually became the official religion of the Roman Empire. Later, Constantine moved the capital of the Roman Empire from Rome to Constantinople (now Istanbul, Turkey), making it the center of the Christian empire and weakening the peninsula. When Julius Caesar came to power, he decided to reorganize Italy, but was stabbed to death before he could carry out his plans. His legal heir Octavian was able to restore order. After Octavian died, several infamous leaders—Tiberius, Caligula, and Nero—controlled Rome and treated the citizens cruelly.

***400 CE–800 CE:*** Various tribes began to invade the weakened empire. The Goths sacked Rome in 410. The Vandals attacked in 435. Romans lost many of their sources of grain and oil. Wealthy families' power and influence began to increase in city–states. Some Roman clergy also gained power and influence; they decided to make Rome the center of Christianity again, leading to two churches: the Eastern Orthodox Church in Constantinople, and the Roman Catholic Church in Rome. The religious and political power of the popes gradually increased, and by 590, Pope Gregory brought a general peace to the peninsula. In 774, Charlemagne finally drove the last tribe, the Lombards, out of Rome. When Charlemagne was crowned, Rome once more became the seat of an empire and the focus of Western religion and culture.

## Renaissance

The Renaissance (rebirth) was a period of curiosity and adventure that began in Italy in the 1300s and eventually spread across Europe. It was a period in which people became interested in improving society. They looked to the ancient societies of Greece and Rome as models for their art and learning. People began to focus less on religion and more on humans and their problems.

Italy was fairly stable in the 1300s and some of its citizens had leisure time to think about art, literature, science, and philosophy. Wealthy families had a lot of power in the city-states, and they wanted to make their cities beautiful. They felt they had a duty to society. In Florence, Milan, and Venice, a handful of wealthy bankers and traders began giving money to artists, intellectuals, and others so that they could create. Architects designed and built elaborate cathedrals, plazas, fountains, and homes. New styles of painting and sculpture flourished. Writers began to use the Italian language in formal writing, and musicians experimented with new ways of composing. Explorers searched for silk, spices, and other exotic products, and found new lands.

By the 1400s, merchants, bankers, diplomats, and scholars who visited Italy from Europe, had shared the new and beautiful Italian art and architecture with their countries. Renaissance ideas spread. In Italy, after this long period of peace and creativity, political stress began again. Some Italians wanted the Catholic pope as ruler, others wanted the rule of stronger city–states, and still others wanted national elections. This brought an end to the Renaissance, but Europe was now different. Italian ideals set enduring standards for art in the Western world, influenced centuries of writers and architects, and encouraged intellectual pursuits.

## Modern History

Modern Italian history dates from 1870, when Italy was unified for the first time under King Victor Emmanuel II. From 1870 to 1922, Italy was governed by the king and an elected parliament. This type of government is called a constitutional monarchy. During World War I, Italy rejected its standing alliances with Austria, Germany, and Hungary. In 1915, Italy joined the Allies and hoped to expand its territory as a reward for fighting.

The time after the war was difficult for Italians. They had expected a generous settlement of postwar land, instead of the small portion along the border of Austria which they received. Veterans and others were having difficulty finding work. While the wealthy feared the growing support for Communism among the lower classes, the majority of Italians wanted change.

In 1922, Benito Mussolini came into power and installed a fascist dictatorship. Although the king remained head of the state, he really had little power. Mussolini wanted to rebuild the glory of the Roman Empire for Italy, and did succeed in helping the country to recover from some of the effects of the war. He put people to work again, built roads and railways, and settled old disputes between Italy and the Roman Catholic Church. On the other hand, Mussolini eliminated former political parties and opponents through murder, exile, and prison camps. He restricted many civil rights and took control of businesses, newspapers, the police, and schools.

To rebuild an empire, Italy needed to expand its territory. In 1935, Mussolini and his armies invaded and conquered Ethiopia. In 1936, they joined in Spain's civil war on the side of the dictator Francisco Franco. By 1940, and the outbreak of World War II, Mussolini had isolated Italy in the world community. The only alliance left was with Nazi Germany. But Mussolini's war efforts ran into problems on all sides. Italy was defeated in North Africa, Greece, and finally in Italy. After several defeats the king forced Mussolini to resign. Italy eventually surrendered to the Allies.

In 1946, after the war, the Italians voted to replace their monarchy—closely associated with Mussolini and fascism—with a republic. Several major and many minor political parties were formed, unlike the United States, where there are only two major political parties. Italy thrived, especially in the north, for many years. In the south of Italy, the country remained poor. Many southern Italians moved north or left Italy for other countries.

Italy set about the task of strengthening itself. The country joined NATO in the 1950s, allying with the United States. This helped sustain the Italian economy until it was able to grow on its own in the 60s. Italy was also a founding member of the European Economic Community, which eventually became the European Union.

The following decades were characterized by political unrest. Governments and leaders came and went, and power shifted frequently. All the while, the Italian people called for improvements and stability.

In recent years, Italy has aided the U.S.-led coalition in Iraq (they withdrew troops in 2006). The global economic crisis has impacted Italy. The country continues to work towards political and economic stability in a changing world.

## Vatican City

The Roman Catholic Church at one time owned a vast amount of property in Italy. In 1870, when Victor Emmanuel II became king, Rome was named the capital city. Church property was reduced to a 100-acre site in the center of Rome. This became known as Vatican City, home of the Roman Catholic Pope.

Vatican City has its own postal system, railroad station, newspaper, and bank. The Vatican's Swiss Guards are ceremonial escorts for the pope.

St. Peter's Church in Vatican City is one of the largest in the world. A huge *piazza*, or open square, is in front of
the church. Nearby are other impressive buildings: the Vatican Palace, where the pope resides, and the Vatican Museum, which is filled with art masterpieces.

## San Marino

San Marino is a small independent republic, which is totally surrounded by Italian territory. It is about 140 miles directly north of Rome and is near the coast of the Adriatic Sea. Monte Titano, part of the Apennines mountain range, covers most of San Marino. On each of Titano's three peaks is a large medieval fortress.

Most of the people of San Marino are Roman Catholic and speak Italian. The majority work on the land, growing wheat and grapes and raising livestock. Others manufacture pottery, weave various textiles, and quarry stone. In 1862, San Marino and Italy signed a friendship treaty which has been renewed several times.

## In Your Classroom

In an encyclopedia or history book, find the traditional story of the founding of Rome. Twin brothers, Romulus and Remus, were abandoned on the bank of the Tiber River. They had nearly starved when a she-wolf found them, fed them, and nursed them to health. A shepherd raised them. When the brothers were grown, they established a stronghold— Rome—on the spot where they'd been abandoned. Read the story to the students and then ask if there are any stories or myths about the founding of their city.

Ask the students to research Charlemagne, known as Charles the Great, who is considered the founder of the Holy Roman Empire. Have them write a paragraph about his life.

Have half of the students choose an Italian hero, such as Octavian, and the other half an Italian villain, such as Nero. Help them discover how each helped or hindered life for the people of Italy.

Have the students list an artistic work by the following Renaissance artist or sculptor:

| Artist | Work |
| --- | --- |
| Fra Angelico | Annunciation |
| Titian | |
| Botticelli | |
| Raphael | |
| Donatello | |
| Cellini | |
| Michelangelo | |

Other interesting Italian natives to discuss are Andrea Doria, Genoese admiral; Christopher Columbus, also born in Genoa; Enzo Ferrari, race car designer; and Sophia Loren, movie actress.

# Daily Life

In Italy, it's all about living the good life, and this mentality is reflected in the day-to-day activities and practices of Italians. Many countries and people are focused on work; in Italy, people are often less concerned with success. Italians enjoy good meals, art and architecture, and time spent with families and friends. It's often said that Italy is a very relaxed culture, and evidence of this can be found in the cities and countryside.

## It's All about Family

In Italy, family is extremely important. Immediate and extended families are very close, and spend much time together. There is no question as to who is in charge – it's mom. Mothers and grandmothers are especially respected in Italy – cross them at your own risk!

It's not uncommon for sons and daughters to live at home well into their 20s. Sometimes, parents will move in with their children in later years; they help around the house and care for their grandchildren. Aunts and uncles aren't strangers in Italy; they often play a large part in their nieces' and nephews' lives.

# Education

Preschool programs are offered in Italy to children from three to five years old. The programs are optional and parents are charged fees. One of the schools of choice is a Montessori preschool. These were developed by Dr. Maria Montessori who taught at the University of Rome in the early 1900s. The program centers on developing a partnership between teacher and pupil. No grades are given and the teacher determines when the student is ready to move on. In addition to Montessori schools, there are many other private preschools, most of which are run by religious orders.

From ages six to 14, children must attend school. Public schools are free, while private schools charge fees. Sometimes the children have classes on Saturdays. Children are up early to get ready for school. The girls wear casual skirts or slacks with blouses and sweaters. They enjoy choosing bright colors. The boys also dress casually. Students who do not live near their school ride a city bus across town. There are about 20 children in each class and the subjects include Italian, English, geography, math, science, history, music, technical training, physical education, and religion—even in public schools. Art classes are sometimes taught in museums if near the school. The students may all call their teacher by his or her first name. And even in Italy, the students know what homework is!

After primary and middle school, students may continue their studies at a classical or a scientific high school; or they may choose from a variety of technical schools which prepare them for specific careers. At the end of these five-year programs, students who wish to continue their studies must first pass an extremely difficult state exam.

Universities are crowded, so after high school, only a small percentage of students continue their studies at a university. The major universities are located in Rome, Naples, Milan, Bologna (bo-lōn-ya), and Turin. The University of Bologna, which was founded in the eleventh century, is the oldest university in Europe.

# Famous People from Italy

Leonardo da Vinci (1452-1519) was an Italian *polymath* (someone who is gifted in many areas). He was, among other things, an artist (painter, sculptor), a musician, a writer, a scientist, and a mathematician. He painted some of history's finest art, including the *Mona Lisa* and *The Last Supper*. He was also an inventor. He came up with ideas for a helicopter, a tank, and even a flying machine. His influence on the world continues to this day.

Galileo Galilei (1564-1642) was an Italian physicist, mathematician, astronomer, and philosopher. Galileo did much of his work in astronomy. He improved the existing telescope and supported *heliocentrism*, the idea that Earth and other planets revolve around the Sun.

Giuseppe (gee-sep-ee) Verdi (1813-1901) was a famous Italian composer. He did most of his work in opera. Many of his operas continue to be performed today. Here are a few of them: *Rigoletto*, *Nabucco*, and *Aida*.

Sophia Loren (1934- ) is a multiple award-winning Italian actress. She became the first actress to win an Academy Award for a non-English-speaking performance in *Two Women*. She has another Academy Award, along with numerous Golden Globes and a Grammy. Some of her most popular films are *Marriage Italian-Style*, *A Special Day*, and *Yesterday, Today and Tomorrow*.

# Language & Expressions

In the fourteenth century two kinds of Latin were spoken in Italy—one by wealthy, educated people and the other by working class people. Shortly after 1300, a famous poet, Dante Alighieri, began writing a long poem, *The Divine Comedy*, in the language of the workers so that everybody could read it. Because the poem was so popular, the working people's Latin became the official language of Italy.

In grammar and vocabulary, today's Italian is much like ancient Latin. But almost every town or region in Italy has its own dialect or speech pattern. At one time, there were as many as 1,500 dialects. These developed because the mountains in Italy kept people isolated from one another. Today, people living in Sicily may still have difficulty understanding what people in Milan say. However, mandatory education, radio, and television broadcasts have led to the widespread use of the Tuscan dialect.

## Know before You Go

Here are some common phrases you will use in Italy, along with the pronunciations. Try them out! Look up some additional ones.

| Italian | Pronunciation | English |
|---|---|---|
| *arrivederci* | (ahr–REE–veh–DAYR–chee) | good–bye |
| *bene* | (BEH–nay) | well |
| *buon giorno* | (BWAWN JOHR–noh) | good day, hello |
| *buono* | (BWAW–noh) | good |
| *Come sta?* | (KOH–may STAH) | How are you? |
| *grazie* | (GRAHT–see–ay) | thanks |
| *il bambino* | (eel bahm–BEE–noh) | child |
| *il restorante* | (eel REE–stoh–RAHN–tay) | the restaurant |
| *la casa* | (lah KAH–sah) | the house |
| *per favore* | (pair fah–VOH–ray) | please |
| *scusa* | (SKOO–sah) | I beg your pardon |
| *si* | (SEE) | yes |
| *Come vi chiamate?* | (KO–may vee kee–AH–mah–tay) | What is your name? |
| *Mi chiamo* _____ | (Mee kee–AH–mow) | My name is _____ |
| *uno* | (OO-no) | one |
| *due* | (DOO-eh) | two |
| *tre* | (TRAY) | three |
| *quattro* | (KWOT-tro) | four |
| *cinque* | (chin-KWAY) | five |
| *sei* | (SAY) | six |
| *sette* | (SET-eh) | seven |
| *otto* | (AU-TOE) | eight |
| *nove* | (NOV-eh) | nine |
| *dieci* | (DEE-eh-CHEE) | ten |

Name _____   Date _____

# II, IV, VI, VIII! Roman Numerals Are Really Great!

When smaller numbers are to the right of larger numbers, they are added:
XII = 10 + 2 (12)    CCCLVII = 300 + 50 + 5 + 2 (357)

When smaller numbers are to the left of larger ones, they are subtracted:
XL = 50 – 10 (40)    XC = 100 – 10 (90)

Some numbers combine both adding and subtracting:
CMXLII = 1000 – 100; 50 – 10; + 2 (942)

Write these Roman numerals in Arabic numbers.

I.   DCXVII   _____     IV.  XCIX          _____
II.  CMLII    _____     V.   MDCCCLXXXVIII _____
III. MMCCLXV  _____     VI.  MMIII         _____

VIII.   What is one advantage of this type of numbering system?

_____

VIII.   What is one disadvantage of this type of numbering system?

_____

Write the answers in Roman numerals.

IX.    What year is it?                                          _____
X.     What year were you born?                                  _____
XI.    How old are you?                                          _____
XII.   In what year did Columbus first sail to the New World?    _____
XIII.  In what year did the Revolutionary War begin?             _____
XIV.   People still use Roman numerals. Where have you seen Roman numerals used?

_____

_____

XV.    Why do you think people still use Roman numerals?

_____

_____

## Famous Italian Proverbs

Here are some famous Italian proverbs. What do you think they mean?

*Give them a finger and they'll take an arm.*

*The dog that barks doesn't bite.*

*Those who sleep don't catch any fish.*

*He who wants too much doesn't catch anything.*

*Mind your own business, and you'll live 100 years.*

*Death will find me alive.*

*Rome wasn't built in a day.*

## Body Language and Etiquette in Italy

When being introduced to a group of Italians, you will meet the oldest person first, followed by the women.

On public transportation (buses, trains, etc.), you should always give up your seat for an older person. Men are expected to give their seats to women, as well.

When greeting a friend, an air kiss is appropriate.

Direct eye contact during conversation is common in Italy. If you look away, it shows that you are disinterested, which is rude.

Italians place a great deal of importance on posture. Do not slouch or lean. Stand straight.

When Italians converse, they do so with a great number of hand gestures. Don't talk to an Italian with your hands in your pockets.

If an Italian interrupts you while you're speaking, don't be upset. This means that they are interested in what you have to say. They might interrupt you several times – this is a good thing!

# Foods

Italians enjoy their meals not only for nourishment, but also as a social part of the day. Breakfast is light and usually consists of a roll and coffee or milk. The main meal, for most Italians, is served at noon. The entire family gathers for conversation, news, and laughter, as well as for food. The meal usually begins with a pasta dish, then fish or meat, vegetables and salad, and finally fresh fruit or cheese, and coffee for dessert. Bread and wine are served throughout dinner. An evening meal could be pizza, fried potatoes, and strawberries. *Espresso,* a rich coffee, is enjoyed after the meal.

The best–known food from Italy is pasta. There are nearly 50 kinds, including fettuccini, cannelloni, ravioli, and spaghetti. *Pasta* is an Italian word meaning paste or dough. Pasta is made with hard–grained wheat, *semolina,* which is mixed with water and eggs to form a dough which is then rolled and cut into various shapes. Many Italians eat pasta every day, and sometimes twice a day. *Polenta* is a mixture of rice and cornmeal. Prosciutto ham, aged and thinly sliced, is also popular. Parmesan and mozzarella are among the many Italian cheeses.

Less than half of Italy's land is fertile. Still, the farms of the Northern Plain and southern Italy provide Italians with grapes, olives, citrus fruits, vegetables, almonds, wheat, rice, and corn. Many of these are sold at outdoor markets.

## History of Pizza

The round, flat circle of dough which is the base of modern pizza has really been used for centuries. Early Romans spread bits of fish on the dough and baked it. Rural Italian women, who baked the family bread in a large community oven, flattened some of the dough and baked a disc. Gradually people began to add ingredients like tomatoes and herbs to the plain dough.

Soon bakers were opening pizza shops in small towns. One of the best bakers was Señor Esposito, who had a shop in Naples. His pizzas were filled with tomatoes and basil. One day Esposito was asked to make a special pizza for Queen Margherita.

The baker decided to include the three colors of the Italian flag—green, white, and red—to honor Margherita. On the pizza dough he spread red tomatoes, green basil, and added a new ingredient—white mozzarella cheese. This combination became popular in Italy, and later in America.

# Recipes – Italian Dishes

Make some Italian dishes that your students are sure to love!

### Macaroni and Cheese

    1 lb. macaroni
    3/4 T. butter or margarine
    3/4 c. Parmesan cheese
    1/3 c. mozzarella cheese
    1/3 c. Gruyère cheese
    1 c. heavy cream
    salt and pepper

Cook the macaroni in boiling, salted water until tender. Drain. Place macaroni in large bowl. Toss with the butter and cheeses. Add salt, pepper, and cream, and toss again. Bake in moderate oven (350°F) uncovered for 20 minutes or until top is browned. Serves six lightly.

### Italian Salad

    1-2 heads of shredded iceburg and romaine lettuce
    1 chopped pimiento
    1 jar artichoke hearts
    3/4 c. olive oil
    1/4 c. vinegar
    1/4 c. Parmesan cheese

Combine lettuce and pimiento in a large bowl. Drain artichoke hearts, cut in half or fourths, and add to the bowl. Combine oil, vinegar, and 1/4 cup Parmesan cheese in a shaker. Mix well and pour over lettuce. Add salt, pepper, and additional Parmesan cheese to taste. Serve immediately.

### Pizza Party

    frozen 12-inch rounds of pizza dough
    tomato paste
    basil or other herbs
    shredded cheeses
    sliced vegetables, sausage slices, and other toppings desired

Allow one pizza per four students. Bake dough until partly browned. Remove from oven and cool slightly. Have students smooth paste on pizza and add herbs, cheeses, and other ingredients. Return to oven and brown carefully. Remove, slice, and enjoy.

# Holidays & Festivals

Italy is a predominantly Catholic country, so many of its holidays have a religious theme. Others mark political or national events.

**Christmas**
*December 25*

This is a religious holiday honoring the birth of Jesus Christ. Weeks before the holiday, the family Christmas tree is selected and decorated with ornaments and lights. Under each tree is a nativity scene with an empty cradle or manger. On Christmas day, the figure of the infant Jesus is placed in the manger. The family attends church and gathers later in the day for a festive meal. Italians say, *"Buon Natale!"*—Merry Christmas!

**Epiphany**
*January 6*

This holiday honors the day when the Three Wise Men, bringing gifts to the Christ Child, arrived in Bethlehem. This has been the traditional day to exchange toys and gifts. Some modern families are beginning to open presents after the Christmas dinner.

**Valentine's Day**
*February 14*

Valentine's Day celebrates friendship, love, and courtship. On this feast day of St. Valentine, Italian children exchange friendly notes and valentines. There are also many notes from Cupid, the mythical son of Venus, Roman Goddess of Love.

**Easter**
*April or May*

This day marks the end of Lent and a Christian celebration of Jesus Christ's resurrection from the dead. Easter is an important religious holiday. Italian families spend much of Easter Sunday in church. On the following day, Easter Monday, families relax and frequently bring their children to a hillside or beach for a picnic.

**National Holiday**
*June 2*

This day is a national political holiday marking the anniversary of the founding of the Italian Republic in 1946. People celebrate with parades and meetings.

**Festival of Unity (Festa di l'Unita)**

This is a three week political festival held in early summer. Every night there are speakers who present different political points of view. The Festival also includes music, open-air theaters, art shows, dancing, booksellers, and food from several restaurants.

Italy - MP5129

**Summer Holidays**
*August*

For two weeks every August, families leave the cities to vacation in the cooler hills or at sunny beaches.

In addition to these national celebrations, there are many religious *fetes* in smaller cities that honor patron saints with processions through the streets. Children are dressed in their finest clothes and the buildings and balconies are decorated with flowers. Bands play festive music and fireworks explode at regular intervals.

### In Your Classroom

Help the students to create their own school festival. Example: When was your school founded? What color decorations would you use? Would you have a parade? Would you invite parents? Would you serve special food?

Find out more about the national political holiday celebrated on June 2. Compare it to the Fourth of July (Independence Day) celebration in the United States.

Create an Italian calendar commemorating these holidays, and research other celebrations or festivals held throughout Italy. Let students discover *La Befana* and compare her to Santa Claus. Read *The Legend of Old Befana* by Tomie dePaola.

Italy has one of the richest traditions of art and literature in the world. In the 1300s CE, the *Renaissance*, a period of rebirth of interest in past art, began and lasted for three very productive centuries. The rivalry between the city-states of Rome, Florence, Naples, Milan, and others encouraged a high quality of artistic work during this time. The Medici (med-ee-chee), a family of wealthy bankers living in Florence during the Renaissance, encouraged and subsidized many authors and other artists, allowing them to create their art.

### Architecture

One of Italy's most famous structures is the Leaning Tower of Pisa, a marble bell tower. Carved on its portal are several monsters and animals. The building of the tower began in 1174 and was finally finished in 1350—175 years later. Soon after the first three stories were built, the ground beneath the Tower began to sink. The structure tipped until it was nearly 17 feet out of line. The base was reinforced with concrete and has only moved about 12 inches in the last century. The top can be reached by climbing up the 294 stairs inside the Tower to a terrace. From this terrace, Galileo conducted some of his famous experiments on gravity. The Tower is also considered one of the Seven Wonders of the World.

An imposing ruin is the Roman Colosseum, one of the largest buildings in the world. It was a huge stadium four stories high which held 50,000 spectators. Three stories of arcades were faced with Doric, Ionic, and Corinthian semi–columns. Dramas, gladiator challenges, and other events took place in the central arena.

Other famous structures in Italy include St. Peter's Basilica in Vatican City, the Arch of Constantine, the paved Roman road known as the Appian Way, and the Cathedral of Florence—built by the Renaissance architect Filippo Brunelleschi.

## Painting and Sculpture

Italian art has been heavily influenced by the country's religion, by the likes and dislikes of its rulers, and by artists' admiration of earlier classical work of the Greeks.

Michelangelo was Italy's most talented sculptor and painter. His marble statue *Pietà* and his paintings on the ceiling of the Sistine Chapel are some of his most famous works. When he was painting the ceiling, Michelangelo spent his day lying on his back in a sling, which was suspended from the top of the building. He did this for several years! In addition to being a sculptor and painter, Michelangelo was also a poet and architect.

Leonardo da Vinci, another world–famous Italian artist, lived in Florence, Italy, where the Renaissance began. He used an effective technique which softly blended colors and texture in his paintings. The *Mona Lisa* and *The Last Supper* are his most famous works. Da Vinci amazed the world with his skill in painting, but he was also an inventor, a scientist, an engineer, and an architect. He was extremely curious, and studied medicine, botany, and astronomy.

Other gifted Italian artists were Donatello and Botticelli. Luca Della Robbia developed the popular glazed terra–cotta sculptures. Modigliani, an artist in more modern times, was famous for his abstract, as well as his traditional works.

## Literature

Specific Italian literature was late in developing because Latin was so widely used in formal writing. Dante Alighieri's *The Divine Comedy* was one of the first poems written in language that could be read by the common people as well as by royalty. Dante's writings helped unite the country with a common Italian language.

Other notable early writers are Francesco Petrarch, Cicero, and Giovanni Boccaccio, who wrote *The Decameron*, a collection of 100 tales about Italian life. Niccolò Machiavelli's *The Prince* has a strong political slant. Among the later well–known writers were poet Umberto Boccioni, novelist Alberto Moravia, and winners of the Nobel Prize for Literature—novelist Grazia Deledda and poet Salvatore Quasimodo. Italian writers throughout the centuries have contributed much to world literature and have greatly influenced later writers.

## Music

In the music world, grand opera is considered to be a product of Italy. Opera, a play set to elegant music, was originally created to entertain royalty. But soon performances were opened to the public. The Italian people immediately accepted the lavish romances, comedies, and dramatic tragedies. *La Scala* or *Teatro all Scala* (Theater of the Stairs) in Milan is the most famous opera house in the world.

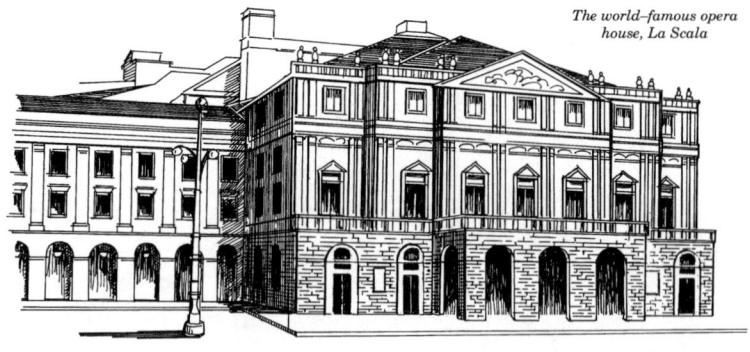

*The world–famous opera house, La Scala*

Guiseppe Verdi, composer of 26 operas, had a long association with La Scala. Verdi became an international figure and his work is still popular all over the world. *Rigoletto* and *La Traviata* are two of his best known operas.

Antonio Vivaldi, born in Venice, was one of Italy's leading composers and violinists. Gioacchino Rossini, a musical genius, created 40 operas. Other talented Italian musicians and composers include Niccolò Paganini, Gaetano Donizatti, Vincenzo Bellini, Giacomo Puccini, Enrico Caruso, a world– renowned tenor, and Arturo Toscanini, one of Italy's principal conductors.

Name _____  Date _____

# Roman Myth Story Frame

Myths were very important in Roman culture and literature. Find and read a Roman myth. Fill in the information below.

Title of myth: _____

Source (title and author of book or internet site where you found it): _____
_____

The main characters were: _____

Briefly describe two of the characters: _____
_____
_____

What was the setting? _____

What problem did the main character(s) have? _____
_____

The character that helped solve the problem was: _____

The solution to the problem was: _____
_____
_____

If I could change the ending to the myth, this is what would happen: _____
_____
_____
_____

Could this actually have happened in real life? Why or why not? _____
_____
_____
_____

I (liked/did not like) this myth because: _____
_____
_____
_____

**In Your Classroom**

Divide the students into groups of four or five. Provide building blocks or Legos® and have each group build a miniature leaning tower. Set a time limit and then measure to find the highest structure. Ask the winning group to explain how they maintained balance.

Have students research the Colosseum. Ask them to compare its size to a modern stadium or arena. Help them discover what kind of sporting events took place in the arena in ancient times.

Organize a class art show. Have each student choose his or her favorite medium—chalk, paint, crayon, colored pencil—and complete a drawing. Hang the drawings around the room and have students vote on a favorite. Invite other classes to the show.

Provide clay for each student and have them create their own sculptures. Older students could design a border or pattern (*frieze*) taken from a famous piece of art.

Have a copy of Carlo Collodi's *The Adventures of Pinocchio* available in the classroom. Read parts of it to the students. Ask them to listen for names, places, or things that suggest Italy (example: the name of the puppet maker, Guiseppi, or the villian Stromboli, named for a volcano near Sicily).

Ask the students if they know any people or organizations that support the arts today as the Medici did in Italy.

# Sports & Games

Soccer is Italy's national sport. It is closely followed by enthusiastic fans. Nearly every city and village in the country has a team and the rivalry is intense. Young people play pick–up soccer in village squares with the hopes of one day becoming professional soccer heroes. In 1982, the Italian soccer team was the best in the world when it won the World Cup championship in Spain. In 1990, Italy hosted the World Cup matches and won third place. Italy won the 2006 FIFA World Cup.

Besides soccer, Italians love racing of all kinds. They have always been strong competitors in the annual Tour of Italy, a two-week bicycle race around Italy, which draws the world's top racers. Sports car racing is also very popular with both school children and adults. The Ferrari and Fiat racing cars, manufactured in Italy, are among the world's best. Formula One, a high-class racing league, is popular in Italy and around the world. Ferrari races its own team in Formula One. The Grand Prix races, a series of international races held on challenging road courses, are held each summer in Imola, Italy. Winning car drivers become instant heroes.

During regular vacations, Italian families spend time visiting Italy's southern beaches. While parents relax under huge, colorful umbrellas, children play in the sand and swim in the clear sea. Wealthier families may spend a winter vacation skiing on the slopes of the Northern Alps.

A popular way for older members of a family to spend a pleasant Sunday afternoon or evening is at a local bocce ball court. The game of *bocce* (or *boccie*) (boch-ee) *ball* originated in Italy and was brought to the United States by Italian emigrants. Bocce is still popular in Italian-American neighborhoods. Bocce ball is similar to lawn bowling but is played on a clay court. Players are divided into two teams, each with up to four players. Four red wooden bocce balls (similar to croquet balls) are given to one team and four blue balls to the other. There is one smaller target ball or *palino*. Play begins when one player throws or rolls the palino out onto the court. Each player's objective is to get his or her ball as close as possible to the palino. Each side has four attempts. After all balls are played, each team scores one point for each of its balls nearer the target than the opponent's. The first team to reach fifteen points is the winner.

**In Your Classroom**

Mark off an area approximately 20 feet by 100 feet in the classroom, gym, or playground for a bocce ball court. Croquet or tennis balls could be substituted for the regulation five-inch bocce balls. Choose two teams of four each. Remind each player that a light touch and finesse are more important than power when rolling the ball. After one game is concluded and scored, eight other students may compete. If there are enough teams in the group, a playoff round can determine the winning team.

Ask students to research Italy's sports car industry. Help them discover answers to these questions: Which car is the most popular? Where are the cars manufactured? What are their top speeds? Who are the best drivers? Where are the races held?

# Spain

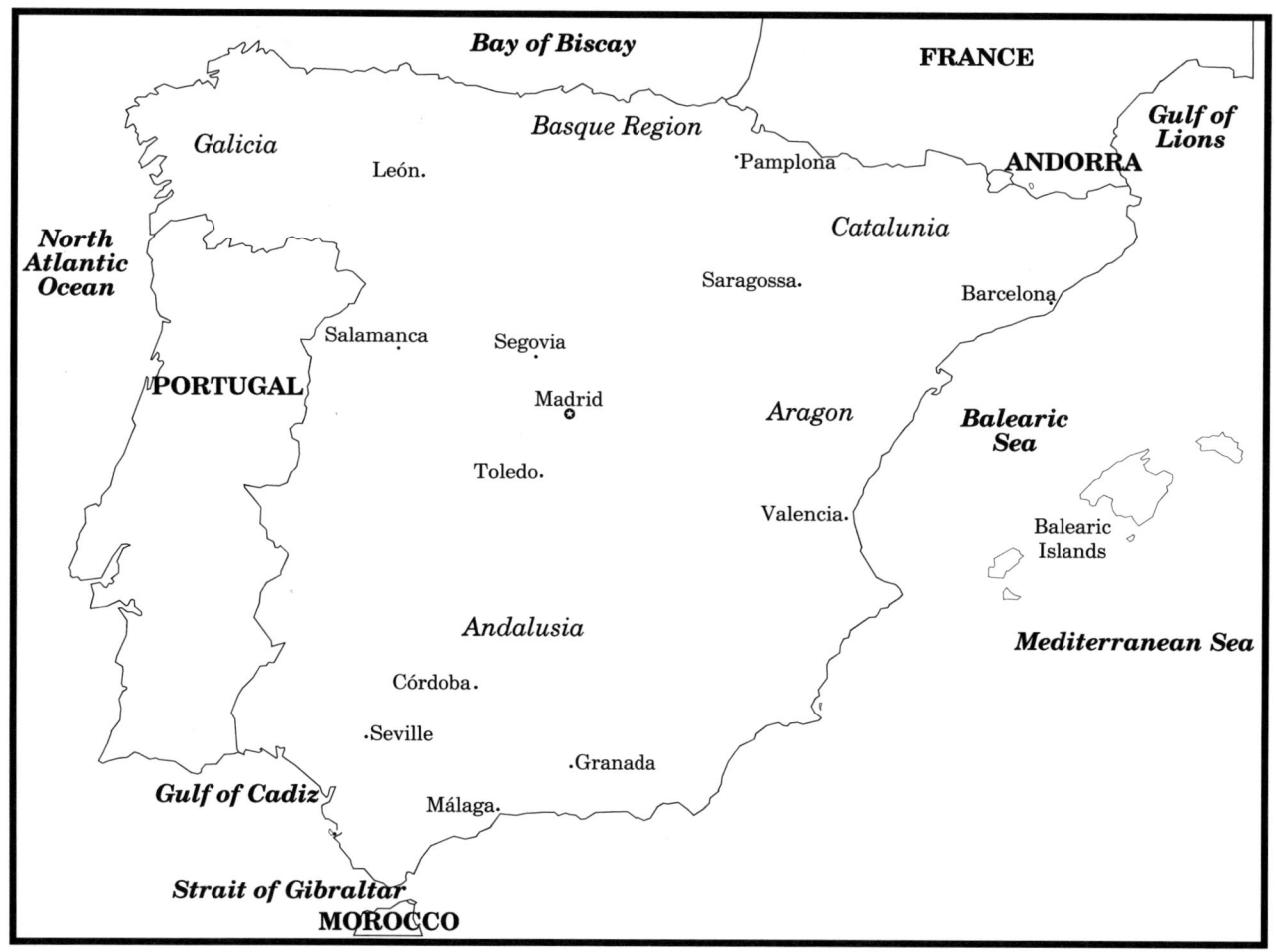

# Welcome to Spain!

Imagine yourself climbing the spires of an impressive cathedral, looking down upon the port from where Christopher Columbus began his journey to the West Indies. Imagine that you are watching a matador lure a thousand-pound bull with sharp horns to within inches of his body. Imagine that you are in Spain, a land full of rich history and colorful people. Exploring the Spanish people's culture and past will help us to understand a country which has helped shape much of the modern world.

## Fast Facts

**Official Name:** The Kingdom of Spain

**Location:** Located in southwestern Europe, Spain is separated from France to the north by the Pyrenees. Spain borders the Bay of Biscay, the Mediterranean Sea, and the North Atlantic Ocean. Portugal is situated to the west.

**Population:** 40,525,002 (2010 estimate)

**Capital City:** Madrid

**Area:** 194,885 square miles; Spain is more than double the size of the state of Oregon.

**Major Language:** Castilian Spanish: 74%
Catalan: 17%

**Major Religion:** Roman Catholic: 94%

**Currency:** Euro; the euro is used in most countries in the European Union.

**Climate:** Spain has a temperate climate. Summers are hot in the interior but moderate along the coasts. Winters in the interior are cold, but cool on the coasts.

**The Land:** Spain is a large, mostly flat plateau surrounded with rugged hills.

**Type of Government:** Parliamentary Monarchy

**Flag:**  The Spanish flag presents three horizontal bands. Top to bottom, the bands are red, yellow, and red. The Spanish coat of arms appears on the hoist side of the yellow band.

**Coat of Arms:**  The coat of arms is quartered to show the four traditional kingdoms of Spain: Castile, Leon, Navarre, and Aragon. A pomegranate at the bottom of the shield represents Granada. Two pillars flank the shield, symbolizing Gibraltar and Ceuta.

**National Flower:** Carnation

**Motto:** "Further beyond"

## Natural Environment

Spain, the second largest European country, occupies 80 percent of the Iberian Peninsula. Bordered by France to the northeast and by Portugal to the southwest, Spain is surrounded by water on three sides. Its geography and its climate vary from one region of the country to another, making Spain a beautiful mixture of mountains, plains, and coastal regions.

The huge Meseta covers most of Spain. A high, flat plateau 2000 feet above sea level, the Meseta is dry and mostly infertile. Most of the country's rivers find their origin in the Meseta. A harsh, dry climate is typical of this region. It is known for its extreme temperatures: sweltering summers and freezing cold winters.

The northern mountains include the Galician Mountains, the Cantabrian Mountains, and the Pyrenees. This area has a temperate climate and receives a good deal of rain.

To the east, one finds the coastal plains, an area known for its beautiful Mediterranean beaches. The summers are hot and dry, while the winters are mild and rainy.

Andalusia, the region in Southern Spain, is home to both the plains of Andalusia and the southern highlands, which include the Sierra Nevada Mountains. Andalusia is the hottest region in Spain and home to some of Spain's most colorful and interesting traditions.

## UNESCO World Heritage Sites in Spain

There are more than 40 World Heritage Sites in Spain. Several monasteries are on the list, including Poblet Monastery and The Royal Monastery of Santa María de Guadalupe. Many Old Town areas of cities are also listed. These include the Old Towns of Ávila, Segovia, and Salamanca.

## In Your Classroom

Make a model of Spain's flag from construction paper. Discuss with your students the significance of the different parts of the flag.

Trace a map of Spain onto a large piece of paper and mount it in your classroom.

Ask children how they would like to live in a country where people in different parts speak a different language.

# A History of Spain

The Iberian Peninsula has been occupied for thousands of years. Drawings that decorate caves along Spain's northern coast are thought to be over ten thousand years old.

We know that Spain's strategic location and wealth of natural resources attracted numerous and diverse groups of people. For hundreds of years, groups such as the Iberians, the Phoenicians, the Celts, and the Greeks fought for control of this precious land. Starting in around 200 BCE, however, the Romans dominated what is now Spain. The Romans brought with them advances in architecture, language, and literature. Many ancient Roman structures still stand—a stark contrast to the modern country that Spain has become. One of the most famous Roman structures is an aqueduct in Segovia. It was built in the third century BCE to bring water into the city from nearby mountains.

In the year 711, Arabs, called Moors, crossed the Strait of Gibraltar from northern Africa into Spain. Within a few years, this people had conquered most of the area, bringing with them a splendid culture and the Muslim religion. The Moors, however, also tolerated the practices of Judaism and Christianity, both of which had existed in Spain for hundreds of years. This lead to a marvelous era of cross–cultural sharing and communication. Muslims, Jews, and Christians lived together in relative peace, exchanging ideas, knowledge, culture, and language. The two centers of this mixture were Toledo and Cordobá, where mosques, synagogues, and churches can still be seen side by side.

## The Catholic Kings

Isabel of Castíl married Fernando of Aragón in 1469, thus uniting two of the most powerful regions in Iberia. Within ten years, Isabel and Fernando were crowned as monarchs, and they ruled together as *Los Reyes Católicos*, or the Catholic Kings. It is interesting to note that they worked as a team: Isabel had the same amount of power and influence as did her husband.

The course of history changed in the year 1492. First, an Italian sailor named Christopher Columbus (*Crístobol Colón*) convinced the Catholic Kings to support his search for a quicker trade route to the Indies. Instead of sailing east around Africa to reach Asia, Columbus intended to sail west. He was convinced that the world was round, not flat, as some people still believed at the time, but he also believed that the world was smaller than it actually is. Spain, under the leadership of Isabel of Castíl, financed Columbus' voyage, a voyage that would lead to the discovery of a continent yet unknown to Europeans. To this day, Columbus Day, or *Día de la Raza*, is celebrated on the 12 of October in Hispanic countries.

*Columbus' ships on his first voyage to the New World*

A second important event that began in 1492 was the expulsion of Jews and Moors from Spain. A religious fervor spread throughout the Catholic community. Anyone who was not Catholic, including Jews, Muslims, and later, Protestants, were considered heathens. These dissidents were either converted, exiled, or executed. This movement, led by the Spanish Inquisition, caused Spain to lose an extremely important and productive part of its population. In addition, the religious fervor of the 15th and 16th centuries served to isolate Spain intellectually and culturally from the rest of Europe.

Although the Spanish Inquisition casts a shadow on this period of history, it did nothing to prevent Spain's rise to power in the 16th century. In 1516, Carlos V, an heir to the Spanish throne, was crowned Holy Roman Emperor. His empire included Germany, Austria, the Netherlands, the Philippines, Spain, and a majority of the newly colonized Americas. With gold and silver pouring into Spain from Mexico and South America, it became one of the richest and most powerful nations in the world. Carlos V saw his people flourish, controlling both land and sea.

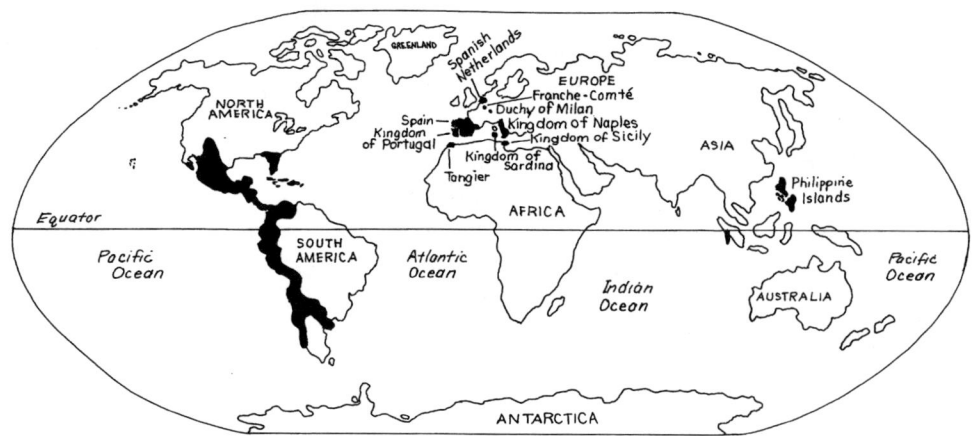

*Spanish empire before 1588*

Unfortunately for Spain, this position as a world power did not endure for long. In 1588, British ships destroyed the Spanish Armada, the premier sailing fleet of the time. From then on, Spanish monarchs watched the slow decline of their country from the splendor and the power of its Golden Age. In 1701, the War of Spanish Succession was fought, as two families vied for the Spanish throne. In 1808, Napoleon's forces invaded Spain from France, and Napoleon's brother Joseph took the Spanish throne. In 1813, Spain's Latin American colonies began to revolt. In 1898, the Spanish–American war freed the Philippines from Spain's power. By the beginning of the twentieth century, Spain's days of glory and riches were merely memories.

## The Spanish Civil War

The early twentieth century found Spain filled with political unrest. The power within the country's government shifted among very different groups. For example, Pedro de Rivera seized power from King Alfonzo XIII in 1923, to become dictator of Spain. In 1931, a liberal Republican Party, tired of centuries of dictatorship, came to power. Radical ideas such as equality for women and land reform marked the Republicans' era in power. A nationalist group of Spaniards preferred monarchy. Led by a man named Francisco Franco, they opposed the Republicans, and that opposition led to civil war.

The Spanish Civil War served as a preview of World War II. The European countries which were gaining power in the 1930s used Spain as a testing ground for their new weapons and strategies. The Nazi party in Germany supported Franco's army, while the Communists from the Soviet Union supported the Republicans. For three years, the civil war raged. Neighbor fought against neighbor, brother against brother. Thousands of Spaniards were killed.

Finally, in 1939, Franco's forces defeated the Republican army. Francisco Franco became the military dictator of Spain, now a country in chaos. Interestingly, the restricted freedom that marked Franco's dictatorship was coupled with a long period of economic growth in Spain. Catholicism was made the state religion. No one could get married except in the Catholic Church. All children were forced to be right–handed. Newspapers and radios were forced to express only the views of the government. On the other hand, Spain's economy grew tremendously during the Franco years. Thousands of tourists began pouring into the country. A strong middle class arose in a country where before there had only been the very poor and the very rich.

Franco died in 1976. Power was immediately transferred to King Juan Carlos, the grandson of Alfonzo XIII, who had been living in exile. Instead of making himself a dictator, however, Juan Carlos created a constitutional monarchy in which the true power lay in the democratic congress.

## Modern Spain

After 1976, Spain emerged as a modern industrial country. In 1985, Spain became a member of the European Economic Community (now the European Union), thus making itself part of Europe rather than remaining isolated. Challenges to the government continued, with occasional violence and retaliation taking place. In 2004, a terrorist group detonated bombs on Madrid trains, killing 191 people. The economic difficulties of the early 21st century have greatly affected Spain and its people.

Spain's rich history is still very evident, both in physical reminders and in the minds of the people. Spaniards, however, do not want to live in the past. Spain is looking toward the future, toward prosperity and leadership in the 21st century.

# Daily Life

The Spanish are a very warm and friendly people. They enjoy spending time with friends and family, talking over a cup of coffee or a glass of wine. When Spanish friends meet on the street or see each other at a party or gathering, they great each other enthusiastically. A man shakes hands warmly with another man, and gives a woman a kiss on each cheek. Women also greet each other with a kiss on each cheek.

## Family Life

Spain has a long tradition of strong families, a tradition that continues today. Many Spanish families are traditional, where the father works and the mother stays at home to care for the family. This is changing, however. As Spain's economy grows, more and more women are taking jobs outside the home. Most children live at home until they get married and start families of their own. Often, grandparents live with their families, as there are very few nursing homes. Care for older people is seen as the responsibility of the family.

Family names in Spain are very interesting. Spanish children have two last names: first, the father's last name, then the mother's. For example, if a child is named Juan Perez Sanchez, this means that his father's family name is Perez and his mother's family name is Sanchez. When he has children, only his father's name will be passed on. If Juan Perez Sanchez marries Marta Martín Lopez, their children's last name will be Perez Martín. Women generally do not change their names when they marry.

## Daily Schedule

The schedule of daily life in Spain is very different. Most businesses and schools begin by 9:00 AM, but close for three hours between 2:00 PM and 5:00 PM for a long lunch break. Lunch, the largest and most important meal of the day, is never served before 2:00 in the afternoon. Traditionally, a siesta, or nap would be taken after lunch, but this tradition is not as prevalent as it once was. Many people return to work between 5:00 PM and 8:30 PM to complete the business day. Dinner is generally served after 9:00 PM.

During the school year, children go to bed immediately after dinner because they have to wake up for school the next day. During the hot months of summer, however, schedules become more relaxed, especially because the nicest part of the day begins after the sun goes down, at about 9:30 or 10:00 PM. It is not unusual for children to stay up until midnight during vacation, or even later for special occasions.

# School

The Spanish government provides education for all children between the ages of six and 18, although law only requires children to attend school until the age of 14. Children attend elementary school from age six to 13 or 14, and begin secondary school when they are 14 or 15. Secondary education lasts for three years, plus an additional year of preparation if a student plans to attend a university. There are 29 state-sponsored universities in Spain, including the famous university in Salamanca, the oldest university in Spain.

Although the state provides education for all students, some still attend private schools. The Roman Catholic Church sponsors most of the private schools, where many children wear uniforms every day. The boys wear blue, brown, or white overalls, and the girls wear brightly colored pinafores that are often striped.

School begins each morning at about 9:00 AM. Many children who go to school near their homes return for lunch every day at 1:00 PM. They return for afternoon classes at 3:00 PM and school is dismissed at 5:30 or 6:00 PM. The grading system in Spanish elementary schools is based on grades ranging from *sobresaliente* (so-bray-sal-ee-en-tay; outstanding) to *muy deficiente* (moo-ee def-iss-ee-en-tay; very unsatisfactory):

| | |
|---|---|
| sobresaliente | outstanding |
| notable | very good |
| bien | good |
| suficiente | satisfactory |
| insuficiente | unsatisfactory |
| muy deficiente | very unsatisfactory |

# Religion

Much of the Spanish population is Roman Catholic. Catholicism was the official state religion of Spain during Francisco Franco's rule. Now, however, although most Spaniards are still Catholic, many do not practice Catholicism as part of their daily or weekly lives.

Catholicism still plays a major role in the country's culture. Most children participate in the ritual of First Communion when they are eight or nine. It is a time for friends and family to gather to celebrate a child's first participation in this sacrament of the Church.

# Famous People from Spain

Isabella I (1451-1504), Queen of Spain, is well known for her role in the expedition of Christopher Columbus. She is also remembered as a great queen for Spain. She and her husband, Ferdinand II, helped unite the kingdoms of Spain, laying foundations for a future of unity and strength.

Miguel de Cervantes (1547-1616) was a Spanish novelist, playwright, and poet. His most famous work, *Don Quixote* (kee-ō-tee), is one of the best known pieces of literature in history. It is recognized as being the first modern novel and is an unquestionable classic.

Spain has produced some of history's great artists. El Greco (1541-1614), though born in Greece, spent a great deal of time working in Spain and was a major figure in the Spanish Renaissance. Pablo Picasso (1881-1973) is known the world over for his efforts in painting and sculpture. He helped found the Cubist art form and was an international celebrity. Salvador Dalí (1904-1989) was a popular surrealist painter and personality. His style and most famous works, including *The Persistence of Memory*, are some of the most recognizable in art history.

Two of *The Three Tenors*, a trio of extremely talented singers popular in the late 20th and early 21st centuries, are from Spain: Plácido Domingo and José Carreras.

Some of today's most popular and talented actors and actresses are from Spain. Penélope Cruz won an Academy Award for her performance in *Vicky Cristina Barcelona* and was nominated for another for *Volver*. Her husband, Javier Bardem, won an Academy Award for his role in *No Country for Old Men*. Antonio Banderas is one of the most popular actors of recent years, and has starred in a great number of films.

## In Your Classroom

Students can have fun discovering what their last name would be if they were Spanish. Have them add their mother's maiden name to their father's last name. They can also figure out what their children's names would be if they were married to another student in the class.

Have your students compare their school day to the school day of a Spanish student. Which starts first? Which ends first? Is one longer than the other? Ask the students if they would prefer the Spanish schedule.

If you have the students prepare any assignments during their study of Spain, use the Spanish grading scale to mark their papers. You may want to post a key to explain what the terms mean.

Castilian Spanish is the official language of Spain. The name of this language, *Castillano*, comes from the name of the region at the center of the country, Castile. Three other languages are spoken in different regions of the country: *Catalan*, in Catalunia; *Gallego*, in Galicia; and *Euskara*, a language unrelated to any other language, in the Basque region. Three hundred million people in the world speak Spanish. Your students can learn to speak Spanish, too!

## Basic Pronunciation of Castilian Spanish

Say *a* as in *car*.
Say *e* as in *egg*.
Say *i* as the vowel sound in *see*.
Say *o* as in *go*.
Say *u* as the vowel sound in *chew*.

Never pronounce the letter *h*.
Both *j* and *x* sound like the English *h*.
Say *ll* as the *y* in *you*.
Say *ñ* as the *ny* sound in *canyon*.
Soft *c* (followed by e or i) and *z* sound like *th*.

## Know before You Go

Here are some common phrases you will use in Spain. Try them out! Look up some additional ones. Review the pronunciations above if you need help.

¡Hola! – Hello!
Buenos días – Good morning/Good day
Buenas tardes – Good afternoon
Buenas noches – Good night
Mucho gusto – Nice to meet you.
¡Adios! – Goodbye
sí – yes
no – no

¿Cómo estás? – How are you?
Bien, gracias – Fine, thank you.
¿Cómo te llamas? – What is your name?
Me llamo _____ – My name is _____
¡Hasta luego! – See you later!

gracias – thank you
por favor – please

## Numbers

| | |
|---|---|
| uno – 1 | seis – 6 |
| dos – 2 | siete – 7 |
| tres – 3 | ocho – 8 |
| cuatro – 4 | nueve – 9 |
| cinco – 5 | diez – 10 |

## Famous Spanish Proverbs

Here are some famous Spanish proverbs. What do you think they mean?

*To where you go, do the things you see.*

*Do not check the teeth of a horse given as a present.*

*A tree that is born twisted never grows straight.*

*The cowl does not make the friar.*

*A bird in the hand is worth more than a hundred flying.*

## Body Language and Etiquette in Spain

Here are some examples of body language and etiquette you'll find in Spain.

*Strangers are expected to shake hands upon meeting. Closer friends may embrace, or, in the case of women, kiss each other on the cheek.*

*If you are a guest, don't sit down until you are invited to do so.*

*For social get-togethers, it is acceptable to be 15-30 minutes late.*

*When invited to someone else's home, be sure to bring a small gift in thanks.*

*Wasting food is frowned upon in Spain. If you are at a meal, be sure to try to finish everything on your plate.*

## In Your Classroom

In order to give students some practice speaking Spanish, pronounce these expressions out loud and ask them to repeat after you. You may want to have students act out a small dialogue between two people meeting on the street.

Prepare a bulletin board entitled *¿Cómo te llamas?*. Give each student a piece of construction paper, and have them write *Me llamo (name)*. They may want to draw a picture of themselves or bring in a photograph. Display them for the class to see.

Place a Spanish/English dictionary in the classroom and allow children to use it to find useful vocabulary, such as words for clothing or classroom items.

Label items in the classroom with Spanish vocabulary cards for the students to see every day. For example: *la puerta* (door), *la pizarra* (chalkboard), *el escritorio* (desk), *la mesa* (table), *la ventana* (window), *el libro* (book), *el cuaderno* (notebook), *el lápiz* (pencil), *el bolígrafo* (pen), *la papelera* (wastebasket), and *la silla* (chair).

English is full of Spanish words. Brainstorm with your students and make a list of Spanish words with which they are already familiar. Ask them about names of food, names of cities, and expressions they have heard.

Research languages spoken the world over. Look at a map of the world. How many countries are Spanish-speaking? How many are English-speaking?

Contrary to the expectations of many, Spanish food is as different from Mexican food as pizza is from stir-fry. The Spanish rely on the resources of their own country—resources such as olives and olive oil, oranges, wheat, wine grapes, fish, sheep, and pork—to provide the staples for their basic, hearty food. And the Spanish love their food!

As mentioned before, the schedule for meals in Spain is very different from our schedule, as are the portions and contents of Spanish meals. Breakfast generally consists of either strong coffee with warm milk (*café con leche*) or hot chocolate, plus rich, sugary pastries. One famous breakfast treat is called *churros*, which are fried dough sticks, slightly similar to doughnuts. Churros are eaten after being dipped in thick hot chocolate.

Lunch is the biggest and most important meal of the day. It generally consists of several courses: a salad or appetizer, the main dish served with bread, a dessert of fresh fruit or flan, and a cup of strong Spanish coffee. Many Spanish adults drink beer or wine at lunch, while children choose water or soft drinks.

Because dinner is served very late, it is usually much lighter than lunch. Dinner often consists of just a main dish, bread, and fruit. Spaniards rarely drink coffee or tea after dinner.

*Tapas* are Spanish appetizers, which are served at bars and restaurants to tide people over between meals. Tapas can consist of anything from olives to octopus. Some favorites include fried calamari (squid), the Spanish tortilla (an omelette made with eggs, potatoes and onion), ham and cheese, or mussels. Many choose to make an entire meal out of tapas—a feat not difficult to achieve!

# Recipes – Spanish-Style Cooking

Below are some recipes that you and your students can study and learn. You may want to try making some of them during a special cooking day, or send the recipes home for the children and their parents to try.

## Paella

Paella (pay-ella), a dish typical of Valencia, consists of a base of rice, chicken, fish, and seafood. It is often cooked in huge pans that look a bit like large pizza pans with handles.

- 1 cup olive oil
- 1/2 pound shellfish (clams, mussels, or others)
- 1/2 pound shrimp
- 1 squid, chopped
- 1 small chicken, chopped
- 4 cups of rice

- 8 1/4 cups water
- 2 medium tomatoes
- 2 cloves of garlic
- 2 laurel or bay leaves
- salt
- saffron or yellow coloring

In a large saucepan, heat olive oil. Add chicken and sauté it slowly over low/medium heat. Peel tomatoes and cut them into medium pieces. Add to saucepan. Allow mixture to heat together for a few minutes. Chop garlic coarsely and add. When the tomato seems to have disappeared, add laurel/bay leaves. Add squid and shellfish and sauté slowly. After ten minutes, add the rice and the water. Allow rice to absorb water (about 25 minutes). Half way through this time, add saffron or yellow coloring and mix gently. Add shrimp after rice has been on for 15 minutes. After 25 minutes, turn off the stove and cover saucepan for five minutes. Serve promptly, and enjoy!

## La Tortilla Española (The Spanish Tortilla)

Regardless of the name, this food bears no resemblance to the flat bread tortillas of the Mexicans. Tortillas españolas are often served as appetizers or side dishes, but they can also be put between two pieces of bread for a fabulous sandwich.

> 6 potatoes
> 6 eggs
> 1/2 an onion
> olive oil
> salt

Peel and chop the potatoes and onions. Sauté them in a bit of olive oil until very tender. Remove potatoes and onions. Pour out excess oil. Beat the eggs, and then add the potato/onion mixture. Add a few pinches of salt. Pour entire mixture into a small to medium frying pan and cook over medium heat, shaking the frying pan occasionally to avoid sticking. When the bottom of the mixture appears to be solid, cover the pan with a plate, and carefully flip the tortilla onto the plate. Slide the tortilla from the plate back into the frying pan so that the other side can cook. Cook until tortilla is solid and not runny. Serve warm or refrigerated.

## Sangría

Sangría is a famous Spanish drink made from wine, soda water, and fresh fruit. Your students can also enjoy it without the wine.

> soda water (flavored if available)
> fruit juice or fruit drink
> fresh fruit slices

Combine the soda water and fruit juice in equal amounts. Add fruit slices and enjoy!

# Holidays & Festivals

Most of the celebrations in the life of a Spaniard revolve around religious festivals. These are usually celebrated with large parades which wind through the streets of the town. All year round, churches take care of huge statues of Jesus, Mary, and the saints, but on a *día de fiesta* (holiday), those statues are carried out into the streets on huge floats, called *pasos*. The floats are usually decorated with candles, fresh flowers, and incense, and it is a great honor to carry them. Many Spaniards dress in traditional costumes to celebrate these special days. A few wear the pointed hoods and robes of the Spanish Inquisition, while others walk barefoot and carry crosses. Almost all businesses and attractions close on holidays, so if you are planning a visit to Spain, make sure you check your calendar!

The most important holiday of the year is *Semana Santa* (Holy Week), which occurs the week before Easter. During that week, activities focus on church services and parades, which silently reenact the events of the Holy Week. Children usually get a few days' vacation from school, and some families take the time to visit the coast or the country.

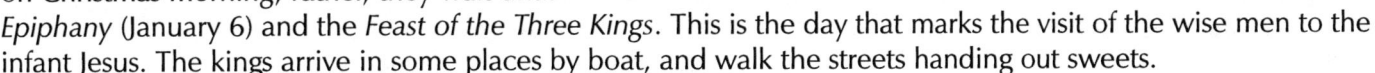

Just before Christmas, many Spaniards celebrate *Santa Llùcià*. A fair is set up around the cathedrals, and people shop for decorations and gifts at the many stalls. The festival day itself is mainly for families to share over a bountiful meal. Christmas is also celebrated, although it is a small celebration shared with family members. Spanish children do not open presents on Christmas morning, rather, they wait until *Epiphany* (January 6) and the *Feast of the Three Kings*. This is the day that marks the visit of the wise men to the infant Jesus. The kings arrive in some places by boat, and walk the streets handing out sweets.

Each city and town has a patron saint, and that patron saint is honored once during the year. Usually, these days are celebrated with songs, dance, and bullfighting. For example, Madrid celebrates their San (Saint) *Isidro* in May. Each day, there are different festivities, and there is a bullfight every afternoon. The northern city of Pamplona celebrates with the *Fiesta de San Fermín* in July. The most famous event in Pamplona is the running of the bulls. Young men line the streets between the corral and the bullring, and run in front of the bulls when they are released each morning.

Sometimes small towns or villages will celebrate with *romerías*, or pilgrimages. Everyone who lives in the town or village sets out together for a remote and sacred place, such as a shrine to the Virgin Mary. The trip may last a full day or more, and it has all the appearances of a large picnic.

At most festivals in Spain, there is much joy, feasting, and wearing of masks. Celebrations begin the night before the feast days and often last until dawn. Larger celebrations may last for several days. There may be fireworks, people wearing giant masks and walking on stilts, music and dancing in the streets and squares, or *castellers*—human towers which are built higher and higher as the crowds cheer for more.

# Creative Arts

From Don Quixote to Pablo Picasso, Spain is home to some of the world's most famous and impressive artists. This country, once the heart of the largest empire on Earth, influenced its colonies with its army, but influenced the world with its art.

## Literature

Many are familiar with Miguel de Cervantes's story of Don Quixote, an old man convinced that he is a knight errant whose most famous fight is against the fierce windmills of La Mancha. Don Quixote, the eternal idealist, and his practical companion Sancho Panza, have become two of the literary world's most recognized characters. This masterpiece by Cervantes is the world's second most widely published work of literature, second only to the Bible. Cervantes lived and worked for much of his life in Madrid, both as a novelist and a playwright.

Lope de Vega (1562–1635), a contemporary and sometimes literary rival of Cervantes, is Spain's most famous playwright from the Golden Age. He was immensely successful during his lifetime and is reputed to have written over 1800 plays. Many refer to Vega as the Hispanic Shakespeare, contending that the works of the two playwrights are worthy of comparison. Vega wrote in a style that common people could understand and enjoy, leading to an incredible level of popularity with the people of Madrid.

## Painting

### *Doménikos Thoetokópoulus – "El Greco" (1541-1614)*

*El Greco*, or The Greek, emigrated from Sicily to Spain at the age of 40, and began an incredible artistic career in the city of Toledo. His works can be seen in the best museums, as well as in cathedrals, churches, and palaces. El Greco's signature style gives his subjects elongated faces and bodies, and many of his works look as if they are reaching up to heaven. This style surprised and shocked a public that was accustomed to realistic paintings. El Greco has been called the first modern painter.

### *Diego Rodriguez de Silva Velázquez (1599-1660)*

Velázquez is known for his portraits of the royal family. His most famous painting, *The Maids of Honor*, has its own room in the Prado (a famous art museum in Madrid), where Velázquez fans can admire his work.

### *Francisco de Goya (1746–1828)*

Francisco de Goya's work ranges from scenes of Spaniards frolicking in the countryside to portraits of the royal family, to the disturbing *black paintings* of his later years. His representations of the royal family are not terribly flattering, showing his attitude towards their life of leisure and wealth.

### *Pablo Picasso (1881–1973)*

Picasso, born in Málaga, studied art in Barcelona, but spent most of his life outside of Spain, in Paris. His innovative styles, such as Cubism, are considered by many to be the first, true modern styles of art. Picasso's most famous painting, *Guernica*, depicts the horror of the Spanish Civil War. It is housed in the Queen Sofía Museum in Madrid, but it has only been in Spain for a few years because Picasso refused to allow this masterpiece to be returned to his country while Franco was alive.

*Salvador Dali (1904–1989)*

Born in Spain, Dali spent his working life in Paris and New York. His style, surrealism, portrays art that looks like photography, but of highly unrealistic situations. His art is also showcased in the Queen Sofía Museum in Madrid.

## Architecture

*Antonio Gaudí (1852–1926)*

Antonio Gaudí's work decorates Barcelona from its apartment buildings to its parks to its cathedrals. His most famous structure is the unfinished cathedral, the Church of the Sacred Family. The spires of this building have often been described as the spires of a sand castle, and they add to the impressive skyline of Barcelona.

## Music and Dance

Spain is a musical nation! In music and dance, regional styles survive. In the northern mountains of Galicia, people sing and dance to well–loved bagpipes and harps. In Catalunia, people join hands together and dance the *sardana* in interlocking rings. Young and old come together in the streets and squares as they move to popular tunes from the 16$^{th}$ and 17$^{th}$ centuries. The tunes are played using flutes, oboes, trumpets, trombones, drums, and other instruments. In Aragon, the song and dance is quite lively. Dancing the *jota* requires joyous and athletic jumping. In Andalusia, and now all over Spain, people dance and sing the world-famous *flamenco*. The heel-stamping, hand-clapping, and finger-snapping rhythms of the flamenco have been influenced by the gypsies for decades. The dancers are generally accompanied by guitarists and singers, some who use castanets. Each performer takes center stage to shouts of encouragement and enthusiasm from the audience.

Spain is also known for dances such as the *fandango* and the *bolero*. The fandango is a lively Andalusian courtship dance with accompaniment by guitars, castanets, and violins. The bolero is a dance with sharp turns, feet stamping, and sudden dramatic pauses with the hand positioned above the head.

Name _____  Date _____

# Discover a Spanish Artist

Choose one of the Spanish artists from page 138. Using an encyclopedia or the Internet, research your chosen artist. Write a short biography on the lines below. Include details like dates of birth/death, childhood, education, and famous works/contributions.

Artist: _____

_____
_____
_____
_____
_____
_____
_____
_____
_____
_____
_____
_____
_____
_____
_____
_____
_____
_____

# Sports & Games

### The Bullfight (La Corrida de Toros)

The bullfight, a spectacle unique to Spain and Latin America, is considered by many to be more of an art than a sport. Steeped in tradition, bullfighting embodies many issues that fascinate Spaniards: bravery, honor, and death.

Visitors to bullfights are often surprised to find that six bulls are killed each Sunday afternoon from March to October in the *plazas toros* across Spain. *Toros bravos*, bulls of four years weighing close to 1000 pounds, charge from the corrals with their angry horns for defense against their human enemies. First, a bull is passed between *toreros* (bullfighters) with large pink capes, allowing the crowd and the *matador* (killer) to size up the bull. Second, men called *bandilleros* drive short stakes into the back of the bull's neck to weaken him. Third, a *picador*, a man on horseback, stabs the bull again in the same area. During the fourth and final stage of the fight, the *matador* fights the bull one-on-one. He passes the bull as close to his body as possible using a *muleta* (small, red cape). After showing his skill and bravery, the matador must kill the bull quickly and expertly. If the crowd approves of the matador's performance, they shout "*¡Olé!*" and wave white handkerchiefs. If the president of the plaza waves back, the matador is awarded one ear of the bull as a trophy. An outstanding matador may receive two ears and a tail. The fight ends as the bull is dragged out of the plaza behind horses, and is then sold for its meat.

### Soccer (Fútbol)

From the sidewalks and the plazas of Spanish towns to the fields of world championships, soccer reigns in Spain. Soccer aficionados appreciate both playing and viewing their sport. Two regional teams, Real Madrid and Team Barcelona, claim fans from all over Spain.

## Tennis

A number of Spanish tennis players have gained international recognition, including Arantxa Sanchez Vicario and Conchita Martinez, in the past. More recently, Rafael Nadal has burst upon the scene. His exciting style of play has earned him the world number one ranking several times. Nadal has also won every major tournament on the tennis circuit (this is called a Grand Slam), and is already being called one of the greatest tennis players of all time.

## Golf

Considering the irrigation systems that must be installed to maintain a golf course in arid Spain, it is no wonder that the game is extremely expensive. However, this game has become more and more popular. In fact, the United States Open was won in 1993 by Spaniard, José Maria Olazabal. Other famous Spanish golfers include Steve Ballesteros and Sergio Garcia. Spain has become famous for its golf courses, and many Europeans come to play there year-round. A portion of Spain's southern coast is even called *Costa Del Golf*.

## In Your Classroom

Discuss bullfighting with your students. Do they think bullfighting is right or wrong? Would they like to see a bullfight?

Ask children about their knowledge of soccer. Did they see any of the World Cup when it was last played?

Ask your students to keep a look out for Spanish sports figures in the news. If you can find enough material in sports magazines, create a bulletin board featuring Spanish athletes.

# Sweden

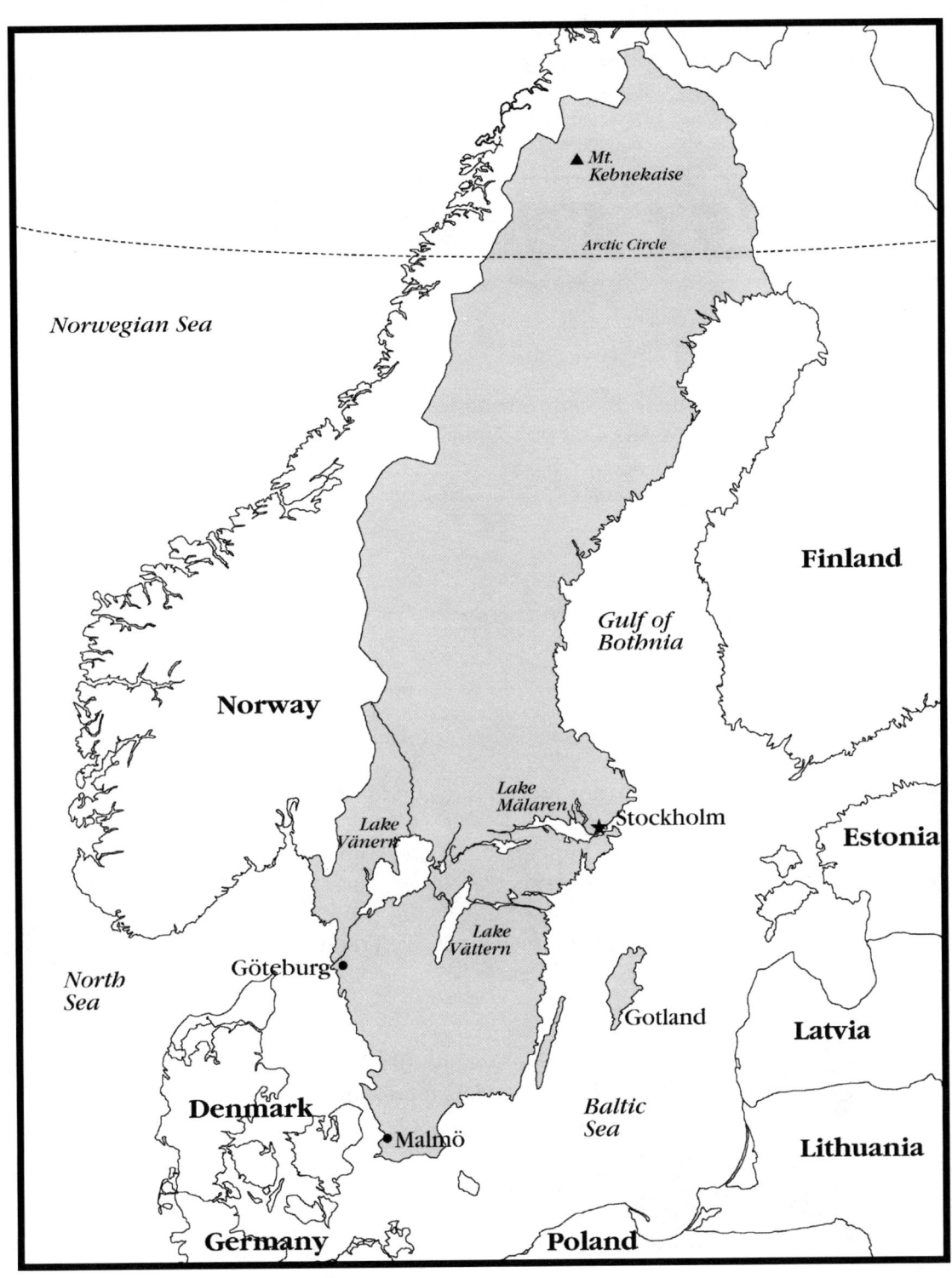

# Welcome to Sweden!

Sweden, a long, narrow country in western Europe, is the largest and most prosperous country in Scandinavia. The country combines both ancient and modern, with a modern, efficient industrial society prospering alongside the slow-paced and simple lifestyle of reindeer herders and craftsmen. Independent and proud, the Swedes take care of themselves by participating in a comprehensive welfare system that is beneficial to all Swedish citizens.

## Fast Facts

**Official Name:** Kingdom of Sweden

**Location:** Situated in northern Europe, Sweden is located between Norway to the west and Finland to the east, across the Gulf of Bothnia.

**Population:** 9,059,651 (2010 estimate)

**Capital City:** Stockholm

**Area:** 173,732 square miles; Sweden is somewhat larger than the state of California.

**Major Language:** Swedish

**Major Religion:** Lutheran: 87%

**Currency:** The main unit is the *krona*, which is divided into 100 *öre* (oo-reh).

**Climate:** Southern Sweden has a temperate climate, with cold winters and cool summers. Northern Sweden has a subarctic climate.

**The Land:** Sweden is mostly made up of lowlands, with mountains to the west.

**Type of Government:** Constitutional Monarchy

**Flag:**  The Swedish flag is blue, with a gold cross. The colors represent the Swedish coat of arms.

**National Animal:** Elk

**Motto:** "For Sweden – with the times"

## Natural Environment

Sweden, the fourth largest country in Europe, is nearly 1000 miles long and about 300 miles wide. It borders Norway on the west and Finland on the northeast. Denmark is just southwest of Sweden. Across the Baltic Sea, on the southeast side, are Russia and Poland.

Sweden is a land of immense forests and shimmering lakes. Half of Sweden is covered by forests, and the country has over 96,000 lakes. In the south, wheat-covered plains can be found. This region is the Skåne (sk -na) province and is known as Sweden's breadbasket because its rich farmland and mild climate produce most of the food for the country. This affluent area boasts many castles and estates, bird wildlife, and coastal resorts. Malmö, Sweden's southernmost city, is located in the Skåne and is known as the gateway to Denmark. Göteborg, the second largest city, is located a little farther up the coast. This large seaport town, which was built for Gustav II Adolf in 1621, is the home of the Volvo car industry and now stages most of the top entertainment events held in northern Europe.

Småland (smō-land), the area in the center of southern Sweden, provides a stereotypically beautiful image of Sweden. Here the plains of the lower south give way to dark green forests, sparkling blue lakes, and cozy red farmhouses. This is also the center of the Swedish glass industry, where some of the world's finest glassblowers work.

Stockholm, Sweden's capital, is on the country's east coast; it looks out onto the Baltic Sea and is one of the most beautiful capital cities in Europe. Known as the Venice of the North, the city is built on a series of 14 islands. There are thousands of additional islands in the archipelago to the east of the city. Some of these islands are the modern suburban neighborhoods of Stockholm, and some are reserved for summer homes. The Royal Palace, City Hall, and the Parliament (*Riksdag*) are all built on small islands within the city. The entire capital is connected by bridges or ferries and there are bus boats to take people around the islands.

Fifty miles off the coast of Sweden is the island of Gotland. It is the largest island in the Baltic Sea and measures 75 miles long and 35 miles wide. Two miles of limestone walls have protected the island since the Middle Ages. Gotland is famous for its charming streets and villages; for cities like Visby, where roses bloom until December; and for plateaus where wild ponies with two toes instead of hooves run free.

Thousands of lakes cover roughly one-twelfth of Sweden. The province of Dalarna is known for maintaining Sweden's ancient traditions. The people often dress in traditional costumes and celebrate many festivals.

Though Norrland, the northern region of Sweden, occupies about half of the country, only a small percentage of the population lives there. The area is important for its iron ore mines and timber industry. Lapland, Sweden's largest province, is an area of unspoiled wilderness where the nomadic Lapp people follow their herds of reindeer. Above the Arctic Circle is the Land of the Midnight Sun, where the sun shines continuously for six weeks in the summer and darkness prevails for six weeks in the winter.

# Lapland

A people known as the Lapps live in the far north of Sweden. The name *Lapp* is Finnish and so are the languages spoken in Lapland. Until recently, the Lapps, also called *sami*, lived very much like their early ancestors. They were nomads who followed their reindeer up the mountains in the summertime and back to the lowland forests in the winter. Lapps lived in tepees called *kåta* (kō-ta) and had to be ready to move with the reindeer. Some families owned thousands of reindeer which they were dependent upon for food and clothing. Entire families packed up and followed their herds, leaving unnecessary things behind. School followed the herd, too. A half-shed, half-tent was erected and the ground was covered with twigs. If students' families were camped nearby, the children would walk or ski to school every day.

*Lapps wearing traditional dress*

If a family's campsite was not close enough, their children slept at school during the week and made the long trek home only on the weekends.

Lapland is beginning to change. Family migrations are shorter now. Some families live in two villages—one in the winter and one in the summer. Other people live in the *jukkasjärvi* (you-kas-yar-vay), a semi-permanent village which operates as headquarters for traveling herders. The village has a school, a church, and even a retirement center. Families often live in town, while only the men follow the reindeer. A few Lapps do their herding by helicopter or snowmobile. Not all Lapps herd reindeer. Some are beginning to settle permanently and farm or fish. Others work in the iron mines which supply ore to the United States and Germany. The people who work in the Lapland mines are some of the highest paid workers in Europe because it is hard to find people who are willing to work in total darkness for several months of the year.

Despite these changes, the Lapps are still known for their traditional bright clothing and caps. Visitors love to buy the caps trimmed in red, yellow, and blue that are popular in Lapland. Tourists come every summer to climb Kebnekaise, Sweden's highest mountain, to hike and fish, to view the melting glaciers and spectacular waterfalls, and to see the Land of the Midnight Sun.

# Midnight Sun

North of the Arctic Circle, in an area shared by Sweden, Norway, Finland, and Russia, the sun seems to shine endlessly during the summer months. This natural marvel occurs because the earth's axis is tilted at an angle of $33.5°$. As the tilted earth revolves around the sun, sunlight shines on different parts of the earth. When the axis is tilted toward the sun, the Northern Hemisphere receives direct sunlight. When the axis is tilted away from the sun, the Northern Hemisphere only receives the sun's rays at an angle. Periods of daylight change with the latitude and seasons. This daylight reaches a maximum of 24 hours in the polar zones for six weeks during the summer. It is not uncommon to see people enjoying activities all night long in the Land of the Midnight Sun.

## In Your Classroom

Using a map of Scandinavia, have students locate Sweden and color it green. Students should find Stockholm and designate it with a red star. Students should then label the following bodies of water: Gulf of Bothnia, Baltic Sea, Atlantic Ocean, Norwegian Sea, Arctic Ocean, and North Sea.

An entire class may want to construct a cardboard castle. Have students bring in milk cartons, round cans, cone-shaped objects, and paper flags. After looking at pictures of castles, let each child contribute in some way to the class castle. Cans and cartons could be papered or painted. Flags could be assembled. Turrets could be glued.

Legend says that years ago a Lapp laid his hunting knife on the ground and had to pull extremely hard to pick it up again. He thought that the mountain was full of magic, but it was really full of magnetic iron ore. There are over two billion tons of pure iron ore in the Lapland Mountains. Have the students look up "magnetic field" and write its definition. See if they can explain what happened to the confused Lapp.

Bring in a large magnet. Let students take turns using the magnet to attract a variety of objects (thumbtacks, paper clips, pencils, erasers, etc.). Make two columns on the board or on a large sheet of paper. In one column list the things that were attracted by the magnet, in the other column list the things that were not attracted. Have the students draw conclusions about magnetic properties and discuss.

Lapp men and boys wear brightly trimmed hats. Have students bring in old stocking caps. Cut thin strips of material (long enough to measure around the hat) and form a band for the hat. Using fabric paint or markers, allow students to design their own trim. Remind them of the blue, yellow, and red colors used in Lapland.

Have students list all the products made from trees that they use each day. Plot the lists on a graph and determine which items get the most use in your classroom. This may lead to a discussion on recycling and conservation.

Locate the Arctic Circle on a globe. Have the students trace the line with their fingers. What other areas does the Arctic Circle cross? Have the students locate Sweden. Then have them locate Alaska. Ask them to make geographic comparisons.

In your science books, look up information on the earth's rotation. See if students can discover the reason for the midnight sun. You may even want to have students demonstrate by walking around a stationary lamp while holding a spinning globe.

# A History of Sweden

## Early History

As the glaciers melted from 7000 to 5000 BCE, hunters and farmers began settling in the area that is now Sweden. A culture including tribes from Norway, Denmark, Finland, and Iceland began to establish itself in the Scandinavian area. At first these people all spoke the same language, Old Norse. By 3000 BCE, the people settled into villages and grew crops.

Around CE 100, Swedes began to distinguish themselves from other tribes and settled in the area around Lake Mälaren. The people of the Malar Valley prospered. A trading post was established on an island in Lake Mälaren and a fortress was erected to protect it.

The Viking Age began around the ninth century. Historians disagree on the origin of the name, but a logical explanation could be that it came from the Old Norse word, *vik*, meaning *battle*. For the next 250 years, Vikings sailed out of the Scandinavian countries and invaded surrounding nations. Most Vikings were expert shipbuilders and sailors; many were also warriors and robbers. In Sweden, however, the Vikings were not as concerned with killing and plundering. Instead, they used their excellent seafaring skills to sail across the Baltic Sea and set up trading posts with what is now Russia.

## A Shaky Union

Throughout the thirteenth and fourteenth centuries, Sweden, Norway, and Denmark often banded together, taking turns at controlling the union. At times the union was agreeable, as was the case when Norway willingly united with Sweden in the early 1300s, and in 1379, when Norway, Sweden, and Denmark signed a treaty to insure a union of the three kingdoms. More often, however, the union was marked by a number of battles among the kingdoms. Usually Denmark was seen as the oppressor and Sweden often battled against them. One of these battles was particularly brutal. Many Swedish noblemen and leaders were murdered by the Danes and a revolt against the Danish king ensued. In 1523, Gustav Ericsson came to power in Sweden as King Gustav I Vasa. Sickened by the bloodshed and murder, King Gustav broke ties with Denmark.

Gustav II Adolphus came to power in Sweden in 1611 and helped defeat Denmark in the Thirty Years War. During this time, Stockholm became a major trading center and was recognized by other European countries. Sweden itself became a major power in the Baltic Sea area. Perhaps because of this newfound power, the small kingdom began to take on the role of the oppressor. In the mid-1600s, Sweden attacked Poland and later, Denmark, gaining small portions of territory in the south part of what is now Sweden.

In the 1700s, Russia established itself as a center of trade and commerce, and Sweden lost control in the Baltic to its Russian neighbors. Shifts in power occurred again in 1814 when Denmark released control of Norway, allowing Norway to reunite with Sweden. The late 1800s was a time of economic and social advances. The Social Democratic Party emerged and new laws were enacted to protect workers.

## Neutrality in Violent Times

In 1914, at the onset of World War I, Sweden declared itself neutral and made an agreement with Norway and Denmark to protect the neutrality of all the Scandinavian states. Although the policy of neutrality was not always wise, as was the case when Germany was allowed to invade Norway, the principle of neutrality was valued. In 1920, Sweden joined the League of Nations. Later, as World War II approached, Sweden again declared its neutrality. Sweden joined the United Nations as its fifty-fourth member in 1946 and continued to maintain its neutral position. The 1950s and 1960s were marked by great strides in industrial advance and social progress. The nuclear reactor and a generous pension plan both developed in Sweden during this time.

On January 1, 1975, Sweden's new constitution took effect. The constitution states that Sweden is a constitutional monarchy on a democratic and parliamentary basis. The constitution consists of three parts. The Act of Succession of 1980 allows the oldest child of the monarchy to succeed to the throne, instead of the previous dictate allowing only the oldest male child to succeed. The Freedom of the Press Act of 1949 was included as a document in the new constitution. And the Instrument of Government formally incorporated any changes in the government which had evolved since 1809. In 1976 and 1979, parliament passed amendments to protect human rights and fundamental freedoms. The new constitution also gave more formal control to the government by reducing the power of the monarchy.

## Modern Sweden

Today, the king and royal family are figureheads without any real political force. The Swedes love their royal family and are just as pleased to see the king bestowing Nobel prizes or opening the first annual meeting of Parliament as they were when the royal family was more involved in politics. After 1991, the government decided that the neutrality policy of 1814 was no longer practical. Sweden began reaching out to other European countries, hoping that associations with other nations would assist Sweden in maintaining its economic and commercial progress. Sweden joined the European Union in 1995, and presided over the EU in 2009.

## In Your Classroom

Have students research Vikings and write a research report. Perhaps several Vikings could be chosen for a follow-up research report. Research Leif Ericson and talk about his discoveries. Have students find out where Vinland is. They could choose to write on specific Vikings, such as Leif Ericson or Eric the Red; or they could discuss subjects including shipbuilding, mythology, and daily life.

Students could design their own dragon head for the bow of a construction paper ship. Mount the heads on the paper ships and display on the board.

Model shipbuilding is a hobby in Scandinavian countries. Let your students make their own version of a Viking ship using materials like Popsicle/craft sticks.

# Daily Life

The Swedes are characteristically hard-working, polite, and proud people who value their independence and lifestyle. Although their tax rate is extremely high, Swedes generally enjoy a high standard of living.

Nowhere else in the world are the social welfare programs as extensive as they are in Sweden. Before a baby is born in Sweden, the welfare program is already acting in his or her interest. The program focuses on preventing problems rather than solving them. Maternity clinics and neonatal care are free, as are all doctors' visits for the expectant mother. The law allows six-month maternity or paternity leave from jobs and a cash grant is awarded to the parents when the baby is born. Extra help is given to single mothers who receive an allowance for their children until the children reach sixteen.

Education is free for all students, and a day at school would include free meals as well as free health care. The policy of education in Sweden aims at bridging the gap between social classes and allows each citizen to develop his or her full potential. Low-income students are often sent to summer camp where room and board is paid for by the government. Students who live in isolated villages or regions are often given traveling expenses and boarding fees so they can attend city schools. The five major state universities in Uppsala, Lund, Stockholm, Göteborg (Goot-a-bor-ia), and Umeå (oo-may- ), all offer low-interest loans and other financial aid.

Swedes enjoy their leisure time, and the government has a part in that, too. There are several paid holidays during the work year, and each employee receives plenty of paid vacation time. Many families have invested in summer houses or *sommarstuga* on lakes or deep in the quiet countryside. There are reasonably-priced summer chalets for people who don't own a summer home.

Housing in the cities is sometimes a problem. Two-thirds of the population lives in apartments and this often leads to overcrowding. Although small in size, the Swedish apartment has many conveniences, causing the demand to be greater than the supply. The local authorities or housing associations keep a waiting list and rent the reasonably priced apartments as soon as they become available. In addition, new suburbs are producing small, modern homes at affordable prices. Low-interest loans are available for purchasing homes and furnishings.

There is an attitude of mutual trust between the government administrators and the people receiving government assistance. No one seems to take advantage of the generous policies. The country has tried to distribute its wealth without causing people to sacrifice their lifestyles. The Swedes are formal people who value rules and etiquette in their daily lives. Perhaps these priorities are partly responsible for Sweden's successful way of life.

## Education

Sweden attempts to give all citizens an equal and excellent education. The academic year starts in late August and ends in early June. Students have spring and winter holidays. School begins at 8:30 AM and lasts until 3:00 or 4:00 PM. The government spends a great deal of money on education and ensures that all national schools, books, and meals are free.

Sweden used to have a very rigid method of education. Schools were places of strict discipline where students memorized tables of facts and numbers and worked through hours of homework. Their exams were extremely difficult and a student had to remember every word that was taught all year. Educators began rethinking the educational process and modern schools are much different. Exams and grades are not given until eighth or ninth grade. Until then, parents meet with teachers to discuss their children's progress.

Very young children stay in daycare while their parents are at work. Children under the age of seven can attend kindergarten, but are not required to do so. School does not formally start for children until they are seven years old. They attend a school called *grundskola*, or comprehensive school, for nine years where they study mathematics, history, music, gym, Swedish, and English. All students must take courses in technology, home economics, and child care. Classes usually last forty minutes, with a ten-minute break between each. Seventh graders may add an additional language course, and most choose German or French. Older students must have six to ten weeks of practical work experience outside of the classroom.

After completing *grundskola*, students may choose from three forms of secondary schools, and are admitted according to the grades they received in eighth and ninth grade. Grammar schools, called gymnasiums, follow the comprehensive schools. They offer three years of study in humanities, social studies, business, technology, and science. Students must earn a certain grade point average there before they can gain admission to one of Sweden's five major universities. A second choice after the *grundskola* might be the continuation school, a two-year program which prepares students for professional or practical jobs. This program does not qualify a student for university. A third choice is a vocational school. The government wants all young people to continue education, and offers study grants and allowances to students under 21 years of age.

There are five major universities in Sweden. The oldest one is at Uppsala, founded in 1477, and the others are at Lund, Stockholm, Göteborg, and Umeå in Lapland. New colleges and universities have been established. As with the lower levels, students receive an allowance while studying.

Swedes take great pride in bettering themselves, and each year about one-eighth of the adult population returns to school for adult night classes. These courses are usually sponsored by local libraries or organizations such as the Workers Education Association.

## Famous People from Sweden

Bridget of Sweden (1303-1373) is the patron saint of Europe. She founded the Bridgettine Order and influenced many Christians.

Ingrid Bergman (1915-1982) was a Swedish actress who became extremely popular in American film. She won three Academy Awards, along with Emmy Awards and a Tony Award. Her most famous and beloved film is the classic *Casablanca*.

Ingmar Bergman (1918-2007) was a Swedish film director. He won three Academy Awards for his work, and was nominated for several more. Some of his films are *Fanny and Alexander*, *Cries and Whispers*, and *Face to Face*.

Ingvar Kamprad (1926- ) is a Swedish businessman and the founder of IKEA. IKEA is a tremendously successful home furnishing company. In recent years, the store has become very popular.

## In Your Classroom

Brainstorm about elective classes. Ask the students to come up with a course they would like to take as an adult. Have them write a paragraph explaining how they would use the course in their everyday lives.

Lead a discussion with students comparing life in Sweden with life in your country. Include topics such as health care, vacations, and housing. Ask students if they would like to live in Sweden and to explain why or why not.

Research the welfare state that exists in Sweden. Have students write a short report explaining their opinions on the idea of government assistance and how it should be paid for.

Have students compare childcare and education in Sweden with that in their country. What are the similarities? Differences? Ask students which system they would prefer and why.

Swedish is the official language of Sweden. Swedish is a Germanic language very similar to Norwegian and Danish. People in Sweden, Norway, and Denmark can usually read and understand each other's languages. Almost everyone in Sweden speaks Swedish except for the Lapps in the north, who speak a language much closer to Finnish.

All children are taught to read and write in both English and Swedish. If they choose to study English for eight years, they may take a third language as well. If a student wants to go into business, he or she must know the language of the country with which he or she is doing business. Sweden lives by its foreign businesses. Many educational and professional books are written in English or German. Because Sweden has a small population, publishers do not want to print large numbers of books in Swedish.

The Swedish alphabet is very much like the English alphabet except that it has three additional letters. The å is pronounced like the *o* in *horn*. The ä is pronounced *ae* as in *end*. The ö is pronounced like the *u* in *turn*. A few pronunciations are different. The *j* is pronounced like a *y* in English. The *w* is pronounced like a *v*, and *skj* and *sj* are pronounced *sh*.

## Runes

Ancient Vikings from Sweden had their own form of writing. In early times, the Vikings had no paper, so they carved their words on stones, wood, or bones. The alphabet used straight lines for letters because they were easier to carve. Rune stones were used to record adventures and great deeds, to establish a person's right to inheritance, to remember and honor a dead relative, and to label personal possessions. Vikings also thought the runes had magical powers. Runes could make enemies' weapons useless, cure illnesses, protect warriors in battle and travelers at sea, and make people fall in love.

Runes from Sweden have been found as far away as Germany, Britain, Russia, Iceland, and Greenland. A controversial stone known as the Kensington Stone was found in Minnesota. The writing starts by proclaiming, "We are eight Swedes and 22 Norwegians on an exploratory journey..." The message goes on to tell of travels and is dated in the year 1362! This indicates that Vikings may have been in the northern part of the United States in the twelfth century. However, language experts doubt the authenticity of the stone because the message is so lengthy.

There are several runic alphabets. One particular alphabet is called *futhark* after its first six sounds: f, u, th, a, r, and k. Writing was done between double or single lines. Dots, instead of spaces, were used between words. Designs were often added.

## Famous Swedish Proverbs

Here are some famous Swedish proverbs. What do you think they mean?

*Angry cats get scratched skin.*

*Shared joy is twice the joy.*

*The one who desires to pretty, has to suffer.*

*The more chefs, the worse the soup.*

*The morning hour has gold in its mouth.*

## Body Language and Etiquette in Sweden

Here are some examples of body language and etiquette you'll find in Sweden.

*When conversing with Swedes, be sure to maintain eye contact at all times. This shows respect and attention.*

*Swedes are very proud of the region in which they live. Never belittle the area you are in or speak more favorably about another region. This will offend local Swedes.*

*If wearing a hat, men should tip their hats to women; they should remove hats when conversing with a woman.*

*Toasting is a formal practice in Sweden. At a dinner, do not drink until the host has given his or her toast.*

*At meals, never put your hands in your lap. Keep them on the table. Also, do not put elbows on the table.*

Name _____   Date _____

# Write Your Own Proverbs

A proverb is a simple statement expressing a truth based on common sense. Some examples are *Haste makes waste*; *Ignorance is bliss*; and *The early bird gets the worm*. Some Swedish proverbs can be found on page 153. Write three proverbs of your own creation below. Explain what each one means.

1. _____
   _____
   _____
   _____
   _____
   _____

2. _____
   _____
   _____
   _____
   _____
   _____

3. _____
   _____
   _____
   _____
   _____
   _____

# Know before You Go

Here are some common phrases you will use in Sweden, along with pronunciations. Try them out! Look up some additional ones.

| English | Swedish | Pronunciation |
| --- | --- | --- |
| Hello. | Hallå | hal-ō |
| How are you? | Hur mår du? | hoo mor do |
| Good morning. | God morgon. | gah mor-ong |
| Good night. | God natt. | gah not |
| What's your name? | Vad heter du? | vah hāt-er do |
| My name is… | Jag heter… | yog hāt-er |
| Thank you. | Tack. | tock |
| one | ett | et |
| two | två | tvō |
| three | tre | tree |
| four | fyra | fear-a |
| five | fem | fem |
| six | sex | sex |
| seven | sju | whoo (like blowing) |
| eight | åtta | ō-ta |
| nine | nio | nee-ū |
| ten | tio | tee-ū |

# Swedish Vocabulary Match

Now that you know something about the Swedish language, can you translate some Swedish words? Draw a line from each Swedish word on the left to its English translation on the right.

|  |  |
|---------|---------|
| STOL | DOOR |
| BOK | PUPIL |
| BORD | CHAIR |
| LÄRARE | SCHOOL |
| DÖRR | WINDOW |
| SKOLA | TEACHER |
| FÖNSTER | FLOOR |
| PENNA | BOOK |
| KLOCKA | PEN, PENCIL |
| ELEV | JUMP |
| GOLV | TABLE |
| HOPPA | CLOCK |

Use a Swedish-English dictionary or the Internet and look up ten more Swedish words. Write the words and their translations below.

_____
_____
_____
_____
_____
_____
_____
_____
_____
_____

# Foods

Swedish people typically start their day with a cup of coffee and a roll. Lunch is usually a cup of coffee and an open-faced sandwich. Dinner is a bit more substantial with coffee and two courses, such as thick potato soup and pancakes. Swedes drink more coffee per capita than any other country in the world.

Cooking varies by region and by season. Skåne cooking is similar to European-style cooking, and goose is a particular specialty. Throughout the forest regions, wild berries and mushrooms are used alone or in creative dishes. Forests also provide a variety of game such as reindeer, elk, and venison.

In a country nearly surrounded by water, it is not surprising that fish is a staple in Sweden. Rivers yield many varieties of fish. Salmon, white trout, grayling, perch, and northern pike are a few of the favorites, but the most common fish served is herring. Herring is poached, steamed, baked, chopped into casseroles and soups, and dried.

Potatoes are also a staple and can be served au gratin, boiled, mashed, or in salads with herring. Potato pancakes with jelly make a light summer meal, while potato soup with sausage makes a heartier winter meal.

The Swedes are best known for their *smorgasbord*, a feast for special occasions. Once or twice a year, the villagers get together and serve samples of their finest cooking. This tradition goes back over two hundred years and some of the same recipes are still used. Usually included are a variety of salads, cheese, hot and cold meats, meatballs, game, dried or smoked fish, anchovies, sausages, eel, vegetables, and breads. Smörgåsbords are served buffet style, with everyone standing, eating, and mingling. This is usually a prelude to dinner, a much more formal affair in Sweden.

# Recipes – A Swedish Smörgåsbord

Have students prepare their own smörgåsbord. Pick a theme. Everyone could bring in a sample of their favorite vegetable or fruit. After the foods are washed, set them on a long table with small paper plates and encourage students to try a sampling of each. Choose finger foods for easier serving. Or try a dessert smörgåsbord, and have each student bring their favorite snack. Serve this smörgåsbord after lunch rather than as an appetizer as the Swedish do. Try these recipes.

## Swedish Meatballs

| | | |
|---|---|---|
| 4 slices of bread, torn | 1/2 lb. ground pork | pepper |
| 3/4 c. hot milk | 2 eggs, beaten | onion |
| 2 lb. ground beef | nutmeg | 2 t. shortening |

Heat shortening in a skillet on medium heat. Mix remaining ingredients together. Shape mixture into balls and brown in the hot shortening (two minutes per side). Reduce heat to low, cover pan, and simmer for eight minutes.

## Swedish Gravy

1 c. light cream
1 T. cornstarch
2 T. cold water

Stir together over moderate heat until thickened. Pour over meatballs.

## Potato Soup

4 potatoes
1 onion
2 c. milk
2 T. butter
1/2 t. salt
1/8 t. pepper
1/2 T. chopped parsley

Chop potatoes and onion into large pieces. Fill a large pot with two quarts of water. Add potatoes and onion and boil for 15–20 minutes. Mash the potatoes and onion and add other ingredients. Simmer on low until mixture has reached soup consistency.

# Holidays & Festivals

The majority of the Swedish population belongs to the Lutheran church. It is understandable, then, that the two major Christian holidays are celebrated with much festivity.

### St. Lucia Day
*December 13*

St. Lucia Day, observed December 13, marks the beginning of the Christmas season. Lucia, whose name means *light*, was a young Italian girl who was martyred. Christians regard her as the bringer of light and the patron saint of the blind. Her feast day happens to coincide with the time of year when nights are long and dark, and so it seems that Lucia brings the returning sun. Very early in the morning, the oldest daughter in the family dresses in a long white gown with a red sash and places a wreath of lighted candles on her head. The other girls in the family dress in white gowns, too, and carry star-tipped wands, but only St. Lucia gets to wear the crown of candles. If a family has no girls, they often invite a neighbor or family friend to act as their St. Lucia. A tray is loaded with coffee cups and sweet buns, called *Lusse-cats*. St. Lucia, followed by a procession of her sisters, carries the tray throughout the house, gently waking her parents and other family members with songs and the smell of coffee. Brothers, called *starboys*, often join the procession wearing tall, white, conical hats with stars. After a big breakfast, the family goes to work or school where smaller versions of the procession are repeated. School hallways and classrooms are lit with candles. Often, there is an assembly where the headmaster of the school talks to the children about their duty to spread tolerance and enlightenment.

*Celebrating St. Lucia Day*

### Christmas Eve
*December 24*

Christmas Eve is a night full of traditions. In farm communities the best sheaf of wheat, saved from the previous year's harvest, is tied to the roof or on top of a pole for the birds. There is usually a big Christmas dinner featuring ham and many other Swedish specialties. Stories are told about *tomte*, the Christmas gnome who lives under the barn and takes care of the livestock. Sometimes, he brings gifts and sometimes the traditional figure, Santa Claus, brings gifts. A Christmas tree is erected, but usually the parents decorate the tree in secret.

### Christmas Day
*December 25*

Christmas Day starts with a candlelit church service called *julotta* (you-lotta). In some places in the country, people race each other home in their wagons or sleds after the service. The winner is said to have good luck with his harvest in the coming year. A traditional smörgåsbord with ham, pickled pig's feet, and many other delicacies is served.

The Christmas season is traditionally celebrated until January 13. On this day, also known as *Knut's Day*, friends gather to take down the tree and eat any edible decorations on it.

## Easter
*April or May*

Another Christian holiday celebrated in Sweden is Easter. Good Friday and Easter Monday are public paid holidays. An old legend says that witches return on Easter Saturday after paying respect to the devil. People all over Sweden used to light bonfires to keep them away. Now young children dress up like witches and visit neighbors, offering decorated cards in return for candy and cakes.

## Swedish National Day
*June 6*

June 6 is Swedish National Day. People all over Sweden celebrate with parades, marching bands, and flags. Stockholm's oldest living museum, Skansen Park, hosts dramatic festivals and many people travel there to take part. Ironically, in a country so liberally paid and rewarded with vacation time, the Swedish National Day is not a public holiday.

## Midsummer
*June*

Midsummer is usually celebrated around June 23, or the nearest weekend. Swedes decorate their homes and churches with flowers, wreaths, and summer branches. Young people like to pick wildflowers, put them under their pillows, and dream about a future husband or wife. Almost every village or town erects a huge maypole, which is decorated with wild flowers, vines, and branches. Traditional costumes are donned, music is played, and everyone dances around the maypole until well into the night.

## Jokkmokk Fair
*February*

About 100 miles north of the Arctic Circle is the town of Jokkmokk (yok-mok), summer home of the nomadic Lapps. Every February the town holds a huge festival featuring handmade crafts fashioned by the Lapps. Baskets made of thin root fibers, carved bowls, and hand-woven ribbons and fabrics are just a few of the items for sale at the fair. Lapps dress in their traditional knee-length coats trimmed with red and yellow ribbon. Reindeer meat is served in a variety of ways. One popular dish is called *renklämma*, a cone-shaped piece of bread stuffed with smoked deer meat. The fair is very well attended and usually guests have to make reservations at least a year in advance.

## In Your Classroom

Choose a season and celebrate one of the Swedish festivals. St. Lucia's Day is always a favorite. Choose a girl and her attendants. Make appropriate costumes (white dresses or cut sheets tied with red sashes). Wreaths could be fashioned out of wire and plastic or silk flowers. Construction paper rolled into a cylinder can be used for candles and pieces of red or yellow construction paper can be cut in the shape of flames. Boys could shape large white construction paper into cones and decorate them with stars. Wands could be made with straws or dowels and foil stars. Each student could carry a wand. Let the students form a procession and go from class to class, delivering cookies to other teachers. In your classroom, discuss the idea of tolerance. Have students give examples of when someone could be tolerant. Talk about how important it is for classmates to be tolerant of other classmates.

# Creative Arts

## Cultural Heritage

Swedes have a passion for preserving their history. Much time and money is devoted to this preservation of culture. Nearly all of the old cottage industries, such as wood carving, textile weaving, and glassblowing, are preserved by organizations such as Friends of Handicrafts and the Home Industries Association, as well as the Swedish government. Many small businesses and companies set up special tax funds to help pay for *heritage farms*. Here men and women dress in traditional costumes and assume occupations like weaving or plowing as their ancestors did. Skansen, an open air folk museum, is just outside of Stockholm and is probably the largest living museum of its type. The museum is open to the public and spectators may walk around inside the village, observing the craftspeople at work with glassblowing, wood carving, lace making, or any number of authentic activities. Local festivals take place on these heritage farms with fiddlers and concertina players, folk dancers, and artisans of every type.

## Theater

Theatergoers in Sweden choose from the best of the old and the new. The Drottningholm Theater, next to the Royal Palace, stages seventeenth- and eighteenth-century plays and ballads. Current plays arrive in Sweden almost as soon as they finish their original run in London or New York. In fact, Swedes have a better chance of seeing a current play than do the people of New York or London. Lower ticket prices, made possible by the government, allow many people to attend the theater in major cities in Sweden. If people cannot get to the theater, the theater comes to them. The government pays dance and theater groups to take their events to areas in the remote north.

## Glass

Sweden is known for its glassworks. Glass was first melted in Sweden in 1556. Kosta, founded in 1742, is one of the oldest remaining glassworks. Fine glassware techniques were taught to the Swedes by Bohemians. Kosta was one of the first to try working with full lead crystal glass. The best known glassworks in Sweden is Orrefors, which was established in 1898. The workers at Orrefors are encouraged to add their creative flair for design to the old methods of glassblowing. Some glass companies are participating in the preservation of culture. Long ago, the glassworks was more than just a working plant. It was a social gathering place for friends from outlying areas. The hot furnace was just right for providing warmth and for baking herring and potatoes. Music was provided by local amateurs and conversation was lively.

## Literature

One of the best loved writers in Sweden is Astrid Lindgren, author of the Pippi Longstocking books. Lindgren is called Aunty Astrid in her country, and she is a symbol of home, family, values, and rural Sweden. Her character Pippi is not, however, the model of Swedish values. Independent and headstrong, the young girl in the books lives without parents, tells wild stories, and does what she pleases. The idea for this bold character came from Astrid's daughter, Karin. Karin was sick in bed and asked her mother to invent a story. "Make up a story about a girl named Pippi Longstocking," she begged. And so her mother did. When the stories were written and published, they won many literary awards and were translated into several languages. Lindgren went on to write over 80 children's stories, most of them about Swedish children growing up in rural Sweden as she did.

Selma Lagerlöf (la-ger-loof), another prominent Swedish novelist, was born in 1858 in rural Varmland. She began a teaching career, but gave it up after ten years in order to write full-time. Her first book, *The Story of Gosta Berlings*, was a collection of Varmland folktales. The characters were usually good, simple, honest Swedes and the settings were typical Swedish countryside locales. Lagerlöf later traveled throughout Egypt and Palestine and returned to Sweden to write *Jerusalem*. This led to a series of Christian stories based on the Bible. Perhaps Lagerlöf is best known for her book designed to teach Swedish geography, *The Wonderful Adventures of Nils*.

Karl Larsson, a beloved Swedish artist, was born in Stockholm in 1853. He began his career as an open-air painter in an artists' colony. He was influential in the Art Nouveau period in Sweden, but is probably best known for his rustic landscape paintings of his native Dalarna. Perhaps the most typically Swedish of all the provinces, Dalarna provides a perfect background of serene forests, lakes, and cottages.

Larsson gained some renown as a book illustrator. His book, *House in the Sun*, was published in 1909. Larsson also tried his hand at portraits and painted a picture of one of his contemporaries, Selma Lagerlöf.

## The Nobel Prizes

*Alfred Nobel*

Alfred Nobel was a Swedish chemist and inventor who was born in Stockholm. In 1867, he developed the formula for dynamite and other explosives. He hoped his inventions would aid in the iron ore mines, but was dismayed to see them used in warfare. Perhaps that is the reason for the instructions in his will. Nobel wanted all his money to go into a fund which would award six prizes internationally for outstanding achievement in physics, chemistry, physiology or medicine, literature, economics, and for the promotion of world peace. The fund is controlled by a board of directors.

## Sculpture

Carl Milles, whose real name is Vilhelm Carl Emil Anderson, was born near Uppsala in 1875. He studied art in Paris under Auguste Rodin. In 1920 he returned to Sweden and became a professor at the Stockholm Art Academy. Milles became known for his stone, bronze, and wood sculptures. In 1929, Milles traveled to the United States and took a position as an art teacher in Michigan; he became a U.S. citizen in 1945. His sculptures are found in both countries. *Playing Bears*, an immense granite statue, was done for the Berzelius Park in Stockholm. His much-photographed Poseidon is the fountain sculpture in front of the Göteborg Museum. His sculptures also adorn the Rockefeller Center in New York and can be found in the Metropolitan Museum of Art in New York City.

## In Your Classroom

Look up *glassworks*. Have the children draw diagrams of the steps involved in glassblowing. Discuss the kind of experience and safety features needed to work in this industry. Have the students make a list of things made of glass in their house. Compile the lists, and determine which are specialty items and which were probably made in a factory. If possible, plan a field trip or show a video of glassblowing.

Secure a list of Nobel Prize winners. Separate the list by decades and assign each decade to a group of students. Have them determine who won awards that year and why. Perhaps the class could come up with a list by countries. Display the results on the board.

Assign students the task of awarding an honorary peace prize to someone they know. It could be a national figure or a personal friend. Have the students write a nomination speech, explaining their choice.

Obtain books of landscape paintings and technique. Provide sketch pads for the students. Take them outside and instruct them to sketch one tree, then another, and then the background. Display sketches.

# Sports & Games

Outdoor life is very important to the Swedes, and they take advantage of their recreational time with a wide variety of outdoor sports. Soccer is the favorite sport and it is played and watched by young and old alike.

Ice hockey is a popular winter sport, as are figure skating, and cross-country and downhill skiing. Snowmobiles and snow scooters are appearing in some places. Snow scooters are similar to motorbikes, but a license is not required to drive them. They are extremely noisy, however, and use a lot of fuel, so some places ban them. A much wiser choice would be the *sparkstottingar*. It's made of two long, thin sticks with steel runners, a sloping seat for the passenger, a handlebar across the top, and a small footplate on the left runner. To operate, one stands behind the seat, puts one foot on the footplate, and kicks off with the other. It takes some practice, but it can be great fun. It is a practical vehicle, too. Many people use them, from mothers with children to mail carriers.

In Lapland, dog sledding is a favorite sport. Siberian and Alaskan huskies are used, and these dogs are eager to perform. A team of four or five huskies can cover quite a distance. The Nordic Marathon is an organized event where dozens of dogsled teams race in a 150-mile competition around Kebnekaise, Sweden's highest mountain.

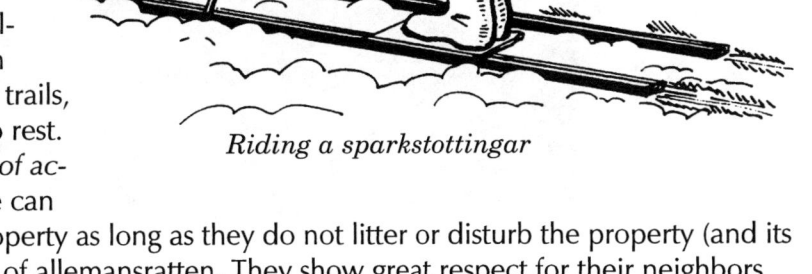
*Riding a sparkstottingar*

Summer activities include sailing, canoeing, yachting, hunting, fishing, and hiking. Sweden's clean environment is especially appealing to hikers. Well-marked trails and paths are kept in good condition year round. Small log cabins are located along the trails, and are used by weary hikers who need a place to rest. *Allemansratten* (al-ā-mon-sret-en) means *the right of access*, and Sweden's hikers take this literally. People can walk freely through forests, reserves, or private property as long as they do not litter or disturb the property (and its owners) in any way. Hikers do not take advantage of allemansratten. They show great respect for their neighbors and their country.

Tennis is another popular summer sport. Björn (byorn) Borg, a tennis superstar, brought much attention to his native Sweden and the sport. Currently there are over 950 indoor and outdoor tennis clubs throughout Sweden.

The government pays for many athletic programs so a great number of people have a chance to participate. Most major companies have a gym or sports club for use by their employees and families.

## In Your Classroom

Tell students to imagine that they work for the Swedish tourist industry. Ask them to design a brochure to attract vacationers to Sweden. Tell them to include points that would interest both the summer and winter vacationers.

Tell students to design their own park. The government will pay for the park as long as it can provide healthy experiences for the people. What will students include in their park? Using a large sheet of paper, the students should map their designs and include a legend and a compass rose.

# Switzerland

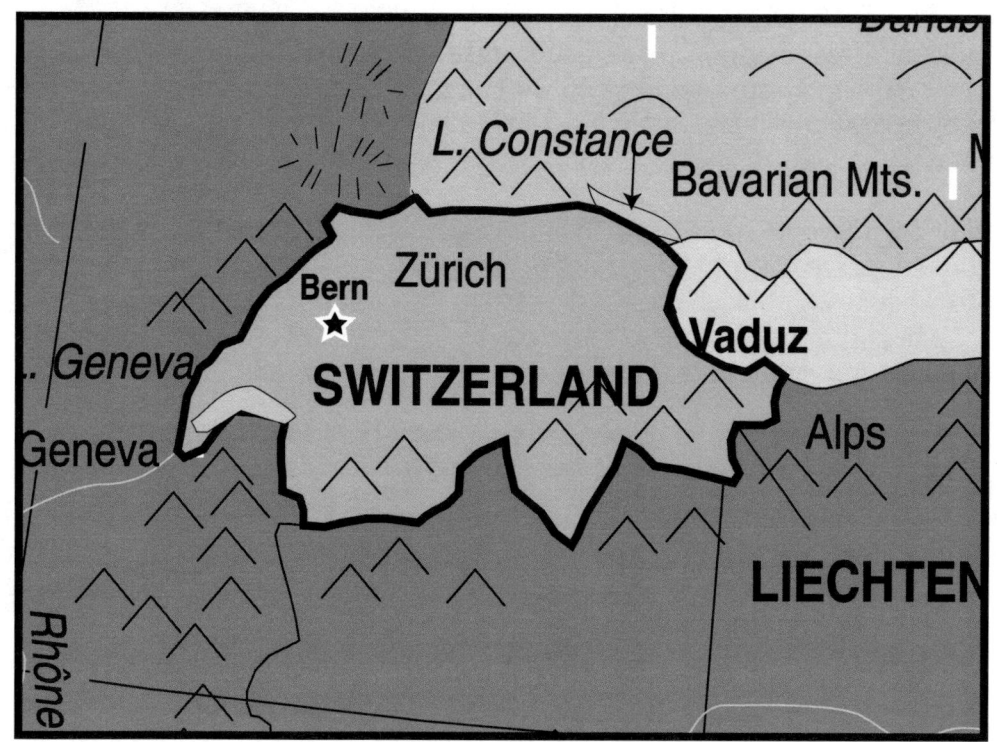

# Welcome to Switzerland!

Switzerland (officially the Swiss Confederation) is a small, land-locked country in Western Europe. Switzerland is bordered by France on the west, Germany to the north and east, Italy to the south, and Austria and Liechtenstein to the west. Switzerland is made up of 26 states or *cantons*, with Bern as the capital. Because of the country's strategic position and diverse landscape, the Swiss people have a unique history and play an important role in Europe as well as the rest of the world.

Because of its central location, Swiss people speak several languages. The four official languages are French, German, Italian, and Romansh, but many people speak English as well. The Swiss Confederation was established on August 1, 1291. Throughout its existence, Switzerland has had a history of neutrality; it has not been involved in war internationally since 1815. Although Switzerland has a reputation for peace and neutrality, it was one of the last countries to join the United Nations after World War I. They are one of the few countries in Europe who have not joined the European Union. The Swiss government divided into three branches, like the US: the executive (Federal Council), legislative (Federal Assembly or Parliament), and judicial (Federal Tribunal.)

Switzerland is one of the richest countries in the world. Two of its major cities, Zurich (a world center for international financial transactions) and Geneva, boast a high quality of life. Along with its neutrality, a strong economy and a high standard of living, Switzerland is well-known for its beautiful landscape: mountains, lakes, and rivers.

## FAST FACTS

**Official Name:** Swiss Confederation

**Location:** Switzerland is located in central Europe, between France on the west and Italy on the east.

**Population:** 7,604,467 (2010 estimate)

**Capital City:** Bern

**Area:** 15,940 square miles

**Major Languages:**
German: 63.7%
French: 20.4 %
Italian: 6.5%

**Major Religions:**
Roman Catholic: 41.8%
Protestant: 35.4%
Islam: 4.3%

**Currency:** Swiss franc

**Climate:** For the majority of Switzerland, a temperate climate is normal. The climate varies some in the mountains.

**The Land:** Switzerland is dominated by mountains, with a central plateau made up of rolling hills.

**Type of Government:** Confederation (though similar in structure to a federal republic)

**Flag:**  The flag of Switzerland is red, with an equilateral white cross in its center.

**Coat of Arms:** The design of the coat of arms is much like the Swiss flag, but on a shield.

**National Flower:** Edelweiss

**Motto:** "One for all, all for one"

## Natural Environment

Switzerland has three main topographical regions: the Swiss Alps in the south, the Swiss Plateau in the center, and the Jura mountains in the north. The Alps are located in the central and southern parts of Switzerland, covering 60 percent of the country's area. Because the southern part of Switzerland is so mountainous, it has much fewer inhabitants than the northern part of the country. This area is popular among tourists who come to experience the majestic beauty of the mountains. The tallest peak in Switzerland is the Dufourspitze (du-for-shpitz-a), at 15,203 feet. Among these mountains are many valleys, glaciers, lakes, waterfalls, and rivers. Some of Europe's largest rivers, the Rhine, Rhône, Inn, Aare, and Ticino flow into the largest Swiss lakes: Lake Geneva, Lake Zurich, Lake Neuchâtel, and Lake Constance.

The Middle Land (or Plateau) contains farmland, forests, and the largest Swiss cities. This landscape is still hilly, but less extreme than the Alpine regions. The largest lake, Lake Geneva (known as Lac Léman in French), is also located here.

Switzerland generally has a temperate climate; however, its weather is difficult to predict as it often varies from year to year and region to region. The mountainous regions experience extreme weather conditions. Sometimes the Alps are exceedingly cold, and other times the southern part of the country has an almost-Mediterranean climate. Summers are warm and humid with moderate rainfall. In the lowlands, winters tend to be cloudy and foggy, and alternately sunny and snowy in the mountains. Throughout the year, a weather phenomenon called the *föhn* (foon) can occur. The föhn brings warm winds from Italy up north into Switzerland. The southern valleys of the Valais canton experience the driest conditions.

Deer, squirrels, foxes, rabbits and marmot colonies can be found throughout the country, as well as golden eagles, ravens, woodpeckers, and skylarks. Most rivers contain trout and other fish. But, sadly much of the wildlife in Switzerland is disappearing. Bears, wolves, lynxes, and bearded vultures used to populate the country, but now hardly any remain.

Farmland makes up about half of Switzerland's terrain, so many livestock graze in these pastures. Cows are particularly abundant as their milk is used to produce famous Swiss cheese and chocolate.

**In Your Classroom**

Make a Swiss flag using construction paper, crayons, or paints. Post this flag in a prominent place in the classroom as you study the country of Switzerland.

Draw a map of Switzerland. Be sure to label all major cities, especially the capital, and indicate mountain ranges, rivers, and lakes.

Discuss the disappearance of bears, wolves, lynxes, and bearded vultures from Switzerland. What are some things that cause animals to leave one region and move to another, or even become extinct? What are some ways to prevent this from happening? How can the students educate others about animal protection?

Name _____   Date _____

# My Coat of Arms

A coat of arms is filled with symbols of a country. History, wildlife, and culture are often included. What symbolizes you? Create your own coat of arms in the template below. Add your favorite colors.

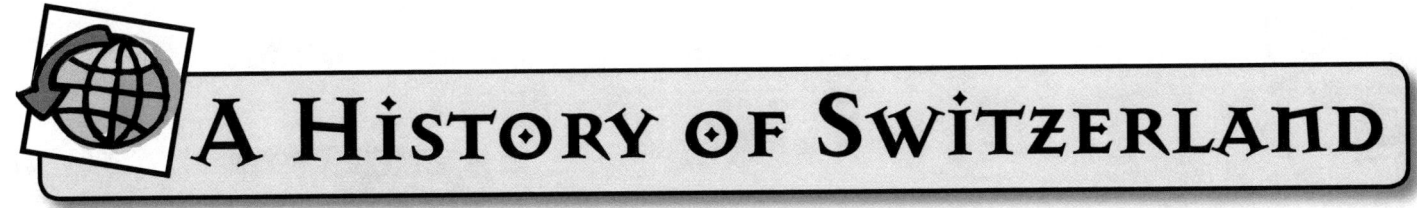

# A History of Switzerland

## Early History

The Celtic tribe called Helvetii and the Illyrian-Celtic tribe called the Raeti used to inhabit the country. The region that is now Switzerland was highly coveted due to its strategic location and its access to Alpine passes. In 50 BCE, Julius Caesar invaded the country, later followed by the Germanic Alemanni, Burgundians, Ostrogoths, and Franks. In the 10th and 11th centuries, the Holy Roman Empire took control of the region. However, feuds broke out, angering the peasants and in 1291 several cantons declared their independence. Although random fighting occurred over the next 200 years, Switzerland continued to maintain its neutrality.

## Internal Struggle

In the 16th century, however, the Protestant Reformation and the Counter-Reformation challenged Switzerland's political stability. Civil war broke out, leaving Switzerland divided by language and religion. During 1618 to 1648, the Thirty Years' War threatened the country, uniting its people in an effort to defend their interests. In 1648 Switzerland was formally recognized as being independent from the Holy Roman Empire. Switzerland remained at peace until the French Revolutionary armies invaded the country in 1798, establishing it as the Helvetic Republic. In 1815, after Napoleon's defeat, Swiss control was restored and its neutrality supported by the powers of Europe. The country has not participated in international war since then. Over the next few decades, Switzerland established its modern government and constitution.

## Home Security

In the 20th century, World War I and II posed a threat to Swiss neutrality, causing political turmoil between the country's French and German factions. During World War II the country feared being attacked by Germany and mobilized a large army of troops to protect its borders. Today they still have a national militia ready to protect their freedom. In fact, Switzerland requires all men between 20 and 50 years of age to serve in the army for a period of time. This is often considered a rite of passage by Swiss males. Swiss citizens are not allowed to serve in foreign armies, except for the special Swiss Guards of the Vatican. This group of Swiss soldiers is known for its discipline and loyalty. They have a long history of serving as guards at foreign European courts.

## Modern Switzerland

Today Switzerland continues to maintain its independence and neutrality, and is home to many international organizations. The League of Nations is located in Geneva, as well as World Health Organization, World Economic Forum, International Telecommunication Union, and the International Red Cross (which originated in Switzerland.)

# Daily Life

## Housing

Houses in Switzerland vary from smooth stone buildings, to house-and-barn combinations, or wooden houses with shingled roofs. The Swiss chalet is a famous type of house made from wood and is usually located in the mountains. Although the country's population is very dense, the houses tend to be quite large. Most people rent rather than own homes because land is scarce and therefore expensive.

## Clothing

Today, the Swiss dress like most Western Europeans—but slightly less casual. They often dress in traditional costumes covered with intricate embroidery for local festivities or parades. In the Gruyère region, herdsmen wear a *bredzon*—a short blue jacket made from canvas or cloth. Women from this region wear embroidered long-sleeved jackets, aprons and straw hats with ribbons hanging from the brim. Gold lace caps and dresses covered in silver ornaments are also traditional women's clothing. *Lederhosen* (lay-der-hō-sen), a type of leather shorts, are a traditional male costume in Alpine regions.

## School

Education is free and mandatory for nine years, but most Swiss children attend at least three more years of additional school. Public schools are under local control. Switzerland has several cantonal universities and federal institutes of technology for post-secondary education, as well as many private schools that attract students from other countries.

In Switzerland, most children attend the public school. Private schools are quite expensive, and those who attend generally are thought of as unable to make it at the public school. Each canton is responsible for their schools, which means education can vary widely. Some are very advanced and begin teaching a foreign language in fourth grade, while others begin in seventh grade. Public schools include *Kindergarten*, *Volksschule* (elementary school), *Gymnasium* (secondary school) and *Universitäten* (universities).

Kindergarten is typically for children ages five and six. It is not required, but most children attend because it helps them acclimate socially and prepares them for a school setting. Elementary school begins at age seven and typically lasts nine years. It is divided into the *Primarschule* and *Oberstufenschule*. Each canton's curriculum varies, but the Primarschule usually la    years with one teacher teaching all subjects. The Oberstufenschule lasts three years and is divided into three levels, the highest being Sekundarschule. The second highest is Realschule, which teaches the same subjects as Sekundarschule but not as in-depth. Oberschule is the lowest level of Oberstufenschule and educates students who have learning difficulties.

After elementary school, students choose to either enter the Gymnasium or to begin an apprenticeship. Once they have finished their apprenticeship, it is still possible for them to continue their education at either a secondary school or a technical college. For those who choose to attend a Gymnasium, the school is divided based on subjects. Some focus on math and science, while others focus on modern languages, ancient languages, sports, art, or economics. All of these last four-and-a-half to six-and-a-half-years. Students who attend the Gymnasium usually continue their education at a university once they have earned something called a federal graduation diploma.

## After-School Activities and Sport

Children sometimes enroll in after-school activities. Many of them join a football club or a multi-sport activity camp where they participate in outdoor games such as archery and climbing during the school holidays. Other after school activities include: cookery, art, and Boy Scouts or Girl Scouts. Swiss families like to spend time together at home, and they also enjoy going to concerts, festivals or the theater.

## Famous People from Switzerland

Many Swiss people have been valuable contributors to society. Two of the Protestant Reformation's greatest leaders, John Calvin and Ulrich Zwingli, were Swiss. So was Jean Jacques Rousseau, the philosopher and writer who influenced the French Revolution and was a forerunner in the 18th century Enlightenment. Hermann Hesse, a Swiss poet, painter, and novelist best known for his works *Siddhartha*, *The Best Bead Game*, and *Steppenwolf*, received the Nobel Prize in Literature in 1946. The playwright Friedrich Dürrenmatt and artists and architects Henry Fuseli, Alberto Giacometti, Paul Klee, and Le Corbusier are also famous Swiss who have influenced the world through their work.

## In Your Classroom

Make your own versions of the traditional Swiss garb. Use paper plates, construction paper, cardboard and tape to make hats. Then tape streamers to the hat brims for ribbons. Use blue construction paper and scissors to make *bredzon* for the boys.

Here are some fun facts about verbal and nonverbal communication in Switzerland.

## Famous Swiss Proverbs

Here are some famous Swiss proverbs. What do you think they mean?

*To every fool his hat.*

*No smoke without fire.*

*Sometimes you have to be silent to be heard.*

*Relax. The lake is not on fire.*

### Body Language and Etiquette in Switzerland

Here are some examples of body language and etiquette you'll find in Switzerland.

You will usually refer to Swiss acquaintances by their proper title (Mister, Miss, etc.). First names are reserved for close friends and families.

Stand up straight! Poor posture is not well-liked in Switzerland.

Never point your index finger to your head. This is considered an insult.

Don't be late – the Swiss take punctuality very seriously.

When dining out, do not wave your hand at a server. This is very rude.

Swiss like to keep their surroundings clean. Never litter. If you do so, you will be publicly scolded by any that witness.

Never put your feet on a chair, desk, or table.

The two most-spoken languages in Switzerland are German and French. For information on these languages, turn to pages 38 and 61.

## Foods

Traditional Swiss cuisine is similar to other European countries, but the Swiss are especially known for their dairy products. They are most famous for their cheeses, named for the valleys where they are produced (Gruyère and Emmental). A popular Swiss dish called *fondue* is made by melting these cheeses and then dipping bread into it using long forks. The Valais valley is famous for its saffron and vineyards. Wine is not only produced in this region, but also throughout other parts of the country. The Swiss are also famous for their chocolate. They invented modern techniques in chocolate making, which improved the quality of chocolate. They are also responsible for the invention of milk chocolate and hazelnut chocolate.

Here are some popular Swiss dishes.

*Quiches* (keesh) are pastry crusts filled with eggs, milk, or cream. Meat, vegetables, or cheese are often added for delicious flavor.

*Papet vaudois* (pap-ā vō-dwa), inspired by French cuisine, is a dish containing leeks, potatoes, and pork sausage. It is a very filling meal. Sometimes, the dish includes cabbage or liver.

*Rösti* is a potato-based dish, very similar to hash browns. Occasionally, the potatoes are flavored with apples.

*Polenta* is made of ground cornmeal, and possesses a texture similar to gruel or porridge. It's usually served with a meat, like sausage or rabbit.

*Bündner Nusstorte* is a sweet pastry filled with caramelized nuts.

*Rivella* is a carbonated beverage that is very popular in Switzerland. It is based on lactose. Other popular drinks are apple juice/cider and Ovomaltine, a cocoa-flavored powder added to milk.

### In Your Classroom

Bring Swiss cheeses and chocolates to class and have the students taste some of each for a snack.

## Holidays & Festivals

Switzerland celebrates Christmas, New Year's Day, and Good Friday. Its other legal holidays are Easter Monday, Ascension Day, *Whit Monday* (in April or May), and *Bundesfeier* (boonds-feer). Bundesfeier, or Swiss National Day, is a patriotic holiday. It celebrates the Federal Charter signed in 1291. Towns celebrate this day with paper lantern parades, bonfires, hanging strings of Swiss flags and displaying fireworks.

The German-speaking Swiss celebrate many religious days and seasons with festivals, depending on their canton or town. Switzerland celebrates over one hundred different festivals of pagan, Christian, and patriotic origins. Its most famous celebration is *Fastnacht* (fast nackt), or carnival, which marks the final days before Lent. For three days, people parade in masks and costumes through the streets, riding on colorful floats and playing loud instruments.

### Whit Monday
*The Day after Pentecost (April or May)*

Also known as *Monday of the Holy Spirit*, this celebrated day used to mark a baptismal season. Special services are often held, and parades sometimes mark the day.

### Swiss National Day
*August 1*

Inspired by the Federal Charter of 1291, this national holiday celebrates the foundation of the Swiss Confederacy. Swiss cities and towns are decorated with the colors and flags of Switzerland. Paper lantern parades and bonfires light up the night. In some towns, fireworks top off the festivities.

### Fastnacht

The celebration of this holiday has a variable date, but is usually very near Ash Wednesday and the start of Lent. In Basel, the celebration begins in the early morning when all of the city's lights go out. People march through the streets in costumes and masks, carrying decorated lanterns. Drummers and pipers march with the group. The festival continues for three days.

### Christmas
*December 25*

Families decorate their Christmas trees on Christmas Eve. Presents and a nativity scene are placed under the tree. A large dinner is served and carols are sung. After midnight mass, gifts are exchanged over hot chocolate and doughnuts.

## In Your Classroom

Have the students use paper plates to make Fastnacht masks. Use scissors to cut holes for eyes, and staple string to the sides of the plate to tie the mask in place behind the student's head. Glitter, construction paper, and paints are excellent materials for decorating.

Help the students research Swiss Bundesfeier holiday.

# Creative Arts

## Crafts and Hobbies

The Swiss are famous for their decorative arts such as embroidery, wood carving (which can be seen on their famous Swiss chalets), weaving, and painting. There is a type of unique painting that originated among Alpine dairy farmers of the early eighteenth century that involves carving and painting farm animals on wood. The Swiss are especially well known for their watch making and are responsible for producing half of the world's watches.

## Folklore

William Tell is a legendary Swiss hero who was an expert marksman with his crossbow. According to the legend, William Tell lived in a town called Bürglen in the canton of Uri during the 13th and early 14th centuries. At this time, the Austrian emperors called the Hapsburgs were trying to overtake Uri. Hermann Gessler, the newly appointed Austrian lord of the canton, set up a pole in the town square, hung his hat from it, and commanded that the people bow before it. William Tell walked by the pole without bowing and was arrested. The Vogt told him that as punishment he would be forced to shoot an apple off of his son Walter's head or both would be killed. If he was able to hit the apple with one shot, he would be free. Tell shot one arrow from his crossbow, hitting the middle of the apple and cutting it in half. But Gessler noticed that Tell had another arrow left in his quiver and he asked why he had brought two with him. Tell replied that if he had not been able to hit the apple, he would have used the second arrow to shoot Gessler. This enraged Gessler, starting a long feud between the two men. It ended when Tell eventually shot Gessler, sparking a rebellion among the people of Uri. With William Tell as one of their leaders, the people eventually formed the Swiss Confederation. As legend has it, Tell died during battle as he was trying to save a drowning child.

Over the years, many different versions of the legend of William Tell have been written and told, so it is difficult to determine what is myth and what is truth. Whether real or fictional, William Tell continues to exist as a hero and maintains a powerful identity to this day. In fact, according to a recent survey, 58% of Swiss believe that he truly existed.

## Music

Yodeling is often associated with Switzerland. This is a form of singing that involves one extended note that quickly and frequently changes pitch, causing the note to transition between low and high. It is a very unique sound that you might have heard. Historically, yodeling was used as a form of communication between alpine villages in the Alps.

The *alphorn*, a long wooden horn, has also become associated with Switzerland. Mountain dwellers use the giant horns, which are nearly as tall or taller than an adult, for communication and cattle-calling. The distinct notes echo off of mountains and can be heard for miles.

**In Your Classroom**

Discuss the legend of William Tell. What is the students' consensus? Do they believe the story or think it is a myth? Discuss other folklore heroes, such as America's Paul Bunyan, England's Robin Hood, or China's Hua Mulan. Compare the different legends and see what the heroes/heroines have in common. What makes these stories so timeless?

In your classroom, discuss the difference between fiction and nonfiction. Give some examples of fictional characters and books versus nonfiction books and characters. Have half of the class write fictional stories and the other half recount nonfiction stories. When they are finished, mix up the stories and read them aloud. Have the students guess which ones are fiction and nonfiction.

Have the students practice yodeling. You might try listening to examples from the Internet.

Discuss the Swiss watch-making tradition with the students. Have each student take a survey of all the clocks and watches in his or her home and bring the list into school the next day. Evaluate the brands and see which ones are Swiss.

# Sports & Games

Many tourists come to Switzerland each year with one purpose in mind: mountaineering. The Swiss Alps attract mountain climbers, hikers, backpackers, and skiers from all over the world. Other winter sports like ice skating, ice hockey and curling are very popular among the Swiss.

*Schwingen* is considered the Swiss national sport and is a form of folk wrestling. The sport originated in the Alps and was traditionally common at public festivities. The two wrestlers wear special shorts and meet in a ring. They proceed to hold each other by the back of the pants where the belt meets and throw their opponent on the ground.

Another Swiss sport called *hornussen* is a cross between golf and baseball. Stone-throwing competitions are also popular traditions throughout the country.

Like most Europeans, the Swiss are enthusiastic football (soccer) fans. They joined with Austria to host the Euro 2008 football tournament. Tennis is another popular sport, and the Swiss are proud of their stars like Martina Hingis and Roger Federer, each multiple Grand Slam singles champions.

Many sports organizations have their headquarters located in Switzerland as well. These include: International Ice Hockey Federation, International Olympic Committee, FIFA (International Federation of Association Football) and the UEFA (United European Football Association.)

A card game called *Jass* (yass) is extremely popular in Switzerland. In the German-speaking regions, the game is played with thirty-six cards divided into four suits of bells, acorns, flowers, and shields. Each suit has an ace, könig, ober, under, banner, nine, eight, seven, and six. In the French-speaking parts of the country, they use the same deck that most Americans use in card games; however, Jass does not require any cards below the number six. When there are trumps, the cards in the trump suit hold different values than those in the other suits.

**In Your Classroom**

Organize a stone-throwing competition outdoors. Make sure the students choose stones that are similar in size.

# Answer Key

## England

The King's English (page 14)

BISCUIT – COOKIE
BOBBY – POLICE OFFICER
BOOT – TRUNK
CHEERS – GOODBYE
CHIPS – FRENCH FRIES
TROUSERS – PANTS
GARDEN – YARD
JUMPER – SWEATER
PLASTER – BANDAGE
LIFT – ELEVATOR
LORRY – TRUCK
PETROL – GAS
QUEUE – LINE
SPANNER – WRENCH
SULTANAS – RAISINS

## Germany

Sprechen Sie Deutsch? (page 63)

red – rot
book – das Buch
blue – blau
yellow – gelb
children – die Kinder
black – Schwarz
green – grün
school – die Schule
white – weiß

## Ireland

Mapping Out History (page 93)

# Italy

II, IV, VI, VIII! Roman Numerals Are Really Great! (page 116)

| | |
|---|---|
| I. | 627 |
| II. | 952 |
| III. | 3,265 |
| IV. | 99 |
| V. | 1,888 |
| VI. | 2,003 |
| VII. | Answers will vary |
| VIII. | Answers will vary |
| IX. | Answers will vary |
| X. | Answers will vary |
| XI. | Answers will vary |
| XII. | MCDXCII |
| XIII. | MDCCLXXVI |
| XIV. | Answers will vary |
| XV. | Answers will vary |

# Sweden

Swedish Vocabulary Match (page 156)

STOL – CHAIR
BOK – BOOK
BORD – TABLE
LÄRARE – TEACHER
DÖRR – DOOR
SKOLA – SCHOOL
FÖNSTER – WINDOW
PENNA – PEN, PENCIL
KLOCKA – CLOCK
ELEV – PUPIL
GOLV – FLOOR
HOPPA – JUMP

# Additional Resources

## England

**Resources for Children**

Cushman, Karen. *Catherine, Called Birdy*. New York: Clarion Books, 1995. An insider's look at the daughter of a minor English nobleman in 1920.

Davison, Brian. *Looking at a Castle*. New York: Random House, 1987. A look and learn book.

Giblin, James Cross. *Chimney Sweeps Yesterday and Today*. New York: Harper & Row, 1987.

Moon, Bernice and Cliff. *Britain*. New York: Hodder Wayland, 1999.

**General Resources**

Ebbutt, M.I. *British Myths and Legends*. New York: Random House, 1994.

Fuller, Barbara. *Britain (Cultures of the World)*. New York: Times Books, 1994.

Fry, Plantagenet Somerset. *Kings and Queens of England and Scotland*. New York: DK Publishing, 2006.

Hart, Roger. *English Life in Chaucer's Day*. New York: W.P. Putnam & Sons, 1973.

Hibbert, Christopher. *Daily Life in Victorian England*. New York: American Heritage, 1975.

Johnson, Gerald W. *British Empire*. New York: William Morrow & Company, 1969.

Kirtland, G.B. *One Day in Elizabethan England*. New York: Harcourt, Brace, and World, 1962.

Lee, Alan. *Castles*. New York: McGraw-Hill Book Company, 1986.

Morgan, Gwyneth. *Life in a Medieval Village*. Cambridge: Cambridge University Press, 1975.

St. John, Jetty. *A Family in England*. New York: Lerner Publication Co., 1988.

Warner, Marina. *Crack in the Teacup*. New York: Houghton Mifflin, 1980.

White, Thomson. *Elizabeth I and Tudor England*. England: Wayland Publishers, 1984.

## France

There is a plethora of books about France available. The public library or any bookstore offers dictionaries, story books, and reference books for children as well as adults. Canadian teacher resources and publishing houses are good resources for books in French. Many favorite authors are translated into French. Children's illustrated dictionaries are excellent tools for research. Enjoy your exploring!

Aliki. *The King's Day: Louis XIV of France.* Thomas Y. Crowell, 1989. (ISBN 0–690–04588–3) An illustrated rhymed history of the Sun King.

Axworthy, Anni. *Anni's Diary of France.* Whispering Coyote Press, Inc., 2000. (ISBN 1-879085–58–5) A journal with drawings and children–referenced activities.

Bemelmans, Ludwig. *Madeline* books. Viking Press. (ISBN 0590–75942–6)

Bjork, Christina. *Linnea in Monet's Garden.* R & S Books. (ISBN 91–29–58314–4) A delightful story with drawings and photos of Monet, his garden, and a French trip.

Blackwoood, Alan and Brigitte Chosey. *Countries of the World: France.* Bookwright Press, 1988. (ISBN 0–531–18186–3) A reference book with photographs.

Brunhoff, Jean de. *Babar* books. Random House. (ISBN 0–394–80576–3)

Cole, Ann et al. *Children Are Children Are Children.* Little, Brown & Co. (ISBN 0–316–15114–9) An activity approach to exploring, Brazil, France, Iran, Japan, Nigeria and the former USSR, and still the best activity and short reference resource for teachers.

Kowalchik and Hylton, eds. *Rodale's Illustrated Encyclopedia of Herbs.* Rodale Press, l998.

Macaulay, David. *Cathedral.* Houghton–Mifflin. (ISBN 0–395–17513–5)

———. *Castle.* Houghton–Mifflin. (ISBN 0–395- 25784–0) Macaulay's books are super for children to explore as they are full of diagrams and fascinating facts.

McCully, Emily Arnold. *Mirette on the High Wire.* Scholastic. ( ISBN 0–590–47693–9) A charming story of Paris, high wires, and a special friendship.

Montaufier, Poupa. *One Summer at Grandmother's House.* Carolrhoda Books, 1985. (ISBN 0–87614–238–2) A book of drawings and text about French families and the French countryside.

Munro, Dixie. *Inside/Outside Book of Paris.* Dutton's Children's Books, 1992. (ISBN 0–525- 44863–2) A book with drawings and text about the French capital.

Saint–Exupery, Antoine. *The Little Prince.* Harcourt Brace and World, Inc., 1943. (ISBN 0- 15-246503–0) A classic French fantasy.

NOTE: *Cinderella, Sleeping Beauty, Little Red Riding Hood, Princess Furball,* and *Beauty and the Beast* are fairy tales of French origin. Search for different versions of the same tale, in English or from different cultures.

# Germany

**Resources for Teachers and Children**

Adler, Ann. *A Family in West Germany.* Minneapolis: Lerner Publications, 1985.

———. *Passport to West Germany.* New York: Franklin Watts, 1986.

Ahlberg, Janet, and Allan Ahlberg. *The Jolly Postman or Other People's Letters*. Boston: Little, Brown & Company, 1986. (A story of a postman's visit to several fairy-tale characters. It includes the letters they receive.)

Bettelheim, Bruno. *The Uses of Enchantment: The Meaning and Importance of Fairy Tales*. New York: Vintage, 1989. (Gives the reasons fairy tales are so important to children as well as recommendations for telling the stories.)

Bradley, John, and Catherine Bradley. *Germany: The Reunification of a Nation*. New York: Gloucester Press, 1993.

Dornberg, John. *The Two Germanys*. New York: Dial Books, 1974.

Hintz, Martin. *Enchantment of the World: West Germany*. Chicago: Children's Press, 1983.

James, Ian. *Inside West Germany*. New York: Franklin Watts, 1989.

Janson, H. W., and Anthony Janson, editors. *History of Art for Young People*. New York: Prentice Hall, 6th edition, 2003.

Kirby, George. *Looking at Germany*. Philadelphia: Lippincott Jr. Books, 1972.

*The Late Middle Ages*. History of the World. Milwaukee: Raintree Publishers Limited Partnership, 1990.

Macaulay, David. *Castle*. New York: Houghton Mifflin/Walter Lorraine Books, 1982.

MacDonald, Fiona. *A Medieval Castle*. New York: Peter Bedrick Books, 1993.

McKenna, David. *Places and Peoples of the World: East Germany*. New York: Chelsea House Publishers, 1988.

Opie, Iona, and Peter Opie. *The Classic Fairy Tales*. New York: Oxford University Press, 1980. (Gives a historical perspective of several popular fairy tales and of changes that have been made to the stories over the years.)

Parnell, Helga. *Cooking the German Way*. Minneapolis: Lerner Publications, 2002.

Pfeiffer, Christine. *Germany: Two Nations, One Heritage*. Minneapolis: Dillon Press, 1987.

Pitcher, Caroline. *Build Your Own Castle*. New York: Aladdin Books, 1985.

Rosenberg, Jane. *Sing Me a Story*. London: Thames & Hudson, 1996. (The stories of several operas are told and illustrated.)

Seger, Gerhart H. *Germany*. Grand Rapids: The Fideler Company, 1978.

Sharman, Tim. *We Live in East Germany*. New York: Franklin Watts, 1986.

Spruyt, E. Lee. *Behind the Golden Curtain: Hansel and Gretel at the Great Opera House*. New York: Four Winds Press, 1987.

Stadtler, Christa. *We Live in West Germany*. New York: Franklin Watts, 1984.

Ventura, Piero. *Great Composers*. New York: G. P. Putnam's Sons, 1989.

———. *Great Painters*. New York: G. P. Putnam's Sons, 1984.

Wright, David K., Rhoda Irene Sherwood, and Scott Enk, editors. *Children of the World: West Germany*. Milwaukee: Gareth Stevens, 1988.

Wright, Lyndie. *Puppets*. New York: Franklin Watts, 1989. (Gives easy-to-follow directions to make a variety of puppets.)

**Fairy Tales**
(Books are listed by illustrator. All tales are stories collected by the Grimm brothers.)

Adams, Adrienne. *Hansel and Gretel*. New York: Macmillan, 1979.

Brett, Jan. *Goldilocks and the Three Bears*. New York: Putnam Publishing Group, 1996.

Burkert, Nancy Ekholm. *Snow White and the Seven Dwarfs*. Translated by Randall Jarrell. New York: Farrar, Straus & Giroux, 1985.

Gag, Wanda. *Tales from Grimm*. New York: Putnam Publishing Group, 1981.

———. *More Tales from Grimm*. New York: Putnam Publishing Group, 1981.

Mayer, Mercer. *The Sleeping Beauty*. New York: Atheneum, 1994.

Ormerod, Jan. *The Frog Prince*. New York: Lothrop, 1990.

Plume, Ilse. *The Bremen Town Musicians*. New York: Dragonfly Books, 1998.

Sanderson, Ruth. *The Twelve Dancing Princesses*. Boston: Little, Brown & Company, 1993.

Sendak, Maurice. *Dear Mili*. New York: Michael Di Capua Books, 2004.

Zelinsky, Paul O. *Rumpelstiltskin*. New York: E. P. Dutton, 1986.

Zwerger, Lisbeth. *The Seven Ravens*. New York: Simon & Schuster Books for Young Readers, 1991.

# Ireland

*The Book of Kells*. Reproduction of the manuscripts. New York: Dover Publications, 1984.

*Celtic Fairy Tales*. Reproduction of 1892 ed. Compiled by Joseph Jacobs. New York: Dover Publishing, 1968.

Cotterell, Arthur. *A Dictionary of World Mythology*. New York and London: Oxford University Press, 1990.

*Early Irish Myths & Sagas*. Trans. Jeffrey Gantz. Penguin Books, 1982.

Fairclough, Chris. **We Live in Ireland**. *Sketches of 26 Irish Men, Women, and Children*. New York: Bookwright Press, 1986.

Fitzgibbon, Constantine. *Out of the Lion's Paw. Ireland Wins Her Freedom*. New York: American Heritage, 1969.

*Folktales of Ireland*. Trans. Sean O'Sullivan. Chicago: University of Chicago Press, 1999.

Foster, R. F. *Modern Ireland: 1600–1972*. New York: Allen Lon (Penguin Press), 1990.

Fraden, Dennis B. *The Enchantment of the World Series. The Republic of Ireland*. Chicago: Children's Press, 1984.

*Great Folk Tales of Old Ireland*. Compiled by Mary McGarry. New York: Bell Publishing Co., 1978.

Jenner, Michael. *Ireland Through the Ages*. New York: Viking Penguin, 1996.

McCaffery, Mary A., et al. *Irish Trivia*. (Original ed.: Queenland Press) New York: Bell Publishing Co., 1990.

O'Brien, Elinor. *The Land and People of Ireland*. New York: HarperCollins, 1975.

O'Brien, Marie and Conor Cruise O'Brien. *Ireland—A Concise History*. New York: Thames & Halloran, Inc., 1985.

Taylor, Alice. *To School Through the Fields. An Irish Country Childhood*. New York: St. Martin's Griffith, 1994.

———. *Quench the Lamp*. New York: St. Martin's Press, 1994.

Wallace, Martin. *The Irish—How They Live and Work*. Praeger Publishers, Inc., 1972.

Yeats, W. B. *Irish Fairy and Folk Tales*. New York: Modern Library, 2003.

# Italy

Adams, Briquebec, Dramer. *Illustrated Atlas of World History*. New York: Random House, 1992.

Adleman, Robert H. and Col. George Walton. *Rome Fell Today*. Boston: Little Brown & Co, 1970.

Church, Alfred J. *Roman Life in the Days of Cicero*. New York: Biblo & Tannen, 1978.

Cowell, F.R. *Life in Ancient Rome*. New York: Perigee Books, 1976.

Deiss, Joseph Jay. *Herculaneum: Italy's Buried Treasure*. J. Paul Getty Trust Publications, 1989.

dePaola, Tomie. *Tony's Bread*. New York: Paperstar Books, 1996.

———. *The Legend of Old Befana*. New York: Voyager Books, 1989.

———. *Merry Christmas, Strega Nona*. New York: Voyager Books, 1991.

———. *Strega Nona*. New York: Aladdin, 1979.

DiFranco, Anthony. *Italy: Balanced on the Edge of Time*. Dillon, 1983.

Haskins, Jim. *Count Your Way Through Italy*. Minneapolis: Carolrhoda Books Inc., 1990.

Hauser, Ernest O. *Italy: A Cultural Guide*. New York: Atheneum, 1981.

Hearder, H. & Jonathan Morris, eds. *Italy: A Short History*. England: Cambridge U. Press, 2001.

Johnston, Tony. *Pages of Music*. New York: Putnam Publishing Group, 1988.

Leech, Michael. *Exploring Rural Italy*. Illinois: Passport Books; National Textbook Co., 1988.

Macauly, David. *City: A Story of Roman Planning and Construction*. Boston: Houghton Mifflin Co., 1983.

Nencini, Franco. *Florence: The Days of the Flood*. New York: Stein & Day, 1967.

Powell, Anton. *Renaissance Italy*. New York: Franklin Watts, 1980.

Powers, Elizabeth. *Nero: World Leaders Past & Present*. New York: Chelsea Publishers, 1988.

Time–Life Books. *Italy: Library of Nations Series*. Amsterdam: TLB, Inc., 1986.

Venezia, Mike. *Da Vinci*. Chicago: Childrens Press, 1989.

Ventura, Pietro. *Venice: Birth of a City*. New York: G.P. Putnam's Sons, 1988.

Whyte, Arthur James. *Evolution of Modern Italy*. New York: W.W. Norton Co., Inc., 1965.

# Spain

**Resources for Teachers and Children**

Biggs, Betsey. *Kidding Around Spain: A Young Person's Guide*. John Muir, 1991.

Christian, Rebecca. *Cooking the Spanish Way*. Minneapolis: Lerner Publications Company, 1982.

Codye, Corinn. *Queen Isabella I*. Austin: Raintree Steck–Vaughn Library, 1991.

Cross, Esther and Wilbur. *Spain*. Chicago: Children's Press, 1985.

Finkelstein, Norman H. *The Other 1492: Jewish Settlement in the New World*. New York: Charles Scribner's Sons, 1989.

Lawson, Don. *The Abraham Lincoln Brigade: Americans Fighting Fascism in the Spanish Civil War*. New York: Thomas and Crowell, 1989.

Leahy, Philippa. *Spain*. New York: Crestwood House, 1993.

Rutland, Jonathan. *Take a Trip to Spain*. London: Franklin Watts, 1980.

Selby, Anna. *Spain*. Austin: Raintree Steck–Vaughn Publishers, 1994.

Shubert, Adrian. *The Land and People of Spain*. New York: Harper Collins, 1992.

Tolhurst, Marilyn. *Spain*. Edgewood Cliffs: Silver Burdett Press, 1989.

Wood, Geraldine. *Spain: A Shining New Democracy*. Minneapolis: Dillon Press Incorporated, 1987.

**Fiction**

Braun, Lutz. *Faster than a Bull*. Austin: Raintree Steck–Vaughn Publishers, 1993.

Koslow, Philip. *El Cid*. New York: Chelsea House Publishers, 1993.

Livingston, Myra Cohn. *Platero y yo (Platero and I)*. New York: Clarion Books, 1994.

Wojciechowska, Maia. *Shadow of a Bull*. New York: Aladdin Books, 1987.

# Sweden

Arbman, Maj. *Looking at Sweden*. Philadelphia: J. B. Lippincott Co., 1971.

Bendure, Glenda. *Scandinavian and Baltic Europe*. Hawthorne, Australia: Lonely Planet Publishers, 1993.

Branston, Brian. *Gods and Heroes from Viking Mythology*. New York: Peter Bedrick Books, 1994.

Caselli, Giovanni. *A Viking Settler*. New York: MacDonald and Co. Ltd., 1986.

Clare, John D., ed. *The Vikings: Living History*. Orlando: Harcourt Brace Jovanovich, 1992.

Clarke, Helen. *Vikings*. New York: Gloucester Press, 1979.

Evans, Idrisyn Oliver. *Flags of the World*. New York: Grosset and Dunlap, 1970.

Hutchings, Jane. *Insight Guide to Sweden*. Insight Guides, 2003.

Innes, Hammond. *Scandinavia*. Alexandria, VA: Time–Life, 1963.

Ansari, Nuha, ed. *Fodor's Sweden*. New York: Fodor's Travel Publications, Inc., 2004.

James, Alan. *Lapps: Reindeer Herders of Lapland*. Vero Beach: Rourke Publications Inc., 1989.

Kaplan, Irma. *Fairy Tales from Sweden*. Chicago: Follett Publishing Co., 1967.

Knowlton, Mary Lee and Mark J. Sachner. *Sweden*. Milwaukee: Gareth Stevens Publications, 1987.

Lewin, Ted. *The Reindeer People*. New York: Simon & Schuster Children's Publishing, 1994.

Lindgren, Astrid. *Pippi Longstocking*. New York: Puffin Books, 1997.

Lye, Keith. *Take a Trip to Sweden*. New York: Franklin Watts, Inc., 1983.

Moberg, Vilhelm. *History of the Swedish People from Pre-History to Renaissance*. New York: Pantheon Books, 1972.

Moberg, Vilhelm. *History of the Swedish People from Renaissance to Revolution*. Minneapolis: University of Missesota Press, 2005.

Nano, Frederic C. *The Land and People of Sweden*. New York: HarperCollins Juvenile Books, 2000.

Reynolds, Jan. *Far North: Vanishing Cultures*. San Diego: Harcourt Brace Jovanovich, 1992.